SCANDINAVIAN INSTITUTE OF
ASIAN STUDIES MONOGRAPH SERIES

NO 16

# Chinese Communism 1931-1934

Experience in Civil Government

Trygve Lötveit

Studentlitteratur

To my father, S. Lötveit

©Trygve Lötveit 1973
Printed in Sweden
Studentlitteratur
Lund 1973
ISBN 91-44-10041-8

# CONTENTS

# ACKNOWLEDGEMENTS

This is, in a somewhat altered form, the thesis for which I received the degree of Ph.D. from the University of Leeds in December 1970. It was originally entitled The Central Chinese Soviet Area: Some Aspects of Its Organisation and Administration, November 1931 - October 1934. The study was an extremely slow process, and I had to draw very heavily on the patience of my sponsors.

The larger part of the work was done at the University of Leeds, where I held a research fellowship, financed through a grant from Leverhulme, from October 1965 to September 1968. I was attached to the Departments of Russian and Chinese Studies, and I want to express my thanks to the heads of these departments, Professor F.M. Borras and Professor Owen Lattimore. Professor Lattimore was my special supervisor, and I am much indebted to him for very valuable comments and corrections, and not least for his encouragement. Dr. Jerome Ch'en acquainted me with the Shih Sou Collection, and he helped to solve a number of problems relating to Chinese language and Chinese society. I also received valuable comments from Mrs. Sybille van der Sprenkel and Mr. James H. MacDonald.

From October 1968 to September 1969 I was a research fellow at the Contemporary China Institute, School of Oriental and African Studies, University of London. I want to thank Professor Stuart R. Schram, from whom I received valuable advice, and also Geoffrey Shillinglaw and John Hall, who corrected my English.

I further want to acknowledge grants from the Norwegian Research Council for Science and the Humanities, which financed my work from October 1969 to December 1970, and also enabled me to publish the thesis. Some alterations in the text have been made during my work at the Scandinavian Institute of Asian Studies, where I am now a research associate.

The responsibility for all the shortcomings of the study is, of course, my own.

Trygve Lötveit

Copenhagen, July 1973

## ABBREVIATIONS

| | |
|---|---|
| AB League | Anti-Bolshevik League |
| CCP | Chinese Communist Party |
| CEC | Central Executive Committee |
| KMT | Kuomintang |
| RSFSR | Russian Socialist Federative Soviet Republic |
| SSC | Shih Sou Collection |
| SW | Selected Works (of Mao Tse-tung) |

# INTRODUCTION

Some years ago the Chinese Soviet Republic, of November 1931 to October 1934,* was in fact a wilderness for the historian. Today the situation ought to be a vastly different one. A landmark in the development of our knowledge on the period was the publication of Hsiao Tso-liang's book Power Relations ... in 1961, and about the same time a vast amount of primary sources was made available. To be sure, the sources are not abundant in every respect; I shall below draw attention to quite irritating loop-holes. But as a whole the material is overwhelming, and the problem which overshadows all others is how to convert the complexity of sources into a readable account.

General narratives of the events leading up to the formal establishment of the Chinese Soviet Republic can easily be found elsewhere.[1] There were the massacres of the spring and summer of 1927, which inevitably made the Chinese Communists enemies instead of allies of the Kuomintang. The same year saw the Autumn Harvest Uprising, led by Mao Tse-tung, and Mao's retreat with a remnant of his defeated troops to the Chingkang Mountains on the border of Hunan and Kiangsi, where, in the spring of 1928, he was joined by additional forces under Chu Te. After a troublesome year of military excursions and disputes with their superiors in the Communist Party, Mao and Chu moved eastward in January 1929, and subsequently established new base areas in southern Kiangsi and in western Fukien. Mao and Chu fought successfully against three annihilation campaigns staged by the Kuomintang, and survived bitter disputes with the party leadership under Li Li-san. After this race through major historical events we arrive at our special period, the period of the Chinese Soviet Republic from November 1931 to October 1934.

In time, the scope of our discussion is thus rather limited; geographically it is equally limited. We shall be dealing only with the Central Soviet Area, i.e. the integrated area in Kiangsi and Fukien which was actually ruled by the Central Government in Juichin. Various other Chinese soviet areas - geographically separate and politically more or less independent - will be left out.

---

\* It is important to mark the new epoch beginning with the Long March, although it should not be ignored that formally the Chinese Soviet Republic continued to exist after October 1934.

## The Central Soviet Area

o = county capital.

_____

It does not seem possible to draw the borders of the Central Soviet Area.
But all names on the map, except the provincial names KIANGSI, FUKIEN
and KWANGTUNG, stand for counties included in its territory according
to one of the following sources: Hung-se Chung-hua 29.4.1933 p.1, 31.8.
1933 p.5 and 15.3.1934 p.1; Hsüan-chü yün-tung chou-pao No. 2 (10.9.1933
p.5; doc.13 p. 2.

Some of the outlying counties were probably only in part controlled by the
Communists.

Not all the soviet counties have been located. As far as the south-western
corner of Fukien is concerned, the map is based on a source of March
1934; at an earlier stage the Communist area definitely extended further
toward the east.

The Central Soviet Area has often been designated as the "Kiangsi Soviet". This is misleading in two respects. Firstly, a soviet is not in itself an area; it is a Russian word for a council, and it may also be used for an administrative organisation of which the council is a part. Secondly, in most of the period of the republic the Central Soviet Area was not confined to Kiangsi; it covered part of Kiangsi and part of Fukien, while it is uncertain whether or not it extended into the northern fringe of Kwangtung.

The population of the Central Soviet Area was rather small: various contemporary sources agree that by the summer of 1933 it counted about three million.[2] It was predominantly a rural population, but not exclusively so; such towns as Juichin, Ch'angt'ing (T'ingchou) and Ningtu (Posheng) were by no means negligible.

There were various important trends in the development of the Central Soviet Area in our period, and it may be useful to sketch some of them very briefly.

There was the development of the administrative apparatus. Starting from very rudimentary soviets which existed before, a rather complex system of local and central government was gradually built up. The two National Soviet Congresses, in November 1931 and in January - February 1934, were of course essential events in this respect, but a tremendous lot of constructive work was carried out at other times.

There was the development of the military situation. In late 1931 and early 1932 the soviet area was relatively free of external threats, as the Kuomintang was preoccupied with the aggression of the Japanese. From the summer of 1932 the Red Army had to be more on the alert, since the enemy was initiating its Fourth Encirclement and Annihilation Campaign, but as far as the Central Soviet Area is concerned the major battles of this campaign did not begin until February 1933. New Communist victories and the revolt of the Kuomintang 19th Route Army again for some time made the military situation look brighter, until the main assaults of Chiang Kai-shek's Fifth Campaign began in January 1934.[3] The rest of the period of the republic was a desperate fight for survival - the Red Army did survive, but its territory was lost.

In addition, there was the development of personal power relations, whose roots are to be found not only in the Chinese soviet areas, but in Moscow and Shanghai as well. We have the rather strange story of a group of Chinese students at the Sun Yat-sen University in Moscow who had sided with Stalin in the Stalin-Trotsky dispute - more than that, they were, according to Sheng Yueh, the enemy of all "anti-Party" factions in the university. The group was nicknamed "the 28 Bolsheviks". These 28 revolutionaries later returned to China, most of them in the year 1930. Their rector at the Sun Yat-sen University, Pavel Mif, was appointed Comintern delegate to China, and travelled to Shanghai probably late in the same year. In January 1931, when the Fourth Plenum* in Shanghai finally condemned the Li Li-san line, leading members of the group, sponsored by Mif, took over control of the central organs of the Chinese Communist Party.[4]

In the present context we need not deal much with the head of the 28 Bolshevik group, Ch'en Shao-yü (Wang Ming) - after some time he returned from Shanghai to Moscow,[5] and he seems never to have been to the Central Soviet Area. In the period under discussion a really important part was played by the "Bolshevik" Ch'in Pang-hsien (Po Ku), Secretary General of the Chinese Communist Party from September 1931 to January 1935;[6] however, in government matters Ch'in was overshadowed by another powerful member of the group, Chang Wen-t'ien (Lo Fu), a name with which we shall become well acquainted later. A fourth "Bolshevik" who must be mentioned is Wang Chia-ch'iang (Wang Chia-hsiang), who was to become the Commissar of Foreign Affairs of the Chinese Soviet Republic. Moreover, some of the group's associates were much more significant than most of its own members. Among these associates was above all Chou En-lai, who was already developing his well-known ability to survive political setbacks; in January 1931 he simply moved over from a dominant position in the preceding, heavily ciriticised, party leadership to a prominent seat in the new one.[7] Another person whom the 28 Bolsheviks made extensive use of was Hsiang Ying; it seems strange that he should obtain a leading role in party and government affairs, since his abilities were reported to be rather low[8] - in contrast to the very impressive intelligence and ability of Chou En-lai.

Having secured for themselves the top leadership of the party, the 28 Bolsheviks and their associates immediately started the process of getting Mao and his apparatus in the Central Soviet Area under control as well. First they dispatched their representatives from Shanghai to Kiangsi - a Central Bureau of the party with Hsiang Ying as secretary** was established with Mao's headquarters in early 1931[9] - and later the Central Committee itself undertook the same journey. It is extremely difficult to determine the time when the Central Committee moved; was

---

\* The Fourth Plenum of the CCP Central Committee.

\*\* Chou En-lai probably took over the secretary post later. (See Dieter Heinzig, The Otto Braun Memoirs and Mao's Rise to Power, The China Quarterly No. 46, April-June 1971, pp. 278-79).

it in 1931, 1932 or in early 1933 ? The available sources do indeed conflict on the issue.[10] However, the transfer of the Central Committee as a formal institution is one thing – the time of that move seems to remain obscure – but the whereabouts of particular party leaders may be something else. We should probably accept Kung Ch'u's account that he personally met Chang Wen-t'ien, * Wang Chia-ch'iang and Chou En-lai in Juichin, at a conference discussing measures to be taken in connection with the Ningtu Uprising of December 1931.[11] Powerful members of the dominant faction of the party leadership thus seem to have been present in the Central Soviet Area virtually throughout the period of the republic.

To Mao Tse-tung the physical presence of the party leaders presented an extremely difficult situation. Some years later, in April 1945, he sponsored a Central Committee resolution which described, in rather general terms, the history of the Chinese Soviet Republic as a struggle between the extremely erroneous "leftist" policy of the 28 Bolsheviks and their associates on the one hand, and the more moderate, correct line of Mao and his men on the other. The "leftists", the resolution said, finally prevailed, and their erroneous line manifested itself in ideology, politics, and in military and organisational affairs. The most catastrophical consequence of the "leftist" policy was that in 1934 the Red Army was defeated and the Central Soviet Area lost to the enemy.[12]

This Mao-sponsored account of events naturally became official and unquestionable in China. Sufficient material should be available for us to examine this version, and possibly to give it more historical content. Such a task can be approached in various ways.

One approach is to study the leading personnel of the party and the soviet government, to establish who were loyal to the 28 Bolsheviks and who were Maoists, and on this basis trace a tendency in the development of power relations by pointing out who were favoured and who were not. The method may lead to results only if it is applied seriously and critically; in actual fact it has sometimes been used rather superficially. Some top cadres are, without any documentation, said to have been positively identified as "Bolsheviks", whereas closer study seems to show that they did not belong to the group.[13] The evidence given for some cadres being Maoists is that they had co-operated with Mao at an earlier stage, or that they were awarded high-ranking positions later, after Mao had brought

---

*    There is a disagreement on the whereabouts of Chang Wen-t'ien in
     1931 - 1932. (See Kung Ch'u, 1954, pp. 264-65 and 303-04; Jerome
     Ch'en, 1969, p. 95; Klein and Clark, 1971, vol. 1 p. 63; and
     Warren Kuo, <u>Analytical Hist...</u>, 1968, vol. 2 p. 481).

the party machine under control.[14] But Li Li-san and Chang Wen-t'ien also held high positions for some time after 1949. And how many of the top leaders condemned during the Cultural Revolution had worked with Mao for some time?

Professor Hsiao Tso-liang has made a very valuable contribution to the clarification of the topic through his annotation of a large number of documents from the period in question. His respect for the source material may well serve as a model for others. Nevertheless, Professor Hsiao's method has its limitations. The breaking up of his record into separate comments on individual documents prevents a systematic pursuit of an overall view.

An attempt is made in this thesis to examine the Maoist version of a gradual penetration of the leftist line, by means of studying the development within various spheres of the policy of the Chinese Soviet Republic - specifically those relating to the administration of justice, the class struggle and finances.

To clarify the penetration of the leftist line will be one of the main problems to be dealt with in later chapters. A further one will be to explore the significance of the very substantial administrative apparatus which the republic built up.

It is easy to point out that the appearance of a complicated apparatus for local administration had, in itself, revolutionary implications. It was a state of affairs vastly different from traditional China. Although the rule of the Chinese emperors was absolute in the sense that nobody could question their decisions, nevertheless, at the local level the government of the imperial bureaucracy used to be very superficial.[15] The administration of southern Kiangsi and western Fukien must also have been superficial in the period between the fall of the empire and the Communist take-over. A tremendous contrast is the vigorous attempt made by the Communists at building up a highly articulated organisational network extending to the very roots of society. They had not sufficient time to carry this scheme fully into effect in every locality of the Central Soviet Area, but in some places their achievements were impressive indeed.

The organisational efforts made by the Communists were of course aimed at putting themselves into close contact with the masses of the people; it is also clear that this aim was to a considerable extent achieved. But having made contact with the masses through this organisational network, the Communists were faced with two diverging possibilities - they could try to direct the masses, and they could listen to the masses. How much

Fig 1.  A preliminary sketch of the Chinese soviet hierarchy.

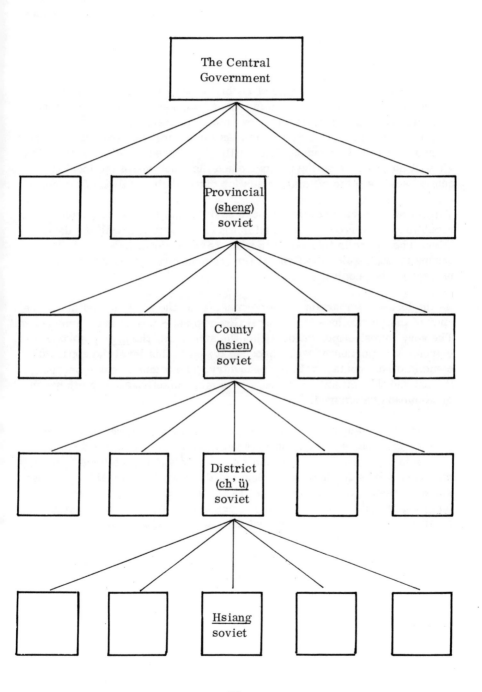

did they actually listen and how much did they direct? A hierarchy of administrative organs was built up, organs which at least theoretically derived their authority from direct or indirect election by the people; but how much real democracy was there in the system? These questions are difficult to answer.

We cannot deal with every type of revolutionary organ in the Central Soviet Area. Various mass organisations, such as poor peasant unions, trade unions, women's organisations etc., will largely be left out, as well as the organs of the Red Army. As far as organic structure is concerned, even the Communist Party will be referred to only peripherally. We will concentrate on the structure and the functions of the local and central soviets – the official organs for civil administration of the republic.

The overall structure of the Chinese soviet apparatus in the period of the republic is very roughly sketched in fig.1. We will deal with the details later. The figure is there only to indicate the several levels of local organs through which the Central Government communicated with the masses of the people.

As the locus of important decision-making for the whole soviet area, the apex of the hierarchy – the Central Government – was of great importance. The very lowest organisation within the structure, the hsiang soviet, was extremely important as well, because it was at this level the apparatus came in direct contact with the peasantry. The organs located between the top and the bottom can be dealt with more briefly, although they can by no means be ignored.

A superficial view of the apparatus as a whole does not reveal any originality whatsoever. The apparatus which had been established earlier in Russia could be sketched in the same way.[16] A closer investigation, however, seems to show that at least at the most local level the Chinese soviet structure to some extent bears the personal stamp of Mao Tsetung's approach. And above all, the originality of the Chinese soviets must be sought, not in their structure, but in their function.

# CHAPTER I.    THE HSIANG SOVIET

The administrative unit of the hsiang* ought to be explored to every possible extent. It existed as a traditional unit in the countryside, but where the Communists found it unsuitable for their purposes, they re-demarcated it, which normally meant that it was reduced in size. There were two re-demarcation drives, one in 1931 – 32 and one in 1933. The standards used are indicated in table 1.

Table 1

A.   Rules for the size of the hsiang population, as laid down by a CEC resolution of November 1931.

|  | Maximum population |
|---|---|
| Hsiang located in hill areas | 3,000 |
| Hsiang located in plain areas | 5,000 |

Source:  Doc. 1 art. 2.

B.   Rules for the size of the hsiang population, as laid down by a CEC resolution of July 1933.

|  | Normal size of population | Absolute minimum | Absolute maximum |
|---|---|---|---|
| Hsiang located in plain areas, especially densely populated | 2,000 | | 2,500 |
| Hsiang located in a mixed area of plains and hills, with medium density of population | 1,500 | | |
| Hsiang located in thinly populated hill areas | 1,000 | 250 | |

Source: Doc. 22.

---

*    The Chinese term has been retained as preferable to the misleading term "township".

Although the hsiang in the period of the republic represented the lowest
self-contained soviet organization, as far as the countryside was concerned
it was not the smallest administrative unit. The village (ts'un) was
smaller. In the late part of the period the regulations said that there should
be from two to five villages in each hsiang. [1] A separate village soviet
which had in some places been established at an earlier stage, was officially abolished in November 1931, [2] but efforts were subsequently made
to build up a network of hsiang soviet branches to permeate the villages.

The unit of the hsiang was suitable as a seat for the basic soviet organisation. It was large enough to prevent fragmentation of the local
government. And it was small enough to facilitate to some extent the
efforts made to establish intimate contact between the apparatus and
the masses of the people.

There were nevertheless tremendous problems involved in creating this
intimate contact - problems which were never fully overcome. Election
to the hsiang soviet was one of the main instruments made use of for
establishing contact, but it was by no means easy to make the election
work as it was intended.

## The Election

It was not an election by the whole of the population. The regime did
not claim to be a democracy without qualifications; it professed to be a
class democracy. It called itself a Workers' and Peasants' Democratic
Dictatorship[3] - a concept first put forward by Lenin in 1905. [4] Allowing
for some generalisation this meant a democracy for those who had
suffered exploitation before the revolution, and a dictatorship against the
former exploiters - a democracy for the vast majority, and a dictatorship against a small minority. To the individual the question of which
of the two groups he belonged to would mean a tremendous lot. This
question was actualised at the time of the hsiang election - the previously
exploited masses had the right to vote, while the former exploiters had
not. The vote was given to workers, poor peasants, middle peasants,
self-employed persons etc.; while those excluded were landlords, rich
peasants, capitalists, Buddhist monks, Taoist priests, police and
bureaucrats of the Kuomintang government, and others. [5]

The regulations on the right to vote were not original; they were modelled
on the rules embodied in Russian constitutions of 1918 and 1925. [6] It is

therefore the more interesting to note that the Mao-sponsored party resolution of April 1945 criticised them, saying that one of the blunders made by the Chinese "leftists" in the early thirties was to deprive all exploiters of political rights.[7] The criticism was made at a time when the Chinese Communists no longer were advocating the Workers' and Peasants' Democratic Dictatorship, but the widely different, Mao-designed, New Democracy.

Mao Tse-tung is probably right in maintaining that the policy of consistently excluding the exploiters from political rights was introduced in the Chinese Soviet Republic by his "leftist" opponents; nevertheless, at the time of the republic he did indeed himself contribute to the execution of the same policy.[8] In this, as in several other respects, he was by no means his own master in those years.

Mao may also have been critical toward another provision, introduced with the electoral regulations of 1933. The issue was this time the ideological dilemma arising from the fact that the peasantry, and not the proletariat, constituted the main force in the Chinese revolution. In an attempt to bring more of the proletarian element into local soviet work it was laid down that the workers' votes should carry almost four times as much weight as those of the peasants at the election on the hsiang level. Whereas normally one regular delegate should be elected for every 50 peasant electors*, the normal ratio for the workers was 1 to 13.[9] A similar arrangement had in principle been suggested at an early stage by a Comintern resolution on Chinese questions.[10] A very feeble protest may possibly be read out of Mao's comment in December 1933 on the introduction of this system in Ch'angkang hsiang – he said that less than one tenth of the population of the hsiang had a correct understanding of the leadership of the proletariat.[11]


There were altogether three elections at the hsiang level in the period of the republic. The way in which the first one, of early 1932, was conducted, was later heavily ciriticised by the Vice-Chairman of the Central Government, Hsiang Ying.[12] Nevertheless, this first election was in Mao Tse-tung's view better than the second one, held in the later part of the same year[13]; various grave errors committed in the second election are recorded in a resolution of the Central Executive Committee.[14] The negative experience seems to have enabled the leadership to get the third and last election, held in late 1933, more under control.

---

\*    Certain other non-proletarian groups in the countryside were treated equally with the poor and middle peasants in this regard.

The local soviets were instructed to establish special committees to be charged with the tasks of preparing and supervising the electoral procedures. It should be noted, however, that in 1932 such election committees in most cases either failed to materialise or were found to be inefficient, so that certain staff members of the soviets had to do the work instead.[15] One of the things supposed to be carried out under the supervision of an election committee was the registration of those among the local population who were entitled to vote, and those who were not[16] – an obvious prerequisite for implementation of the class line in the election.

Another task to be carried out before the election was to nominate the candidates. We are here indeed at a crucial point – we know that in late 1932 the nomination in many cases made a sham of the whole hsiang election, since everything was decided beforehand.[17] According to Mao's report this happened even in the model hsiang of Ch'angkang as late as the autumn of 1933; the hsiang party branch nominated exactly as many candidates as were to be elected, formal discussions of the list of candidates in the trade unions and the poor peasant union meant no alteration, and the list was finally voted upon and adopted unaltered by the local electorate.[18]

The Central Government made efforts to introduce a more democratic procedure than this. It laid down regulations that the local election committee should draw up the list of candidates, after having consulted various mass organisations such as trade unions, the poor peasant union, the women's association and others. It was recommended that the list should contain twice as many names as delegates to be elected, to enable the people to have a real choice. The list was to be made known well in advance of the election, so that it could be fully discussed by the masses.[19]

It is interesting to record Mao Tse-tung's account from late 1933 of how the inhabitants of Lower Ts'aihsi in Fukien made their comments on the result of the nomination. Copies of a list of candidates containing somewhat more than 160 names, from whom 91 might be elected, were pasted up in the various villages of the hsiang, and many local people expressed their opinions by writing underneath the individual names. "Some", Mao noted, "wrote two characters, some five or six characters and some more than ten characters. The minors (erh-t'ung) wrote also. Most often were written the words "good" or "not good". There were also some who wrote "approve" or "passive", and under one name was written "bureaucrat"."[20]

We are here touching the most interesting point of all so far as election is concerned. How much real influence did the popular voice have? It is, however, very much easier to raise such questions than to answer them. How common was the practice of writing on the list on the wall? Report of this has been found only from the hsiang of Lower Ts'aihsi. What about those wo did not master the art of writing? And to what extent were the mass organisations actually consulted for the nomination? How much did the masses speak through the mass organisations, or how much were the same organisations influenced or dominated by the local party branch? For reason of source material we have to leave the questions, and proceed from the preparatory election work to the election itself.

The election differed very much from most Westerners' image of a poll. The election meeting* in the Central Chinese Soviet Area was a sort of mass meeting; it was a selective mass meeting where only those entitled to vote were admitted.[21] There was no secret casting of a ballot - every one voted simultaneously by a show of hands.[22] The electoral regulations of 1931 allowed for a very summary procedure, saying that the participants at the election meeting might, if the majority among them so wanted, vote upon the list of recommended candidates as a whole.[23] This option was done away with through the regulations of August 1933; henceforth the candidates must be submitted and voted upon one by one.[24] Finally, the 1933 regulations required that separate election meetings should be held for the workers;[25] this was in order to give effect to the provision granting extra weight to the proletarian votes.

How much did the voice of the masses count? Unfortunately we cannot penetrate very deep into this cardinal problem. From the election of 1933 we do have some very brief reports of candidates who failed to be elected after having been heavily criticised by the people. These reports are scattered, deriving from various hsiang. And what were the reasons for the rejections? Among the unfortunate candidates were one or two who had deserted from the Red Army, there was one woman who came from a landlord family, there were some cadres who had been passive in their work or had been vacillating in the struggle against class enemies, and so on.[26] What should be noted is that the reported mass criticism of candidates conformed very well to the party line. It may indeed also have represented the voice of the people - in the struggle against common enemies the intentions of the party and the masses might very well to a large extent converge. However, the desires of a people tend to be more

---

\* According to the electoral regulations of 1931 one election meeting should normally be held for every village. (Doc.2 art.18). The 1933 regulations said that, as far as the peasant population was concerned, one election meeting should normally be held for every wu-tzu, which in this connection meant a group of houses within a village. (Doc.4 art.11).

diversified than the line of a Communist party. There must even have been some anti-party tendencies among the masses of the Central Soviet Area; the large numbers that fled from certain soviet districts[27] are sufficient evidence of that. But anti-party tendencies were not supposed to be brought to bear on the election of soviet delegates.

Apart from the election of delegates there was another device supposed to help in channelling the will of the masses into the hsiang soviet: this was the motion (t'i-an) discussed and adopted by the local electorate. Such a motion was drafted by the election committee[28] - in this connection we may note that at least by 1933 the committee would as a rule include local representatives from the soviet organisation, the party and the mass organisations.[29] The draft was supposed to be discussed and altered by the masses at the election meetings, and the formal motion should finally be submitted to the newly elected soviet congress of the hsiang.[30] We know fairly well the contents of two such motions, both carried in 1933; they called for increased recruitment to the Red Army, economic mobilisation, building of roads, etc.[31] If we search for evidence of the democratic functioning of the system, we may to some extent be disappointed - the contents of the reported motions reflected a little too closely the aims of the party and the Central Government. What would have happened if the masses had wanted to carry a motion for the building of Buddhist temples in connection with a religious revival, for example a revival of the type which some soviet districts saw in the winter of 1933 - 34 ?[32]

The masses could not be left unguided. The regime aimed at mobilising the resources and energies among them for struggle against the enemy and for safeguarding the people against a resurrection of the old class exploitation. There was undoubtedly a great deal of genuine support among the population for such a policy, and this support was to be canalised and organised through the soviets. But the regime would not give way to tendencies among the people which it deemed ran contrary to the above aims. The masses should be listened to, but they must also be led.

To lead the masses was in fact a very important function of the election movement. The movement included large-scale propaganda campaigns, with the aim of educating the people in the revolutionary significance of the soviets and of the soviet election, and to raise morale in the mobilisation for struggle against the enemy. In Mao Tse-tung's view, propaganda work was of cardinal importance - it was decisive for the outcome of the whole election.[33]

The masses should be listened to, and they must also be led. We are here touching a principle which was supposed to run through the whole political system - the Leninist concept of Democratic Centralism.[34] This principle meant that the will and opinions of the people should find their way upward through the hierarchy of the soviet apparatus, right to the top; while the same apparatus simultaneously was to be used for communicating the directives of the central organs downward, right down to the masses of the people. Our discussion of the electoral procedures does show that some efforts were made to carry the principle into effect; let us attempt to examine its implementation further through a study of the organic structure and the functioning of the hsiang soviet.

The structure and the functioning of the hsiang soviet are fields where there is a serious shortage of material. This is especially so for the early part of the period under consideration - even at that time there seem to have been some hsiang soviets which were fairly well organised,[35] but on the whole the situation was apparently fairly bad. In April 1932 Hsiang Ying complained that in some places the elected soviet delegates only met to choose a chairman for the hsiang, and after that they did no more.[36] However, it is clear that a most significant development of the system took place later.

An attempt to describe in some detail the structure and the functioning of the hsiang soviet must be based almost exclusively on sources from late 1933 and early 1934. Unfortunately the material presents more instructions and regulations than reports on how the system functioned in actual fact. The reports are not totally lacking. Mao Tse-tung's surveys do permit some interesting glimpses of the actual life of three model hsiang soviets in Kiangsi and Fukien, but the state of affairs in these model hsiang cannot be expected to be representative of the general situation. We cannot do very much more than describe how the hsiang soviet was supposed to be organised, and how it was expected to function, in the late period of the republic.

The Staff

The various institutions of the hsiang soviet are shown in fig.2. At the top of the structure stood the representative congress, which derived its authority from election by the people. Beneath this were two other bodies, elected directly or indirectly by the congress - the presidium and the staff. The latter was a small body, made up of the chairman, the vice-

Fig. 2. The structure of the hsiang soviet in the late period of the republic.

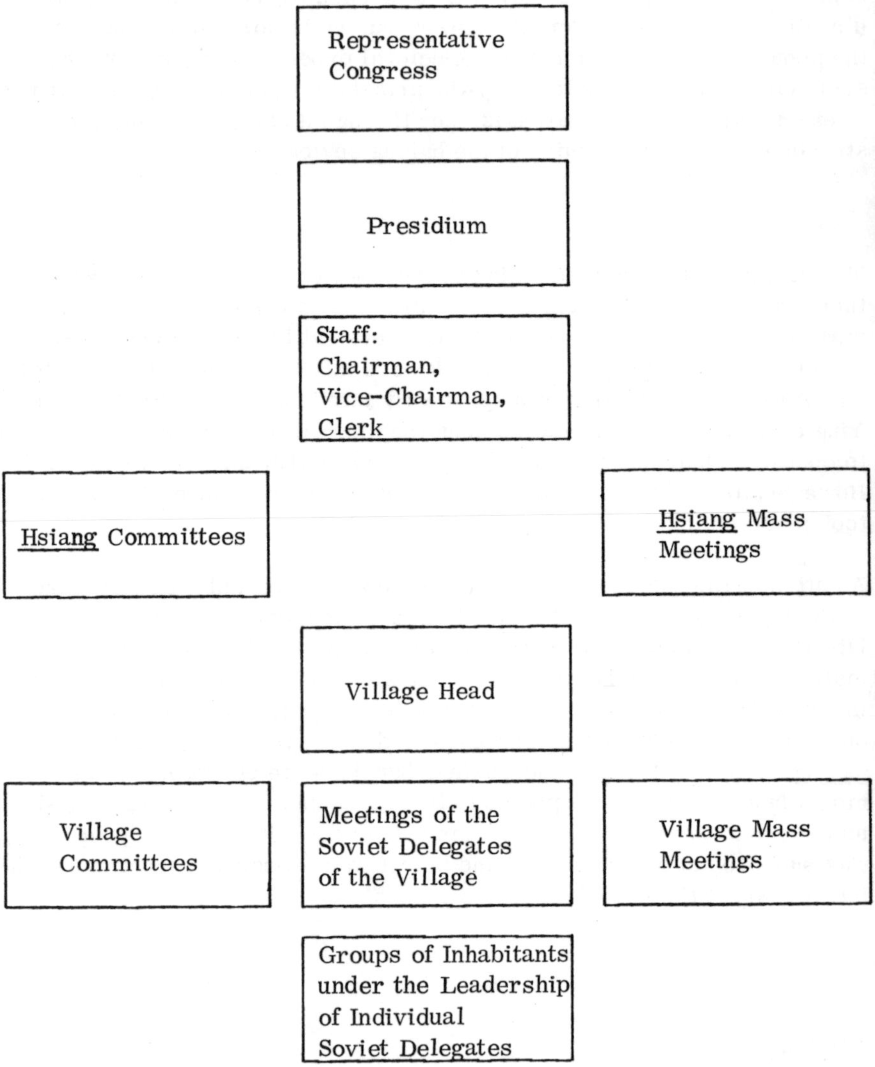

```
                    ┌──────────────────────┐
                    │  Representative       │
                    │  Congress             │
                    └──────────────────────┘

                    ┌──────────────────────┐
                    │                       │
                    │  Presidium            │
                    │                       │
                    └──────────────────────┘

                    ┌──────────────────────┐
                    │  Staff:               │
                    │  Chairman,            │
                    │  Vice-Chairman,       │
                    │  Clerk                │
                    └──────────────────────┘

┌──────────────────┐                        ┌──────────────────┐
│                  │                        │  Hsiang Mass     │
│ Hsiang Committees│                        │  Meetings        │
│                  │                        │                  │
└──────────────────┘                        └──────────────────┘

                    ┌──────────────────────┐
                    │                       │
                    │  Village Head         │
                    │                       │
                    └──────────────────────┘

┌──────────────────┐ ┌──────────────────────┐ ┌──────────────────┐
│                  │ │ Meetings of the       │ │                  │
│ Village          │ │ Soviet Delegates      │ │ Village Mass     │
│ Committees       │ │ of the Village        │ │ Meetings         │
└──────────────────┘ └──────────────────────┘ └──────────────────┘

                    ┌──────────────────────┐
                    │ Groups of Inhabitants │
                    │ under the Leadership  │
                    │ of Individual         │
                    │ Soviet Delegates      │
                    └──────────────────────┘
```

chairman and the clerk, and was the real nucleus of the whole hsiang soviet. *

The chairman and the clerk were full-time soviet employees, which would imply that they were entitled to a subsistence allowance. In larger hsiang the vice-chairman worked full time as well.[37] Formally the staff derived its authority from the representative congress - either through a direct election by the congress,[38] or through an indirect election via the presidium.[39] We may well ask how real the election was. Generally speaking, it was often the local party branch that in actual fact decided important political issues, and the choice of staff members for the hsiang soviet was of vital importance.

With regard to the work of the staff we have to rely almost wholly on the instructions which Mao Tse-tung put forward in April 1934. The lack of information on how this nucleus worked in actual fact is very regrettable.

According to Mao's instructions the chairman had to supervise the whole soviet apparatus of his hsiang, and to deal personally with the daily running of administrative work. He may in practice have had to decide himself on many minor affairs, and on questions which were too urgent to wait for a presidium meeting.

An important task for the chairman was to take care of the liaison of the hsiang soviet, both upward and downward. He was from time to time summoned to take part in conferences called by soviet institutions at a higher level, and he had to keep himself well up to date with instructions from above. As for downward liaison he was supposed to attend meetings which the hsiang soviet arranged at the village level, meetings of various soviet committees, and finally meetings arranged by various mass organisations not included in the soviet structure.

Armed with instructions from above and detailed information from below, the chairman was equipped to guide and strengthen soviet work throughout his hsiang. Within his sphere of responsibility were recruitment to the Red Army, preparation for defence against enemy attacks, detecting and combatting counter-revolutionaries, elections, promotion of agricultural production, food supply, collection of taxes, road building, educational schemes, organisation of co-operatives, improvement of sanitation, etc.

---

*   A hsiang soviet might also employ one or two persons to take care of communications and to supervise local guard posts, but they had nothing to do with the guidance of the apparatus as a whole.
    (Doc. 6 art. 51; doc. 9 A pp. 10-11; doc. 34 art. 10).

He was charged with drawing the attention of the presidium and of the representative congress to the special problems of, and also to the experience gained by, the various villages. If a village lagged behind in any respect, the chairman had to see to it that efforts be made to solve the difficulties. [40]

The tasks of the vice-chairman were very similar to those of the chairman. He might be allotted one or two villages as his special area of responsibility; but he also had to keep himself well acquainted with the affairs of the whole hsiang, to be able to take the place of the chairman if the latter was absent. In the daily running of soviet administration, the amount of work allotted to the vice-chairman naturally depended on whether he was a full time worker of the soviet apparatus or not. [41]

The clerk was to assist the chairman and the vice-chairman in taking care of liaison with village meetings, committees and mass organisations. In addition to that he was charged with keeping records on landholdings and population, taking care of the registration of births, deaths and marriages, providing for liaison with other localities, dealing with passports, dispatching instructions and messages from the hsiang soviet to the various villages, helping illiterate dependants of Red Army soldiers to write letters, etc. [42]

Mao Tse-tung then gives the following revealing instruction:

> "------- if the chairman and the vice-chairman are illiterates (pu chih-tzu), [the clerk shall] read aloud the documents from their superiors for them; at the meetings of the presidium and the representative congress [he shall] read the important items of the documents, write the record of the meetings, inform the chairman and the vice-chairman of matters which have not caught their attention." [43]

It seems not to have been unusual that even the chairman and the vice-chairman of the hsiang soviet were illiterates. The clerk, however, not only had to be a literate, he had to be able to read and write fairly well.

Surveys carried out under the leadership of Professor John Lossing Buck, the results of which were first published in 1937, have supplied some interesting data on the rate of literacy in China. In rural districts investigated in South China, 49.1 per cent of the males and 2.6 per cent of the females above the age of seven had attended a school to any extent. However, only 34.6 per cent of the males and 1.6 per cent of the females were classified as literates. [44]

We cannot tell how representative these figures are for the situation in the rural districts of the Central Soviet Area in the period under consideration. On one hand one might expect that the rate of literacy here toward the end of the period was rather above the average, as a result of the efforts made by the Communists in the educational field. On the other hand the very extensive recruitment to the Red Army drew heavily on personnel possessing the highly valued combination of education and a social background of non-exploiting class origin.

A difficult problem in choosing leading personnel for the soviet administration must have been whether emphasis should be placed on education or on a sound social background according to Communist standards. After the Red Army, from which the exploiting classes were excluded, [45] had levied its heavy toll on the resources of literates among the workers and the poor and middle peasants, the people with the highest level of education would very often be found in landlord and rich peasant families - it was mainly these families that in the old society could afford the luxury of sending their children to school. In such circumstances it might have been very tempting to relax the demand for a non-exploiting class background when choosing persons for certain jobs within the soviet apparatus, among them that of hsiang clerk.

On the other hand, the Communist Party, with its network of local branches, would of course be anxious to prevent the employment of not wholly reliable personnel in important positions in the soviet apparatus. Obviously it must have been very dangerous to trust for instance a former landlord - whose property had been confiscated under the new regime, and whose relatives had perhaps been shot - with the clerical work of a hsiang soviet under the control of illiterate superiors. The position would have been an Eldorado for a saboteur.

The Presidium

The presidium (chu-hsi-t'uan)[46] was positioned between the staff on the one hand, and the representative congress on the other. Of the three, the representative congress was theoretically the most powerful, [47] after which came the presidium - designated as the highest political organ of the hsiang when the congress was not in session[48] - and in spite of its importance the status of the staff must formally have been a subordinate one. With regard to the amount of real work carried out by the three bodies, the relationship was, however, reversed. The daily burden of administrative work was carried by the staff, the presidium was called for sessions relatively frequently, while the large representative congress met at somewhat longer intervals.

The presidium counted from five to seven persons, chosen by and among the representative congress.[49] Mao Tse-tung took for granted that the soviet chairman was a member of the presidium, and that he presided over its meetings.[50] Mao has also recorded the following composition of this body in Ch'angkang hsiang in Hsingkuo county of Kiangsi:

The soviet chairman
The vice-chairman
The clerk
The local branch secretary of the Communist Party
The local branch secretary of the Communist Youth League[51]

There was evidently nothing accidental about the composition of the presidium in this particular case - it was the staff supplemented by the party and the youth league secretaries.

The presidium was supposed to meet quite frequently, once in five days, and it was authorised to take decisions on issues which either were not of primary importance, or were too urgent to wait for a meeting of the representative congress. And probably more important than that, the presidium was trusted with preparing and guiding the meetings of the congress, which must in practice have meant that many issues formally decided upon by the latter were in actual fact determined by the former. Moreover, the presidium was to follow up the decisions taken by either of the two organs, to ensure that they were actually carried out, and this required close contact with those responsible for work at the village level, and with the masses themselves.[52]

The Representative Congress

The representative congress of the hsiang soviet was a rather large body. In Ch'angkang hsiang it was in late 1933 reported to be composed of 55 delegates.[53] As a result of the new electoral regulations of that year the number in Lower Ts'aihsi increased from 73 to 91, while Upper Ts'aihsi for the same reason saw an increase from 53 to 75.[54] It is not clear whether or not the alternate delegates (hou-pu tai-piao) are included in the figures - the regulations said that one of these should be elected for every five regular delegates.[55] We know that the alternates had the right to take part in the discussions of the congress,[56] and even persons not elected at all might occasionally be present at its meetings.[57]

The extra weight given to the proletarian votes by the electoral regulations of 1933, as well as the broad interpretation given to the term "worker", had much effect on the social composition of the congress. Of the 75 delegates elected that year in Upper Ts'aihsi, as many as 35 represented workers.[58]

Another interesting aspect is the ratio of delegates for the two sexes. In January 1934 it was reported that female delegates in the majority of cases constituted more than 25 per cent of the total.[59] As for more specific data we are informed that the election of November 1932[60] resulted in slightly more than 30 per cent of female delegates in Upper Ts'aihsi, and slightly less than 29 per cent in Lower Ts'aihsi. Really surprising is the development in the two hsiang in the period between this election and that one year later, resulting in a ratio that would very rarely be found in local representative bodies in western countries, and which it is even more astonishing to find in China against the background of the low position of women in traditional Chinese society. In the intervening period the number of female delegates had, through by-elections, increased so as to constitute slightly more than 62 per cent of the total in Upper Ts'aihsi and slightly less than 59 per cent in Lower Ts'aihsi. The cause of this development was that large numbers of males left the locality in order to join the Red Army or to take up civil appointments.[61]

The hsiang congress – a relatively large body of representatives from the toiling masses – was, at least formally, made the most powerful political organ of the locality. Moreover, the delegates to the congress were supposed to serve as cadres for the regime in a broad sense, in that a number of tasks were given to them individually. The system was new and unfamiliar to the people, and it was by no means easy to make it work properly. Mao Tse-tung was well aware of the problem, and pointed out that the delegates must be disciplined and educated by the presidium:

"If there are among the delegates some who are working actively, and also some who are passive and retarding the work (tai-kung), then one must praise the model work of the active ones, so that the passive ones can learn from them. Toward the passive ones one must apply criticism, some of them must be named at the meetings of the representative congress in order to lead all [the others] to struggle against them. In this way one can educate the whole number of delegates and make the passive ones active."[62]

The quoted passage shows that not much authority was left to the individual delegate when facing the apparatus as a whole. He was to be educated, led, and if necessary urged to work for the common good. The passage deals mainly with problems relating to the work of delegates as individuals; elsewhere Mao complains of unsystematic proceedings at the meetings of many hsiang congresses – confused discussions leading to no result. [63] His instructions of April 1934 show much concern for making the congress work in an orderly and effective way.

A meeting of the hsiang congress was normally to be held every ten days. [64] Mao thought a systematic procedure could best be obtained if the soviet chairman, with his particular experience and insight, presided over the meeting. [65] A representative from the superior district soviet ought to be present, to convey instructions from above. [66] The items on the agenda might have been raised through directives from soviet organs on a higher level – what was then left to be discussed were the methods of execution – or they could be raised locally. [67] The tilling of land, road building, military and economic mobilisation – these are examples of matters which might be dealt with. [68] Not more than two or three items should be discussed at one meeting, said Mao. [69] He also pointed out that a meeting ought not to last for more than two or three hours, and within this time there should be a certain balance between reports and discussions. [70]

At one essential point we are left ignorant – it is not clear whether or not there was any voting over the issues at the meetings of the hsiang congress "The result of the discussion becomes decision (t'ao-lun ti chieh-kuo ch'eng-wei chüeh-i)," said Mao Tse-tung in his instructions. [71] This may seem to imply that he had no voting in view whatsoever, and that the decisions were supposed to be reached in the way that the chairman guided and summed up the discussion. But we cannot draw any definite conclusion based on this single sentence.

To reach a decision was one thing, but at least as important was to ensure that the decision was carried into effect. One of the tasks of the congress was to investigate the work actually carried out in the various villages of the hsiang; from Ch'angkang hsiang it was reported that half of the meetings were devoted to such investigations. [72] Reports of the village heads on what had so far been done, were essential on these occasions. Lessons were drawn from the process of work in the various villages, the problems were discussed in this new light, and persons responsible for failures might be criticised. [73]

Our discussion of the three leading organs of the hsiang soviet will have shown that the centralist aspect of the system was considered to be of great importance – the leading role of the staff and of the presidium was strongly emphasised. Nevertheless, communications were supposed to go in both directions. The ordinary soviet delegates were regarded as bearing the mandate of the people, and they were supposed to be listened to by their superiors in the local soviet organisation.[74]

### Groups of Soviet Delegates and Work at the Village Level

The duty of a soviet delegate was by no means confined to his participation in the meetings of the hsiang congress. His tasks outside these meetings were many, and taken together extremely important. The most direct contact between the soviet apparatus and the masses of the people was supposed to be attained, not through any of the hsiang institutions described so far, but through devices at a lower level.

One of the institutions on a lower level, referred to by sources of December 1933 and January 1934, is a rather obscure one. It was laid down that the delegates should be organised in small groups, each of them made up of from three to seven persons and having its own leader. The leader was supposed to take care of the liaison between the hsiang presidium and the group, to guide his group of delegates in their work, and to arrange for mass meetings on a small scale.[75] Strangely enough, in his instructions of April 1934 Mao Tse-tung does not even mention this institution, but describes instead in some detail certain others, those working within the unit of a village.

The regulations said that there should be from two to five villages (ts'un) in each hsiang, [76] but in actual fact there were some soviet hsiang where the village did not even exist as an administrative unit.[77] From Mao's reports of late 1933 we find that the average number of inhabitants of each village was 446 in Ch'angkang hsiang, 580 in Upper Ts'aihsi and 653 in Lower Ts'aihsi.[78]

A village head (ts'un chu-jen) was supposed to guide all local soviet work. The people of the village might agree to till his fields for him without any charge, so that he could devote his time wholly to his administrative duties. According to Mao's instructions he was to be assisted by a deputy head, and both the head and his deputy had to be chosen from among the

29

delegates to the hsiang congress. Normally every ten days the head was to call the delegates from his village for a meeting, in order to solve certain local problems, to sum up the experience of soviet activity in the locality, and finally to discuss preparations for mass meetings in the village. [79)]

Mass meetings were to be arranged twice a month. Normally two meetings were to be held simultaneously in the same village, each of them comprising about half of the population*; the village head presided over one and his deputy over the other. [80)] The village mass meeting was one of the means used for educating the masses and for raising their spirit in the struggle for the revolution and for economic reconstruction. Here, as in all instances where the soviet apparatus and the masses met, communications were supposed to go in both directions; soviet decisions were to be made known and explained to the people, and the opinions of the people were to be communicated to the soviets. However, on at least three occasions Mao Tse-tung found it necessary to stress that the masses should be led or urged to bring forward their opinions, [81)] thus revealing that free communication from the roots of society upward was not always, and perhaps seldom, easy to realise.

### The Soviet Delegates and Groups of Villagers

As far as the most advanced districts of the Central Soviet Area were concerned, probably the most important type of meeting for the common people came to be held at a level still lower than that of the village. Here we reach an institution which more than any one of those described above was a vehicle through which intimate contact between the soviet apparatus and the masses could be effected. The delegates to the hsiang soviet were instructed to work separately. The village population was divided into groups, each of which was placed under the guidance of a delegate**. According to one document these groups should normally comprise from 30 to 70 persons, [82)] but Mao Tse-tung reports that in Ch'angkang they sometimes numbered less than 30, [83)] and in Ts'aihsi in some cases even less than 20. [84)]

---

\* If the population was very concentrated, one meeting would be held for the whole village. Occasionally mass meetings might even be arranged for the whole hsiang. (Doc. 9 A pp. 26 - 27).

\*\* There may be some sort of relationship between these groups and the old pao-chia system.

According to Mao Tse-tung's instructions a delegate was supposed to call a meeting of his group every 10 days. The purposes of the meetings can best be described in Mao's own words:

"----- investigate the way in which every family is performing the soviet work, discuss the tasks that should be carried out at present, announce agreements on competitions, report the decisions of the hsiang soviet, collect the opinions of the masses and report them to the representative meetings of the village and the hsiang."[85]

"At these meetings one must lead the people to bring forth mutual criticism, for instance if one family harbours a deserter who will not return to his unit, one family is not industrious in the spring ploughing, one family is not making efforts to help the families of the Red Army men in tilling their fields, one lonely (ku-lao) family is in need of help and nobody pays attention to it, one family does not urge sons and daughters to study, one family does not pay attention to sanitation, etc."[86]

The delegate was furthermore supposed, within the group of people under his guidance, to persuade activists to join the Red Army, people generally to join co-operatives, and uneducated adults to start learning at night schools. He should also lead the people in watching the activities of the landlords and the rich peasants.[87] And his work in the group was not limited to the meetings.

"Apart from these meetings every delegate must also take some time for visiting every person under his leadership, to see whether they have some problem that needs to be solved, and whether they have carried out the soviet decisions. In the first place he should visit the homes of the Red Army men's dependants and of the poorest people. He also must go to have a look in the homes of landlords and rich peasants, to see whether they are doing something which is not right."[88]

A small group of villagers, with its regular meetings, led and supervised in various social activities by a representative of the local government - it would be hard to imagine an institution through which intimate contact between the apparatus and the people could be carried further. If one takes this group system at its face value, one important question will be to what extent it was used for directing the people, and to what degree it was used for communicating the will of the people to the local soviets in order to form their policy. Another essential problem, related to the first one, concerns the degree to which the local soviets directed, or were directed by, the top agencies of the state and the party.

31

The discussion of these questions must be deferred. Here, however, we ought to state that we know very little about the extent to which the system of grouping the villagers was in actual fact implemented in the Central Soviet Area. As late as April 1934, not very long before the Communist forces had to pull out, the scheme had in many places not even begun to be introduced.[89] On the other hand we know that it really was carried into effect in some places, while having to admit that even there we are ignorant on how far it was developed.[90]

## Committees

The committees constituted another very important part of the soviet network designed to permeate the small localities. In membership they were not so comprehensive as the groups led by soviet delegates; nevertheless they engaged a large number of local people, and their work affected everybody. An impression of their scope of activity can be obtained from Mao's report of December 1933 from Ch'angkang, where the following committees had been established at the hsiang level:[91]

1. The Committee for Red Army Expansion.

2. The Land Committee (had not been operative since September 1933).

3. The Land Registration Committee (had been active from July to September 1933).

4. The Committee for Hills and Woodlands

5. The Construction Committee. (Mao thought this committee was superfluous).

6. The Watercontrol (shui-li) Committee.

7. The Bridge Committee.

8. The Committee for State Property.

9. The Granary Committee.

10. The Confiscation Committee.

11. The Land Investigation Committee (was by December 1933 a thing of the past).

12. The Education Committee.

13. The Sanitation Committee.

14. The Committee for Protection Against Air Attacks and Poison Gas.

15. The Committee of Arrangements (charged with arranging commemoration meetings).


This list may look impressive as it is, but it by no means gives the whole picture. A number of the committees in Ch'angkang - most of which counted from five to nine members - had their five-man strong subcommittees within each of the four villages of the hsiang. The chairman of the subcommittee in the village was a member of the hsiang committee as well. Mao strongly approved this type of network, but he criticised one strange phenomenon which illustrates very well the difficulty of obtaining organisational uniformity in the soviet area. Even in this model hsiang the committees were regarded as "mass organisations" (ch'ün-chung t'uan-t'i) - comparable, for instance, to the trade unions and the poor peasant union - and not as components of the soviet apparatus.[92]

Of course the committees were supposed to be part of the local soviet organisation. Mao Tse-tung said that their members, as far as the hsiang level was concerned, should be nominated by the presidium and appointed by the representative congress; whereas the village head and the meeting of soviet delegates from the village were entrusted respectively with the nomination and the appointment of the members of the subcommittees.[93] Every soviet delegate was supposed to be a member of one or two committees,[94] and these delegates would presumably to a large extent take care of the committees' liaison upward, to the representative congress. However, Mao Tse-tung emphasised the necessity of a direct liaison between the committees at the hsiang level on the one hand, and the presidium and the staff on the other; at every meeting of a hsiang committee, he said, a member of the presidium should be present.[95]

The committees were indeed supposed to be an extremely significant part of the soviet apparatus. Whereas the groups of villagers led by each soviet delegate should organise the masses in the very broadest sense, the committees were to organise the work of the "activists" (chi-chi fen-tzu) among the population. Apart from the local soviet delegates, representatives from various mass organisations ought to be committee members.[96]

The committees were specialised agencies for the work of the activists. An idea of the specialisation can be obtained from the above list of 15 committees in Ch'angkang; we may also note that the draft bill for local soviets, of December 1933, suggested altogether 31 permanent or temporary committees at the hsiang level.[97)] Moreover, according to Mao's instructions there should be a sort of specialisation within each of these specialised institutions – one of the duties of the committee chairman was to allot special tasks after the meetings to be performed by each of the members.[98)] We can again discern the finespun web of soviet organs designed to permeate everything at the roots of society.

## The Blueprint and the Reality

As already pointed out, our description of the organisation and functioning of the hsiang soviet is to a very large extent based on instructions and re‐gulations. How far did the institutions develop in actual fact?

We know that by late 1933 they operated rather successfully in three hsiang – namely Ch'angkang in Kiangsi and Lower and Upper Ts'aihsi in Fukien – in spite of some peculiar shortcomings. Implementation in these localities of early instructions from the Central Government must have been part of the reason for this success, but to a considerable extent the relationship was apparently the other way round: Mao's general instructions of April 1934, and perhaps also the draft bill for local soviets of December 1933, may have been partly based on the experience gained in the three hsiang. However that may be, we know that these three hsiang soviets had in actual fact grouped the inhabitants around the individual soviet delegates, that they had a number of committees, that each of them had a presidium (although this institution was called by other names), and that their representative congresses met regularly.[99)]

On the other hand, some local soviets were extremely bad. This fact is illustrated very well by the following open letter, printed in Hung-se Chung-hua of January 1st 1934, and addressed to the soviet chairman and the clerk of a hsiang soviet in Menling county in Yüehkan:

> "Under your bed there is a big rice basket. It is full of documents from superior organs (shang-chi). When the documents arrive, you neither read them nor discuss them, but just drop them under the bed. If anybody points out this error of yours, you even say: "I am illiterate." "[100)]

Between the good ones and the bad ones there were presumably all grades of hsiang soviets. The situation was summed up at the Second National Soviet Congress in January 1934: The local soviet work proceeded rather smoothly in a number of localities, but in many places it did not.[101)]

34

## Democracy or Centralism?

When reviewing the hsiang apparatus which the Communists made efforts to build up, and which they managed partially to carry into effect, one is struck by the great emphasis laid on establishing an intimate contact with the masses of the people. The staff was told to pay constant attention to keeping itself in close contact with work at the lower levels, as were the presidium and the representative congress. At mass meetings of the village, and occasionally of the whole hsiang, the local leaders and the people were to stand face to face. In addition we have the ingenious scheme of grouping the inhabitants around the single soviet delegates, a system which was to affect everybody. Likewise the specialised work of the committees was intended to permeate society almost totally.

Yet this is only the soviet apparatus. Although no attempt can be made here, this picture ought ideally to be completed with a description of the party, the Communist Youth League, the militia system and the mass organisations (the poor peasant unions, the trade unions, the women's associations etc.).

The ingenious organisational web designed to establish a close relationship with the masses is one thing. The purpose to which this intimate relationship was put is another. Having built up such an apparatus the top leaders could try to use it for developing a very high form of democracy, or they could attempt to use it for controlling the people completely. Officially the whole system was one of Democratic Centralism, but was it the democratic or the centralist aspect which should be stressed? In contemporary Communist sources both aspects are emphasised.

There should be no reason whatsoever for doubting the sincerity of the statements stressing the centralist aspect of the soviet system at the hsiang level. They were directly based on the needs of the revolutionary struggle.

"----- rely on the firm leadership in the village by the people's
own delegates to the hsiang soviet, by the village committees and
by the mass organisations, make the people of the whole village
organise like a network under the soviet, to carry out all kinds of
soviet work, --------". [102]
(Mao Tse-tung, toward the end of 1933).

"The central task of the soviets is to mobilise the broad masses to
take part in the revolutionary war, through the revolutionary war to
defeat imperialism and the Kuomintang, to spread the revolution to
the whole of China, to evict imperialism from China. To lead the

35

revolutionary war is the central task of the soviets -----."[103)
(Mao Tse-tung at the Second National Soviet Congress in January
1934.)

Examples of stressing the democratic aspect of the soviet system are
frequently found in Chinese Communist documents. It is true that Mao
Tse-tung's statement at the Second National Soviet Congress that
"every problem is discussed and decided upon in accordance with the
will of the people", [104) could, by itself, easily be dismissed as empty
propaganda. The declaration by the same congress that the soviets
must "swiftly and properly solve the difficulties of the masses", [105) is
open to the question of who was supposed to decide what constituted,
and what was the right way of solving, the masses' difficulties. Neverthe
less, there must have been some sincerity in the many pronouncements
stressing the democratic side of the system. Exhortations, such as to
"adopt (hsi-shou) the opinions of the masses"[106) or to "enable the masse
fully to express their opinions toward the soviet work", [107) were
evidently meant as practical instructions for those in charge of the management of the local soviet apparatus, and not as mere propaganda move

An ingenious framework was gradually being built up at the hsiang level,
supplying the organic base upon which a democratic system might be
developed. We may assume that a certain amount of democracy in local
matters actually did evolve in the wake of this building-up process. But
unfortunately other factors were simultaneously working in an opposite
direction - working toward filling the framework with a content quite
different from democracy. One of these factors was the tightening of the
military situation, another was the general radicalisation process which
will be dealt with in later chapters.

Soviet - China and Soviet Russia

Various problems will arise in an attempt to compare the Central Chines
Soviet Area and Russia, with respect to local administration. It seems
to be impossible to draw up a complete picture for either. The local
administrative units of the two countries were of course not identical,
and as far as Russia is concerned, it is not clear which period ought to
be chosen for the comparison.

It does not seem very appropriate to compare the Chinese soviets of
1933-34 with the contemporary ones in Russia. The Russian soviets were

about ten years older than those in China, and what may be more important is that Russia had from 1929 gone through a period of enforced collectivization, which profoundly affected the local administration of the countryside. It may be more correct, although likewise open to questioning, to compare the Chinese soviets of 1933-34, six to seven years after the start in 1927, with the Russian ones in 1923-24, six to seven years after the October Revolution.

A unique source of information on Russian local administration is Professor Merle Fainsod's Smolensk under Soviet Rule (based on a collection of documents covering the province centered in the city of Smolensk). The following is his general evaluation of soviet administration at the lowest level around 1924:

"Beneath the surface of sovietization, the life of the peasant flowed on in its accustomed way relatively untouched by the great political and social overturn which the revolution engendered in the cities. The key personage in the village, the chairman of the village soviet, more often than not, was a non-Party man far closer to the needs and aspirations of his peasant neighbors than to the demands and outlook of the far-off Soviet Power in Moscow or even Smolensk. He had to collect the taxes that higher Soviet authorities demanded, furnish recruits for the army, manage the primitive rural public services, and try, so far as was possible, to settle land quarrels and other disputes among the peasantry; but for the rest the directives which rained in from the center were largely ignored, and the village remained more or less impervious to change in the world outside."[108]

The general condition of the local rural soviets in Russia of the same period is given no higher evaluation by Professor E.H. Carr:

"The primitiveness and inefficiency of the rural district organization was multiplied tenfold at the level of the village Soviet."[109]

However, Professor Carr allows for some "active" village soviets in the Soviet Union, but they were rare. And he musters no evidence of any ideal soviet organisation at the time, not even for the model villages.[110]

It cannot be denied that the efficiency of the local Russian soviets improved in the years to come. For a short period this was to some extent brought about by utilising the administrative abilities of the kulaks, subsequently more emphasis was laid on the training of poor and middle peasants, and finally it became more usual that key positions in the villages were filled by politically trained members of the party or Komsomol. But it was mainly a development of administrative efficiency and of the centralist aspect of local government. During the hard years following the initiation of the collectivization campaign, there could not be much room for the democratic process. [111)]

In Soviet-China the development of local administration was very uneven. Even in the Central Chinese Soviet Area of 1933-34 there must have been cases of hsiang government resembling the state of affairs in the villages of Smolensk province around 1924, as represented by Professor Fainsod. But it would be tempting to challenge experts on Russian history by finding evidence in any village in the Soviet Union of 1924, or even from the following decade, of so fine an apparatus for intimate relations between the leadership and the masses of people as that reported from three modern hsiang in China in late 1933. The task might very well turn out to be impossible. And the systematic efforts made in Soviet-China, especially by Mao Tse-tung, to further develop these relations, are probably without parallel in the Soviet Union.

# CHAPTER II.  THE INTERMEDIATE SOVIETS

Within the category of local soviets we have to distinguish between two essentially different types. First there was the basic (chi-pen) soviet[1] at the hsiang level- through its own institutions it stood in contact with the masses of the people. Secondly there were the intermediate soviets of the district, the county and the province, being positioned between the basic soviet on the one hand and the organs of the Central Government on the other. The intermediate soviets had only indirect contact with the people, their main task being to supervise the soviets at the level, or the levels, below.

## Towns and Cities

A town soviet might be of either of the two types. The draft bill for local soviets of December 1933 distinguished in this regard between small and large towns. The soviet of a small town, with no more than 4,000 inhabitants, had a structure which was much similar to that of the hsiang, and accordingly it was of the basic type. However, larger towns and cities were to be divided into urban districts (shih-ch'ü) with their own separate organisations at the basic level; the soviet for the whole town or city was in this case to supervise and coordinate the work of the various urban district soviets, and therefore it was of the intermediate type.[2]

The basic urban soviets were not very different from their rural counterparts. In some cases they might be allowed a slightly larger permanent staff, and they might have some committees required in towns only.[3] It may be added that "urban" soviets were not always strictly urban; they might also have jurisdiction over small rural areas adjacent to the town.[4]

The urban soviets of the intermediate type were for towns and cities placed on a higher level than that of the hsiang; it appears that in actual fact none of them ranked higher than the district.[5] Theoretically larger cities could be placed on the same level as a county or even as a province,[6] but no evidence has been found showing that any city in the Central Soviet Area actually ranked so high.

Fig.3. The general structure of district, county and provincial soviets,
and of the soviets of towns and cities at the district level or above.

Representative Congress

Executive Committee

Presidium

Chairman
Vice-chairman(-men)
Inspectors
Clerical staff

Labour Department
Land Department
Military Department
Finance Department
Dept. of Economy (kuo-min ching-chi)
Food (liang-shih) Department
Department of Education
Department of Internal Affairs (nei-wu)
Judicial Department
Committee of the Workers' and Peasants' Inspection
Local Office of the State Political Security Bureau
Audit Committee
Department of General Affairs (Tsung-wu-ch'u)

Labour Committee
Land Committee
Finance Committee
Committee of Economy
Food Committee
Committee of Education
Committee of Internal Affairs
Judicial Committee
Committee of the State Political Security Bureau

<u>Notes to fig.3</u>

The figure is based on the draft bill for local soviets of December 1933 (doc. 6 chapters 2, 3 and 4), but an edict of November 1931 (doc. 34) had already provided for largely the same structure.

With regard to the provisions of the 1933 draft bill the following should be noted:

1.  There is an ambiguity as to whether a town with less than 50,000 inhabitants should or should not have its executive committee. (See art. 8, note to art. 9 and art. 10.)

2.  Inspectors were to be employed only by the soviets of the county and the province.

3.  The audit committee was for the provincial soviet only.

4.  Under the provincial soviet there was no military department, as military affairs at this level were to be taken care of by a special agency of the corresponding military zone (<u>chün-ch'ü</u>).

5.  In the soviets of the districts, and of towns and cities placed on the district level, the State Political Security Bureau was to be represented only by a special commissioner (<u>t'e-p'ai-yüan</u>).

6.  In addition to what is shown in the figure, it should be noted that each department was supposed to have its subdivisions (<u>k'o</u>), and in some cases several specialised committees.

---

Our sources do not supply much information on the soviets of larger towns and cities. Their structure can best be dealt with in connection with other soviets of the intermediate type.


## The Intermediate Soviets - General

The main organisations of the intermediate levels were: 1) The district soviet, supervising the work carried on in several hsiang; 2) the county soviet, supervising the work in several districts; 3) the provincial soviet, supervising the work in several counties. A clear understanding of this hierarchy, which was modelled on the system in Soviet Russia, is an indispensable prerequisite for a study of the local government of the Central Chinese Soviet Area.

The internal structure of the soviets at each of the three intermediate levels was basically the same, although the higher soviets had more staff than the lower ones. We will here first deal briefly with the organisational characteristics common to them all, and later look more specifically into the soviets at each level.

The full title of the most detailed source on the intermediate soviets is The Provisional Organic Law for Local Soviets of the Chinese Soviet Republic (Draft). [7] The document was published by the Central Executive Committee on December 12th 1933, and it is referred to in this thesis as the "draft bill for local soviets". The word "draft" makes its evaluation rather problematic - the text of the formal law has so far not been brought to light. However, since it was published by the CEC, and as Mao Tsetung referred to it as an authoritative document very shortly after that, [8] I think we can safely assume that the draft bill represents the program of the Central Government with regard to administration at the various local levels.

We also have some regulations of an earlier date. The structure of the intermediate soviets, as sketched in fig.3, is in fact basically provided for by a CEC edict already adopted in November 1931. [9]


The highest political organ of each of the intermediate soviets was naturally the representative congress. Between the rare sessions of this body the highest political authority was vested in the executive committee, which was elected from the members of the congress. However, even the executive committee met rather infrequently; and when it was not in session, the highest political organ was the presidium, which was elected from the members of the executive committee. The presidium met relatively often.[10] The presidium selected from among its own members a chairman and one, or in some cases two, vice-chairmen.[11]

So much for the central institutions of an intermediate soviet – institutions charged with coordinative work and with tasks of a general nature. A glance at fig.3 will show that there were also a number of specialised institutions, the most important of which were the departments.

In fact most of the soviet work was carried out by the departments.[12] So important was the role assigned to the departments that it would appear that little coordinative work was left to the central institutions. A department was not primarily placed under the authority of any organ of the soviet to which it belonged, it was in the first place subordinated to the corresponding department at the level above. * To take labour administration as an example, the labour department of the district soviet was primarily subordinated to the labour department of the county soviet, and the latter was subordinated to the labour department of the provincial soviet. In turn the labour department of the province owed its obedience to the Commissariat of Labour of the Central Government. In this vertical relationship it was required that instructions from above be carried out promptly.[13]

It is in fact difficult to see what real leadership was then left to be carried out by the central organs within a given soviet. Nevertheless the draft bill of December 1933 laid down that the departments also were subject to guidance and control from the executive committee and the presidium of the soviet to which they belonged.[14]

However, the presidium had no right to prevent a department of the same soviet from carrying out instructions from a corresponding department at a superior level. The only thing it could do was to protest to the executive committee or the presidium on the level above, and a reply must be received before any action could be taken.[15] It is reasonable to assume, by implication, that the competence of the executive committee and of the representative congress in this respect was meant to be restricted in the same way as that of the presidium.[16]

With much emphasis laid on the vertical relationship between superior and subordinate departments, it was quite natural that the Chinese Soviet Republic should see a lack of coordination within the single soviets. In

---

*     The department of general affairs was an exception (Doc. 6 art. 145).

April 1934 Chang Wen-t'ien complained that such coordination at the district level often tended to be neglected altogether.[17]

Organs, not for coordination, but for a sort of horizontal relationship, were provided for at a level lower than that of the department. It will be seen from fig.3 that most of the departments had under them corresponding committees. It is true that the personnel in responsible positions in a given department were heavily represented in the committee attached to it, and that the head of the department was the head of the corresponding committee as well. But at the same time the committee included representatives from other institutions or organisations with related fields of work. Most often not only one, but several of the departments of the soviet were represented. Accordingly the committee would be able to discuss the particular branch of administration from various points of view.[18]

The principle of subordinate organs owing obedience to superior ones did not only apply to the departments. Even such organs as the representative congress, the executive committee and the presidium must promptly carry out orders from their counterparts at a higher level. If a subordinate soviet organ opposed instructions from a superior one, the latter could partly reorganise, or even completely dissolve it.[19] It should, however, be emphasised that communications were supposed to go, not only from the top downward, but also from the bottom upward. Through a system of reports[20] and in other ways information was to be carried from lower soviet organs and upward through the hierarchy. And the higher soviet organs were supposed to take account of such information from below when giving their instructions.

The system of election for the representative congresses of the intermediate soviet organisations was similar to, although not identical with, that of the RSFSR before 1936.[21] According to the electoral regulations for the Chinese Soviet Republic of November 1931 and August 1933 the general pattern was as follows:

The representative congress of the district was composed of delegates elected by the representative congresses of the hsiang and the towns[22] of the district, plus elected representatives from the Red Army units attached to the district.

The representative congress of the county was composed of delegates elected by the representative congresses of the districts, and by those

of the towns and cities directly attached to the county, plus elected
representatives from Red Army units attached to the county.

The representative congress of the province was composed of delegates
elected by the representative congresses of the counties, and by those
of the cities directly attached to the province, plus elected representatives
from Red Army units attached to the province.[23]

The draft bill for local soviets of December 1933 provided for another step
in the pyramid. It required that the representative congresses of towns
and cities placed on the district level or above, were to be composed of
delegates elected by the representative congresses of the urban districts.[24]

We have here indeed a considerable number of stages of indirect representation. It may be useful to simplify the system and look at the path
which the mandate of the common people in the countryside was supposed
to follow in order to reach the top level. It had to pass elections at the
following stages: (1) the hsiang - (2) the district - (3) the county - (4) the
province, and continuing at the central levels, - (5) the National Soviet
Congress - (6) the Central Executive Committee - (7) the Council of
People's Commissars.

Was it possible for the will of the people to pass all these steps? The
French sociologist, Maurice Duverger, would give a negative answer.
In the passage quoted below he deals with indirect representation in political parties, but it should not make too much difference if we apply it to
the system of soviet representation, especially when considering that this
system was to a large extent controlled by a party of the type M. Duverger has in view. He writes:

"Now indirect representation is an admirable means of banishing
democracy while pretending to apply it. Rousseau was aware that
sovereignty cannot be delegated: all the legal artifices concerning
the representation of the mandator by the mandatory cannot conceal
this fundamental truth: that the mentality of the delegates is never
the same as that of those who delegate them, with the result that
every additional stage of delegation increases a little more the gap
between the will of the base and the decision of the apex."[25]

M. Duverger is probably to a large extent right. Neither can we completely dismiss Rousseau's tenets that "la souveraineté est inaliénable"[26]
and "A prendre le terme dans la rigueur de l'acception, il n'a jamais
existé de véritable Démocratie, et il n'en existera jamais."[27]

We are here dealing with abstract concepts, and nothing can be proved. Yet, if we define democracy as rule by the will of the people, it would appear that the democratic form of government is not much safeguarded by any electoral system. And it also seems reasonable to assume that such safeguards as might exist are further reduced through each step of indirect representation.

One might then argue that the lower Chinese soviets, because the election to them had passed through fewer stages, were more democratic than the higher ones. To some extent this may be true, especially for the directly elected soviets of the basic type; but then we must remember their strict subordination within the soviet hierarchy, and also party control.

I have, however, accepted that the leaders of the party and of the Central Government sincerely wanted the regime to listen to the will of the masses. The question is then if there is not after all the possibility for a regime, which is anxious to keep itself in close contact with the masses, to channel, to some extent, the will of the people through several stages. For the Chinese soviets this transmission of opinion might be effected partly through the elections, and partly through the report system and other means of communication.[28] To me it seems reasonable to assume that such a possibility exists, but that it can materialise only if the men of the apparatus at all levels support it actively. It is a difficult process, and it may easily be distorted to the extent to which the men of the apparatus allow themselves to be led by other considerations than that of carrying out the will of the masses. With regard to the Chinese soviet regime other considerations were indeed likely to count during the life and death struggle with the Kuomintang forces.

## The District

The size of the administrative unit of the district (ch'ü) in the Central Soviet Area underwent changes. The resolutions passed by the Central Executive Committee in November 1931 and July 1933, referred to above in connection with regulating the size of the hsiang, also dealt with the extension of the district.

In 1931 it was laid down that a district in the relatively thinly populated hill areas must not comprise more than 9 hsiang, and that it must not

(Cont. p. 51)

Table 2

Number of inhabitants qualifying for one delegate to the representative
soviet congresses of the intermediate and central levels, according to
the electoral regulations of December 1931 (Doc. 2 arts. 36 - 39).

| | | | | | |
|---|---|---|---|---|---|
| District soviets | | 400 inh. for 1 del. | | | |
| County soviets | Urban population | 500 " | " 1 | " | |
| | Rural " | 1,500 " | " 1 | " | |
| Provincial soviets | Urban population | 5,000 " | " 1 | " | |
| | Rural " | 25,000 " | " 1 | " | |
| The National | Urban population | 10,000 " | " 1 | " | |
| Soviet Congress | Rural " | 50,000 " | " 1 | " | |

Notes

1. The election was indirect. (See this thesis pp. 44 - 45).

2. It is not clear whether the word "inhabitants" (chü-min) in this
   connection does or does not refer exclusively to the enfranchised
   part of the population.

3. With regard to over-representation of the urban population the
   regulations followed the example of Soviet Russia (See Istoriya
   sovetskoy konstitutsii, pp. 539-40). The over-representation should
   also be seen in conjunction with what is said in the thesis (p. 17)
   on extra weight given to the votes of workers in hsiang elections.

Table 3

Number of inhabitants qualifying for one delegate to the representative soviet congresses of the intermediate and central levels, according to the electoral regulations of August 1933 (Doc. 4 arts. 23, 26-29 and 31).

| | | | | | |
|---|---|---|---|---|---|
| Soviets of towns placed on the district level | Workers | 20 | inh. | for 1 del. | |
| | Others | 80 | " | " 1 | " |
| District soviets | Urban population | 50 | " | " 1 | " |
| | Rural " | 200 | " | " 1 | " |
| County soviets | Urban " | 400 | " | " 1 | " |
| | Rural " | 1,600 | " | " 1 | " |
| Provincial soviets | Urban " | 1,500 | " | " 1 | " |
| | Rural " | 6,000 | " | " 1 | " |
| The National Soviet Congress | Urban " | 1,500 | " | " 1 | " |
| | Rural " | 6,000 | " | " 1 | " |

Notes

1. The election was indirect.

2. It is not clear whether the word "inhabitants" does or does not refer exclusively to the enfranchised part of the population.

3. One alternate was to be elected for every five regular delegates.

4. Regarding over-representation of the urban population see note 3 to table 2.

Table 4

Number of Red Army men qualifying for one delegate to the soviet
congresses of the intermediate and central levels, according to the
electoral regulations of August 1933 (Doc. 4 art. 37).

| | | |
|---|---|---|
| District soviets | 25 persons for 1 del. | |
| County         " | 100    "    "  1 del. | |
| Provincial    " | 400    "    "  1 del. | |
| The National Soviet Congress | 600    "    "  1 del. | |

Note

One alternate was to be elected for every five regular delegates.

Table 5

System of reports from the soviets of the district, county and province,
according to the draft bill for local soviets of December 1933.
(Doc. 6 arts. 65-67, 78-80 and 91-93).

I    The District Soviet

The executive committee of the district was bound to deliver reports
on its own work as follows:

(1)  to the executive committee of the county at least once every
     month

(2)  to the representative congresses of the various hsiang within
     the district at least once in two months

(3)  to the representative congress of the district (presumably at every
     session of the congress).

## II    The County Soviet

The executive committee of the county was bound to deliver these reports on its own work:

(1)  to the executive committee of the province at least once a month

(2)  to the representative congresses of the various districts within the county (presumably at every session of the congresses)

(3)  to the representative congress of the county (presumably at every session of the congress).


## III    The Provincial Soviet

The executive committee of the province was bound to deliver these reports on its own work:

(1)  to the Central Executive Committee once in four months

(2)  to the representative congresses of the various counties within the province (presumably at every session of the congresses)

(3)  to the representative congress of the province (presumably at every session of the congress).

The presidium of the provincial soviet was bound at least every month to deliver a report on its work to the Council of People's Commissars.


## Notes

1.  The reports delivered at the soviet congresses were naturally made orally, while those sent upward to higher soviet organs almost certainly were in written form.

2.  It is rather peculiar that a report from the county executive committee to the provincial executive committee should be required at least every month, while the normal frequency of plenary sessions of the former body was once in two months (See this thesis p. 56, table 7). Presumably the explanation is that the presidium was supposed to submit reports in the name of the executive committee.

————————————

extend further than 45 li* in both directions. With regard to plain areas it was merely stipulated that the extent of a district must not exceed 30 li in both directions, [29)] but it seems reasonable to assume that the number of hsiang it comprised normally was somewhat larger than in hilly areas. The 1933 resolution set the average number of hsiang within a district at 7, and this figure could be adjusted upward to 9 in plain and especially densely populated areas, or downward to 5 in hilly and thinly populated areas. [30)]

These regulations give us only very incomplete information regarding the size of the population of the district. By using them together with the information we have on hsiang population**, we may suggest - with a large margin of uncertainty - an average district population of 10,500 under the 1933 regulations, [31)] while under the 1931 regulations it may possibly have been more than double that figure.

The district soviet had a rather large permanent staff, though it was small compared with that of the county or that of the province. With regard to the central positions in the district apparatus, the draft bill for local soviets of December 1933 mentions one chairman, one vice-chairman, one secretary (mi-shu) and one or two clerks (wen-shu). [32)] However, most of the personnel was engaged by the various departments. From Juichin we have some interesting data with regard to the total number of employees. It was reported that during the economising campaign in early 1934 the number of staff members (kung-tso jen-yüan) of the district soviets within this county was cut down as follows: [33)]

| Period | Number of staff members in large districts | Number of staff members in small districts |
|---|---|---|
| October–December 1933 | 60 | 40 |
| January–February 1934 | 43 | 35 |
| March 1934 | 32 | 22 |

It is to be noted that we are again in the situation that a very large part of our material consists of laws and regulations, while there is a lack

---

* One li is approximately 630 yards.
** See this thesis table 1, p. 15.

Table 6

Some data on the representative congress, the executive committee
and the presidium of the district soviet.

|  | Number of full members | Number of alternates | Normal frequency of meetings | Intervals at which the organ should be re-elected |
|---|---|---|---|---|
| The rep. congress |  |  | Once in 3 months | 6 months |
| The executive committee | 21–35 | 5–7 | Once a month | 6 months |
| The presidium | 7–11 |  | Once in 3 days |  |

Note

Nearly all the data are taken from the draft bill for local soviets of
December 1933 (Doc. 6 arts. 57–60 and 64). The only exception is
the information concerning the frequency of elections to the representative congress, which has been found in Mao Tse-tung's report to
the Second National Soviet Congress in January 1934 (Doc. 5C, p. 56).
(In actual fact there is no sign that any election to soviet congresses
at any level was carried out after the Second National Soviet Congress.)

---

of information on how the machinery worked in actual fact. We have,
however, at least one very important report from actual life. In an
article published on April 21st 1934, Hsieh Jan-chih, Head Secretary
of the Council of People's Commissars, describes the soviet work in

Shangshe district in Hsingkuo county.[34] But it must be pointed out that this was a model district situated in a model county, and that the district moreover included the model hsiang of Ch'angkang, which has been referred to above. It is certainly to be regretted that the small amount of information available on the actual functioning of the local machinery is so much focused on the models, while the bad soviets, and still more the average ones, to a very large extent are left in the dark.

Hsieh Jan-chih tells us that the soviet chairman in Shangshe district played a very essential role in supervising the daily work of the soviet apparatus. His right-hand man seems to have been the head of the department of general affairs, while no mention is made of a vice-chairman. This chairman appears to have discharged his duties well, although he was far from being a scholar. The desperate lack of educated personnel is demonstrated in a glaring way by the fact that when written instructions arrived from superior soviet organs, the head of the department of general affairs would always read them aloud, but "some of them the chairman could read and understand all by himself". And this was the head of the soviet apparatus of a model district, one of the very best, if not the best, in the Central Soviet Area.

One of the main duties of the chairman was, according to Hsieh Jan-chih's report, to keep himself in touch with, and to guide the work of, the various departments. He used to attend the departmental meetings,[35] and also the meetings of the committees. Some of the problems brought up by the departments the chairman could solve personally, while others had to be taken to the presidium for discussion.

The heads of the departments in Shangshe district were required to attend the meetings of the presidium,[36] which were held at least every five days.[37] At these meetings they received their instructions, and were at the same time acquainted with the work of the whole soviet apparatus.

It is thus clear that the role of the presidium and its chairman in guiding and instructing the departments was intended to be a really active one. As pointed out earlier, this may seem contradictory remembering that a department at the same time owed obedience to corresponding departments at higher levels. It is shown above (p. 43) how disputes between these two separate sources of authority should be solved. But would there not be too many clashes? One way of avoiding such clashes was for the presidium and the chairman to neglect their role in guiding the work of the departments, and this was reported very often to be done in the various districts of the Central Soviet Area.[38] Another way of avoiding disputes, which obviously was regarded as the correct one, was for both kinds of authoritative organs to be led by an organisation separate from the soviet hierarchy, an organisation supposed to have a clearcut and uniform political line - the Communist Party.[39]

No doubt is left about the leadership of the party in respect to the work of the soviet presidium of Shangshe. We are informed that before a meeting of the presidium the issues to be dealt with were always brought up at a meeting of the party committee of the district, where they were reported on by the party secretary. After having there been "concretely decided upon" (chü-t'i chüeh-ting), the issues were taken to the "party fraction of the district soviet", and from the party fraction they were "reflected" (fan-ying) to the meeting of the presidium.

The basic task of the district soviet was naturally to supervise the hsiang soviets under its jurisdiction.[40] There would always be a representative from the Shangshe district soviet attending the meetings of the soviet congresses of the various hsiang, to convey instructions and to investigate the work of the hsiang soviet. The latter job was made easy because every second meeting of the hsiang congress was an "investigation meeting". On these occasions the work which had been carried out in the hsiang was reported upon, and the representative of the district soviet was there to listen and to make his comments.

Another way of investigating the work of the hsiang soviets, practised by the presidium of Shangshe district, was to send out inspectors. The district inspector first went to ask various people among the inhabitants of the hsiang about their opinions on the work of the soviet apparatus. He listened carefully to what the local agent(s) of the Workers' and Peasants' Inspectorate and some group leaders in the local party apparatus had to say. After that he attended a meeting of the representative congress of the hsiang, and voiced his opinions and his criticism.[41]

So much for Hsieh Jan-chih's report from Shangshe - soviet work did not proceed so smoothly everywhere. A couple of weeks before the report appeared Chang Wen-t'ien had complained of two wrong tendencies prevailing in many district soviets. The first one was for the district soviet to limit its activity to the mere transmitting of instructions from above (from the county, the province or the Central Government) to the hsiang under its jurisdiction, and thereafter let things drift as best they would. This might of course lead to an impasse, in which the instructions were not carried out. If no other way out was found, the district soviet would then give way to the other wrong tendency. It would "dispatch men to the various hsiang to convene mass meetings over the heads of the leading organs of the hsiang soviet, to mobilise the masses directly, and even force and command the responsible comrades of the hsiang soviet and the masses of the locality."[42)

It was obviously not easy to get the soviet organisations at the two lowest levels to function as they were intended to - to make the district soviet carry out active leadership while not preventing the hsiang soviet from fulfilling its own mission.

Severe criticisms of shortcomings in certain district soviets are also to be found in the journal Hung-se Chung-hua, criticisms which may well be exaggerated, but are nevertheless interesting. A notice of May 25th 1932 says that in the soviet of a district in Ningtu it was only the chairman, the clerk (wen-shu) and the cook who carried out any work; the rest of the personnel had gone home. Almost all the departments were nominally functioning, but in fact totally dormant.[43) In some other cases the soviet secretary (mi-shu) was reported to have - by virtue of his literacy - made himself a dictator; an example was the secretary in a district in Huich'ang, who had even got the soviet chairman locked up.[44)

The majority of district soviets were probably neither like the model one nor like the bad ones especially selected for attack, but somewhere in between. Unfortunately it does not seem possible to come nearer to the truth than this.

The County

The county (hsien) was a traditionally well established administrative unit in China. It used to comprise a considerable rural area, and had a main town or city as its centre. It was natural that initially the new soviet counties should as a rule be co-extensive with the traditional ones. At a later stage, however, many of the old counties were found to be too large, and were accordingly divided up.

A report published in November 1932 gives us the size of population of some counties in the soviet province of Kiangsi. The disparities are quite large. We are informed that Ningtu (later renamed Posheng) had 273,652 inhabitants, Hsingkuo 231,826, Kanhsien 159,164, Yungfeng 115,252, Kunglüeh 104,128, Anyüan 94,120 and Want'ai 79,175.[45) Unfortunately no such figures have been found from later dates.

Many counties were reduced in size during the summer of 1933. At meetings on July 22nd and on August 16th the Council of People's Commissars decided that altogether 13 new counties should be created, all of them within the Central Soviet Area, [46] and more were probably added on other occasions. [47]

It should be noted that the county of Juichin, which included the Chinese Soviet Republic's capital of the same name, was in a special position. It did not belong to any province, but was placed directly under the authority of the Central Government. [48]

Table 7

Some data on the representative congress, the executive committee and the presidium of the county soviet.

| | Number of full members | Number of alternates | Normal frequency of meetings | Intervals at which the organ should be reelected |
|---|---|---|---|---|
| The rep. congress | | | Once in 6 months | 1 year |
| The executive committee | 35–55 | 7–11 | Once in 2 months | 1 year |
| The presidium | 9–15 | | Once in 5 days | |

Note

Nearly all the data are taken from the draft bill for local soviets of December 1933 (Doc. 6 arts. 69–72 and 77). The only exception is the information on the frequency of elections to the representative congress, which has been found in Mao Tse-tung's report to the Second National Soviet Congress in January 1934 (Doc. 5C p. 56).

The draft bill for local soviets of December 1933 names the following central positions in the apparatus of the county soviet:[49]

1 chairman
1 - 2 vice-chairman (-men)
1 - 2 secretary (-ies) (mi-shu)
1 - 2 clerk(s) (wen-shu)
2 - 5 inspectors (hsün-shih-yüan)

Most of the staff members of the county soviet were, however, working in the various departments. Adding up all the employees of all grades within the apparatus, a considerable total would result.[50] The following numbers of soviet employees in the county of Juichin were reported by Hung-se Chung-hua, not because of the large figures, but as a model for the cut-down during the economising campaign:[51]

| Period | Empl. in the county soviet | Empl. in the soviet of a large dis-trict | Empl. in the soviet of a small dis-trict | Empl. in the soviet of a large hsiang | Empl. in the soviet of a small hsiang | Total number of employees in all soviets of all levels within the county |
|---|---|---|---|---|---|---|
| Sept.-Oct.1933 | 302 | - | - | - | - | - |
| Oct.-Dec.1933 | 245 | 60 | 40 | 4 | 3 | 1,340 |
| Jan.-Feb.1934 | 143 | 43 | 35 | 4 | 3 | 1,114 |
| March 1934 | 116 | 32 | 22 | 3 | 2 | 831 |

There is a serious lack of information on the functioning of the soviet apparatus of the county. We do have a report from the much praised Hsingkuo, but it is not nearly so detailed as those from the model hsiang or the model district referred to above. The county soviet of Hsingkuo was in rather general terms commended for its good planning, for the investigations it made in order to assure that instructions were carried out, and for its good relations with the masses of the people.[52]

We know from various sources that some county soviets worked largely to the satisfaction of the Central Government and the party leaders, while others did not. Some of them fulfilled their tasks, for instance with regard to economic reconstruction and recruitment for the Red Army, while others lagged behind.[53] On the negative side we have also some reports of a quite different type.

One such is from Yütu, where in early 1934 the county chairman, and many other employees in the county soviet and in soviet organs at lower levels, were found guilty of having borrowed or taken money belonging to the government, and in some cases used it as capital in private business. They were said in particular to have engaged in a very lucrative trade with white areas, by which they exported grain and imported salt. In their anxiety to make a profit they had neglected their duties, and the soviet work had accordingly fallen into decay. For such reasons a terrible clean-up followed in the soviet apparatus (and in the local party organisation as well).[54]

A little later, on April 3rd 1934, an extremely reproachful letter was sent by the Council of People's Commissars to the presidium of the county soviet of Want'ai. From this county it had been reported that in the month of February the same year 2,600 people among the masses had fled to white areas, and the flow of refugees had further increased during the month of March. The letter said that the relations between the masses and the hsiang and district soviets within the county were extremely bad. The soviet work in various fields, and on the different levels, was very ineffective. The county soviet issued orders and instructions, but did not see to it that any real change was carried through. Accordingly the Council of People's Commissars told the county presidium:

> "We have to point out that for the backwardness of the work in Want'ai, for the occurrence of large scale flight of the masses of Want'ai, it is in the first place the Want'ai county soviet that should bear full responsibility. The county soviet of Want'ai is all day until the night (i-t'ien tao wan) shouting into the air (k'ung-han) that the tasks given by the Centre shall steadfastly be carried out, but we do not see THE REAL WORK of steadfastly carrying out the tasks given by the Centre."[55]

We may, however, be misled if we take accounts like this on their face value. The judgement may have been too harsh. The Central Government and the party leadership undoubtedly ought to have taken a large share of responsibility for the highly unsatisfactory state of affairs in a number of localities - in later chapters we will show that there was a radicalisation of the policy of central organs which affected the local levels very severely.

The local party organisation was naturally supposed to play an important role in guiding the soviet work at the county level. However, some grave errors are reported to have been committed in this respect. Lo Fu (alias of Chang Wen-t'ien) wrote in an article dated August 1st 1933:

"In our party there obviously still exist two tendencies in relation to soviet work. Either the responsible comrades of our party give direct orders to the soviets and want the soviets to carry out the orders of the party; even to the extent that at the meetings of the county soviet or the district soviet the secretary of the county committee or the district committee of the party takes part and makes a report, and decides upon the work of the county soviet or the district soviet. Or the party pays no attention whatsoever to the soviet work, and regards it as unimportant (wu-kuan chin-yao); it even sends over to the soviet government comrades in the party who have committed errors in the past."[56]

Evidently the party was supposed to lead the soviets without directly commanding them. This was not an easy thing to do, and some of the local party organisations failed to find the right course.

The firm hand of the party seems to be visible in some reports from soviet congresses at the county level. Both at a congress in Ningtu in April 1932,[57] and at one in Juichin presumably in May of the same year,[58] all resolutions are reported to have been carried unanimously. At the Ningtu congress there "was not a single person who opposed or was doubtful". Probably this could be obtained only because the draft resolutions were backed by party authority.

The congresses of the county soviets are reported to have discussed various matters which were deemed to be urgent – for instance recruitment to the Red Army, economic reconstruction, finances, education – and they carried out the elections of the executive committee and of delegates to the representative congress of the province. Delegates to some county congresses voiced criticism with regard to the soviet work of the past, and this criticism could be very harsh indeed.[59] Presumably it was usually sponsored by the party, which had here a method of purging the soviet apparatus.

But that the local party leaders could not always do what they liked to, is shown by an interesting report from a soviet congress in the county of Hsichiang in December 1933. A member of the county party committee criticised, and reportedly with good reason, the report delivered by the soviet chairman. But after he had finished this, he also roundly cursed various delegates to the congress. Then the delegates' criticism was turned against this party committee member, who was found guilty of bureaucratic manners and of other faults. At last he confessed that he had committed errors.[60]

---

Obviously the county soviet was a very important link in the administrative apparatus of the republic. Judging from the results that were obtained in military and economic mobilisation, the county soviets generally did not serve the Central Government badly, although many of them were bitterly reproached for lagging behind in fulfilling the plans.


## The Province

The oldest among the soviet provinces relevant for the present discussion were Kiangsi and Fukien; their territories were at an early stage separate, but joined together through expansion in late 1931 or in early 1932.[61] The former covered a southern part of the traditional province of Kiangsi, and the latter a western part of the traditional province of Fukien. If not otherwise stated, I shall use the names Kiangsi and Fukien as designating the soviet provinces, and not the traditional ones.

As Kiangsi was found to be too large for administrative purposes, the Council of People's Commissars decided on August 16th 1933 to divide it in two; the southern part of it became a new soviet province under the name of Yüehkan.[62] Some months earlier, on April 26th, it had been decided to form a soviet province to be called Minkan*, out of the Communist-controlled areas on the border between the traditional provinces of Kiangsi and Fukien, to the north of the soviet provinces of the same names.[63]

After these regulations the Central Soviet Area had four provinces. Kiangsi was by far the most important one - by September 1933 it seems to have had 20 or 21 counties.[64] Hung-se Chung-hua of March 15th 1934 gives a list, which may or may not be complete for that time, of seven counties in Fukien **.[65] Seven counties are likewise listed for Yüehkan;[66] while the extension of Minkan is difficult to establish.[67]

One indication of the relative economic potential of these provinces ought to be recorded. In September 1933 the Preparatory Committee for the Second National Soviet Congress appealed to the people of the Central Soviet Area to make 300,000 pairs of straw sandals and present them to the Red Army. This job was to be shared by the various provinces and

---

\*    Minkan means Fukien - Kiangsi, and Yüehkan stands for Kwangtung - Kiangsi.

\*\*   At earlier dates the soviet province of Fukien definitely extended much further than to these seven counties.

the county of Juichin (which was placed directly under the authority of
the Central Government) in the following way:[68]

|  | Number of<br>straw sandals | Percentage of<br>the total |
|---|---|---|
| Kiangsi | 150, 000 pairs | 50. 0 % |
| Fukien | 70, 000 " | 23.3 % |
| Minkan | 30, 000 " | 10.0 % |
| Yüehkan | 30, 000 " | 10.0 % |
| Juichin | 20, 000 " | 6.7 % |
| Total | 300, 000 pairs | 100.0 % |

The draft bill for local soviets of December 1933 names the following
central positions in the apparatus of the provincial soviet:[69]

1 chairman
2 vice-chairmen
5-9 inspectors
1-3 secretary (-ies) (mi-shu)
1-3 clerk(s) (wen-shu)

There was a large number of other jobs, most of them connected with
the various departments. For March 1934 the provincial soviet of
Yüehkan budgeted for altogether 220 employees, but the Central Audit
Committee found this figure too high. [70] An article dated February 9th
the same year reports 265 persons to have been engaged by the soviet
of Fukien province, but of these only 146 were working at the provincial
headquarters; most of the rest had either been dispatched to various localities, or had deserted. [71] Unfortunately no figure has been found for
Kiangsi, the largest and most important of the soviet provinces.

The available reports on the work of the provincial soviets are, generally
speaking, by no means flattering. But they must be used critically. They
seem to reflect the dissatisfaction of the party leadership, and to some
extent that of the Central Government, with the work of local cadres. It
is true that the reports include a certain amount of recognition of results
achieved, but their main thrust is critical. We do not really see the
problems from both sides, since the record is silent on arguments which
the provincial cadres may have offered in defence of themselves.

Lists of Counties in the Soviet Provinces of Kiangsi, Fukien and
Yüehkan.

A. Counties in Kiangsi according to a source of September 10th 1933.
(Hsüan-chü yün-tung chou-pao No. 2 p. 5).

| | | |
|---|---|---|
| Posheng | Yangyin | Kuangch'ang |
| Ch'angsheng | Kanhsien | Shengli |
| Lok'ou | Want'ai | Nanfeng |
| Ch'ihshui | Loan | Ch'ungjen |
| Shihch'eng | Ihuang | Hsinkan |
| Lungkang | Kunglüeh | K'angtu |
| Hsingkuo | Yungfeng | |

Note

The list does not include T'ailei, which was one of the counties the
Council of People's Commissars had decided to create at its meeting
of August 16th 1933. (See Hung-se Chung-hua August 31st 1933 p. 5
and February 9th 1934 p. 2).

B. Counties in Fukien listed in Hung-se Chung-hua of March 15th 1934.

| | |
|---|---|
| Ninghua | Shanghang |
| Ch'angt'ing | Hsinch'üan |
| Chaocheng | Wup'ing |
| T'ingtung | |

C. Counties in Yüehkan listed in Hung-se Chung-hua of August 31st
1933 and February 18th 1934.

| | | |
|---|---|---|
| Yütu | Hsichiang | Hsink'ang |
| Huich'ang | Hsünwu | |
| Menling | Anyüan | |

Table 8

Some data on the representative congress, the executive committee
and the presidium of the provincial soviet.

|  | Number of full members | Number of alternates | Normal frequency of meetings | Intervals at which the organ should be re-elected |
|---|---|---|---|---|
| The rep. congress |  |  | Once in a year | 1 year |
| The executive committee | 55–95 | 11–19 | Once in 4 months |  |
| The presidium | 13–19 |  | Once in 7 days |  |

Note

Nearly all the data have been taken from the draft bill for local soviets
of December 1933. (Doc. 6 arts. 82, 83, 85 and 90). The only exception is the information concerning the frequency of elections to the
representative congress, which has been found in Mao Tse-tung's report
to the Second National Soviet Congress in January 1934. (Doc. 5C p. 56).

Among the sources of information in this regard we have first of all
the reports from the provincial soviet congresses. A session of such
a congress could last for 3-4 days, [72) or as long as 9 days;[73) and the
procedure was largely the same as that followed at the county level.
The most interesting thing reported from the provincial congresses
is the criticism of the soviet work of the past. For example, the second
representative congress of Kiangsi, held in December 1933, was
reported to have "severely blamed the presidium of the provincial
soviet that its leadership with respect to the revolutionary war for the
last one and a half years was not satisfactory, that a deep-seated
(nung-hou) bureaucratism existed in the organs of the provincial soviet
and that there were individual cases of opportunism. ... Moreover, the
provincial soviet did not in the past clearly understand the situation at
the lower levels and the concrete demands of the masses, it only
incessantly sent out empty, long and superfluous (jung-ch'ang) documents,
it failed to supply concrete leadership, it did not fully carry into effect
soviet democratisation. ..."[74)

Was this really spontaneous criticism from the delegates? The answer
must be that it was not. Another report from the same congress reveals
that the delegates were by no means left to themselves:

> "Under the leadership of the party and the Central Government the
> congress resolutely revealed these faults of the provincial soviet,
> and achieved complete success."[75)

The essence of what happened at this congress seems to be clear enough.
The party leadership was forcing a shake-up in the provincial soviet apparatus. One of the dominant figures at the congress was Wu Liang-p'ing,
who obviously was closely associated with the 28 Bolshevik group, and
who more than once served the group well in contributing to political
reorganisation.[76)

So much for the provincial soviet of Kiangsi. The men responsible for
the apparatus in Fukien did not fare better. Once in early 1934, probably
slightly after the Second National Soviet Congress at which members of
the 28 Bolshevik group seem to have secured for themselves nearly
complete control of the state apparatus, the Central Government decided
partly to reorganise the soviet of Fukien province. In this connection
Wu Liang-p'ing wrote an article in Hung-se Chung-hua, bitterly criticising the soviet, saying that it had been extremely ineffective in various
fields of work and that it had failed to supply real leadership for the
work at the lower levels.[77)

Kiangsi and Fukien, whose soviets were so bitterly criticised in late 1933 and early 1934, were the most important among the provinces of the Central Soviet Area. As for the others, the soviet of Yüehkan was accused by the Central Audit Committee of having neglected, or of having been too slow in carrying out, certain instructions from the Central Government, [78] and Minkan was definitely the part of the Central Soviet Area where soviet power was least firmly established. [79]

We would certainly be unjust to the provincial soviets if we did not try to balance this criticism. To some extent it is, in fact, modified by our sources. Even one of the reports from the second representative soviet congress of Kiangsi says, before letting loose the wave of criticism referred to above, that the congress "correctly estimated that the provincial soviet had obtained great results in leading the revolutionary war." [80] In August 1933 the Council of People's Commissars had several positive things to say on the results of soviet work in Fukien, although the main thing was also in this case sharp criticism. [81] If we go back to May 1932, we find that the first representative soviet congress of Kiangsi passed a resolution giving the provincial soviet considerable credit for the efforts it had made to improve work at the various levels, but the criticism of continuing shortcomings was even here harsh and included a long list of items. [82]

This, then, is the picture which emerges from the general reports on the functioning of the provincial soviets. Although they allow for a limited recognition of achievements, the weight of the estimates found in these documents is very much on the negative side. But our sources are not yet exhausted. In the last chapter of this thesis we will deal with the results obtained with regard to economic mobilisation; some of the credit for these results must belong to the soviet of the province.

CHAPTER III.    THE CENTRAL GOVERNMENT

The preceding general studies of soviet organisation at the most local and the intermediate levels lead naturally up to a study of the highest organs.

The apparatus of Central Government of the Chinese Soviet Republic, which is shown in fig.4, was closely modelled on the contemporary system in Soviet Russia. There was the very large National Soviet Congress, which was elected by the people indirectly through a number of stages; and there were the much smaller bodies of the Central Executive Committee (CEC), the Presidium and the Council of People's Commissars, elected directly or indirectly by the Congress.

The National Soviet Congress

The National Soviet Congress was convened only twice. The first congress met in November 1931 and the second in January 1934, and on both occasions the session was rather short. The congresses were largely based on the local soviet organisations – a base which naturally changed or developed to a considerable extent from 1931 to 1934. The base being different, the elections to the two soviet congresses had also to be somewhat different.

Of the election to the First National Soviet Congress we do not know very much, but we are informed that in what was then the Central Soviet Area it was carried out indirectly for the civil as well as for the military delegates. The election of the civil representatives was carried through three stages – at the hsiang, district and county levels.[1] The fact that the local soviet organisations were at that time not well established must undoubtedly have caused difficulties for the electoral campaign.

At the First National Soviet Congress there were reported to be altogether 610* delegates, and they by no means came exclusively from the Central

---

*    Another source gives the figure 651. (See Warren Kuo, Analytical Hist..., 1968, vol. 2 p. 379.)

Fig. 4.  Organs of Central Government, February 1934.

| National Soviet Congress |
| --- |

| Central Executive Committee |
| --- |

| Presidium |
| --- |

| Council of People's Commissars |
| --- |

- People's Commissariat of Foreign Affairs
- People's Commissariat for Land
- People's Commissariat for Food
- People's Commissariat of Education
- People's Commissariat of Military Affairs
- People's Commissariat of Finances
- People's Commissariat of Justice
- People's Commissariat for the Workers' and Peasants' Inspection
- People's Commissariat of Labour
- People's Commissariat of National Economy
- People's Commissariat of Internal Affairs
- State Political Security Bureau

Sources: Docs. 37 and 38.

Soviet Area. There were also representatives from the soviet areas of Western Fukien[2]), Hsiangokan (Hunan-Hupei-Kiangsi), Hsiangkan (Hunan-Kiangsi), Hsiangohsi (Western Hunan and Western Hupei), Yütungpei (Northeast Honan) and Hainan. We are even informed that there was one, or perhaps more, representative(s) from Korea.[3]) Various units of the Red Army had their own delegates, and so had the National Labour Federation and the Seamen's Union.[4])

The Second National Soviet Congress had a more solid base, since the local soviet organisations had developed in the meantime. With regard to its election we need not do much more than quote the official regulation for the last step of the process[5]) (since the various steps of election to local soviets have been dealt with earlier):

> "The National Soviet Congress is composed of delegates elected
> by the representative congresses of provincial soviets, delegates
> elected by the representative soviet congresses of counties directly
> attached [to the Central Government], delegates elected by the
> soviets of cities directly attached to the Central Government*,
> and of delegates elected by the Red Army."[6])

It should be noted, however, that this provision cannot have covered completely the election at the top level of delegates to the Second National Soviet Congress. It says nothing about the 48 cadres from the "Centre" or about the delegates from the local militia, the white areas and the "national minorities", all of whom, as table 9 shows, had their seats at the congress.

With regard to social background and geographical grouping of the delegates to the Second National Soviet Congress we can mainly refer to tables 9 and 10. It may be added that quite a few Kuomintang-dominated areas were represented, and that there also were delegates from Manchuria, Taiwan, Korea and Annam.[7]) Ch'in Pang-hsien said in a speech that even Java was represented, while displaying some ignorance by stating that this island was under the yoke of British imperialism.[8])

The two national soviet congresses were large bodies, and they met for relatively short sessions. Were they really effective in forming the policy of the Chinese Soviet Republic? Further, were the delegates really in control of the congresses or were the delegates themselves being

---

\* In actual fact there was no city directly attached to the Central Government, while one county was in this position, namely Juichin. (See this thesis p. 56.)

Table 9

Grouping of delegates to the Second National Soviet Congress according to Hung-hsing of January 28th 1934 (p.1) and Hung-se Chung-hua of January 24th 1934 (p.3).

| Delegated from | Number of Regular Delegates | Number of Alternate Delegates |
|---|---|---|
| Kiangsi | 196 | 26 |
| Fukien | 79 | 8 |
| Yüehkan (Kwangtung-Kiangsi) | 63 | 12 |
| Minkan (Fukien-Kiangsi) | 37 | |
| Red Army | 117 | 28 |
| Local Militia (ti-fang wu-chuang) | 13 | 9 |
| Hsiangkan (Hunan-Kiangsi) | 43 | |
| Minchekan (Fukien-Chekiang-Kiangsi) | 45 | |
| Hsiangokan (Hunan-Hupei-Kiangsi) | 30 | |
| Oyüwan (Hupei-Honan-Anhwei) | 1 | |
| Szechuan | 1 | |
| White areas | 17 | |
| National minorities | 3 | |
| From the "Centre" (Chung-yang) | 48 | |
| Total | 693 | 83 |

Number of visitors attending the congress: About 1,500.


Notes to Table 9

1. The regular and alternate delegates from the county of Juichin, which was directly subordinated to the Central Government, are presumably included in the figures for Kiangsi.
2. The soviet provinces Kiangsi, Fukien, Yüehkan and Minkan belonged to the Central Soviet Area, while Hsiangkan, Minchekan, Hsiangokan, Oyüwan and part of Szechuan were separate soviet areas.
3. The term "national minorities" (shao-shu min-tsu) seems in this connection - strangely enough - to have been used for the peoples of Korea, Annam and Taiwan. (See Hung-se Chung-hua of January 19th 1934, p. 2 and February 1st 1934, p. 3).
4. It is here, as quite often, difficult to establish what the word "Centre" (Chung-yang) stands for. It sometimes means the Central Government, and sometimes the central party organs.

## Table 10

Grouping of delegates to the Second National Soviet Congress according to Hung-se Chung-hua of February 3rd 1934, p. 4.

A. **Social Background**          **Number of Delegates**

| | |
|---|---|
| Industrial workers | 8 |
| Handicraft workers | (Figure illegible) |
| Coolies | 53 |
| Workers employed in shops | 12 |
| Farm labourers | 122 |
| Poor peasants | 303 |
| Middle peasants | 25 |
| Petty traders | 4 |
| Others | 64 |

B. **Membership of the Communist Party and of the Communist Youth League**

| | |
|---|---|
| Members of the Communist Party | 628 |
| Members of the Communist Youth League | 116 |

### Note

If, with regard to section B, we add the number of league members to the number of party members we arrive at a total figure of 744. A comparison of this figure with the total figures given in table 9 seems to make it clear that section B includes alternates as well as regular delegates. But then this must be the case for section A as well, since both sections are based on the same source.

———————————

controlled? In an attempt to solve these problems we have to put together the available pieces of information concerning the proceedings.

The First National Soviet Congress met in Juichin on November 7th 1931. To mark the occasion a parade of the Red Army was held in the morning and a torchlight procession in the evening. Subsequently the congress discussed and unanimously adopted a labour law, a land law, general principles of a constitution and resolutions on the Red Army and on economic policies, all introduced by the Central Committee of the Communist Party.[9] A political program was also passed,[10] and apparently the congress further adopted a resolution on national minorities[11] and regulations for the Workers' and Peasants' Inspectorate.[12] On November 18th the Central Executive Committee was elected, and this election is reported to have been the last act of the congress.[13]

It is evident that the party leadership had drawn up a program for the congress beforehand. On October 30th the journal Hung-ch'i chou-pao published an article by Chang Wen-t'ien, which in Hsiao Tso-liang's opinion "disclosed practically all the major decisions the congress was to make."[14] Eight days before the opening ceremonies Chang, representing the party leadership, informed the world, not of proposals which were to be discussed, but of laws and resolutions which were to be adopted. Can we then conclude that the congress had no influence on policy-making whatsoever, and that everything was decided beforehand? Such a conclusion would be premature. Two questions have first to be discussed.

How did Mao Tse-tung, following the First National Soviet Congress, obtain his unique position in the state apparatus? The congress elected a Central Executive Committee (CEC), which in turn elected Mao as its chairman. The CEC also elected a Council of People's Commissars, likewise headed by Mao.[15] Neither was it only a question of the chairmanship - Mao's followers as a whole apparently attained a very strong position in the top state organs elected directly or indirectly by the congress.[16] How could all this occur? Why did not Mao's opponents, who dominated the top organs of the party, prevent it?

Two possible replies can be imagined:

## Hypothesis No. 1

The party leadership wanted, but had not the power, to bar Mao and his followers from the leading positions in the state apparatus. Mao's supporters at the First National Soviet Congress were in this respect stronger than the central organs of the party.

## Hypothesis No. 2

The party leaders did not want to ignore the machinery which Mao had built up in the Central Soviet Area. As a group they possessed an expertise in handling the theories of Lenin and Stalin, and they had some experience of underground activity from their base in Shanghai, but they had not yet sufficient confidence in their ability to deal with the administrative tasks of the new republic which was to be built up under unfamiliar circumstances in the Chinese hinterland. They therefore wanted, not to replace, but to make use of Mao and his supporters, who were experienced in organisational work in the soviet areas.

Hypothesis No. 1 does not seem to be very plausible. The party leadership was powerful indeed. Its grip on the cadres in Kiangsi is manifested in abundance through the resolutions passed by the First Party Conference of the (Central) Soviet Area, held in November 1931 – probably shortly before the First National Soviet Congress.[17] It is true that these resolutions gave some credit to Mao's apparatus, but after that they let loose a deluge of criticism. The conference referred to its own organisation, i.e. the party organisation of the Central Soviet Area, in the blackest terms.[18] There is no doubt that it was the central party leadership that got the conference to make such abject self-criticisms.[19] If the party leaders could do this, they must also have had the power to control the elections made directly or indirectly by the First National Soviet Congress.

The answer to our problem will probably mainly lie in hypothesis No. 2. This hypothesis needs, however, to be deepened. The party leadership had an extremely strong loyalty to Moscow; and the Comintern presumably did not want to remove Mao Tse-tung from power. Although to a large extent critical of Mao's work, the International apparently at the same time appreciated his organisational achievements.[20] Moreover, Moscow as well as the leaders of the Chinese Communist Party probably saw in Mao's supporters among the cadres and the masses of the Central Soviet Area a mighty force – a force which was indispensable in the revolutionary struggle, and which should therefore not alienated. But if it should not be alienated, then it must be given a certain outlet and a scope of activity. If the skill and experience of Mao and of the cadres who supported him was indispensable, then they after all had a certain power.

We may conclude that Moscow and the leaders of the Chinese Communist Party could have prevented the First National Soviet Congress from putting the Maoist faction into a such prominent position in the state apparatus, but at a too high cost. They chose not to.

Why did some of the laws and resolutions adopted by the First National Soviet Congress differ somewhat from the corresponding drafts introduced by the Central Committee of the party? Such discrepancies are found with regard to the Land Law, the Labour Law, the Resolution on the Problem of the Red Army and the Resolution on Economic Policies, and in some cases they are rather significant. [21] A very poorly composed draft on the organisation of the Workers' and Peasants' Inspectorate seems to have been cut out altogether, and replaced by a completely new edict on the subject. [22] Have we here proof that the First National Soviet Congress was to some extent effective in policy-making?

There is no proof, there is only a possibility. According to a Russian source most of the drafts were published in Hung-ch'i already in March 1931. [23] We know the Chinese texts as they are reproduced in a pamphlet, undated, but published some time before the opening of the congress by the political department of the Third Army Corps of the First Route Army. A very short preface to the pamphlet is of interest, as it invites "all comrades" to "express their opinions towards these drafts and to discuss them. All opinions can be formed into articles and sent to "Chan-tou", the organ of the Central Bureau of the Chinese Communist Party, for publication." [24]

We know at least one other example of a similar procedure in the Chinese Soviet Republic [25] - a top organ of the party or of the government would make drafts, and party members and possibly others would be invited to suggest changes. In the present case the party leadership, on the basis of such suggestions, may have made the final revision before the opening of the congress, or the bills may have been altered by the congress itself. Unfortunately we have not sufficient information to decide the issue.

With regard to the Labour Law we have a partial clue. Hsiang Ying, who as secretary of the Central Bureau [26] presumably acted as a spokesman for the party leadership, suggested in a report to the congress some alterations in the draft, [27] and these alterations were finally effected. Yet, even with regard to this particular law we do not know whether the party ledadership had ready-made concrete proposals for all the changes which were enacted.

Considering the many things which we do not know it may be unwise to speculate too much over these issues. On the one hand the party leaders were very powerful; it cannot have been impossible for them to carry through the laws and resolutions in the form which they wanted. On the other hand the cadres of the soviet areas, many of whom must have been delegated to the congress, were extremely useful, and in view of their usefulness they may have been awarded a certain influence on policy-making.

The Second National Soviet Congress met in Juichin on January 22nd 1934, and lasted until February 1st. Its proceedings can be sketched as follows:

## 22 January

### The Morning

There was a military parade.[28]

### Afternoon and Evening

Mao Tse-tung declared the congress open and made a brief speech.

One of the delegates from Kiangsi submitted a list containing the names of 75 persons proposed to make up the presidium of the congress. The list was adopted.

There were brief speeches by Ch'in Pang-hsien (Po Ku), Liu Shao-ch'i, Ho K'o-ch'üan (K'ai Feng) and Chu Te.

The following six committees were elected:

1. Committee for Investigation of the Credentials of the Delegates.
2. Committee for the Resolution on the Work Report of the Central Executive Committee.
3. Committee for the Resolution on Red Army Construction.
4. Committee for the Resolution on Economic Construction.

5.  Committee for the Resolution on Soviet Construction.
6.  Law Committee.

Liang Po-t'ai was elected head of the secretariat of the congress.

The congress passed the agenda.

The congress decided to send telegrams to Red Army men at the front, workers and collective farmers of the Soviet Union, the volunteer army in Northeast China (Manchuria), and to the revolutionaries who were in Kuomintang prisons.

Stalin, Kalinin, Molotov, Thälmann and Okano were elected members of an honorary presidium of the congress. None of them was present.

There were meetings of celebration.[29]


23 January

This is reported to have been a day of rest for the delegates.[30]


24 January

There was apparently no official activity of the congress in the morning.

In the afternoon Mao Tse-tung produced the first part of his long report on behalf of the Central Executive Committee and the Council of People's Commissars.[31]


25 January

Mao continued and ended his report, which altogether lasted for 10 hours.[32]


26 January

The delegates were organised in groups. The groups discussed separately Mao's report and problems related to it.[33]

## 27 January

The congress continued the discussion of the previous day, in a body.

Mao Tse-tung made his concluding remarks in relation to his report and to the following discussions.[34]

## 28 January

Chu Te delivered a report on the Red Army.

A report by Hsiang Ying on Red Army recruitment, and a ceremony of awarding banners to acknowledge extraordinary achievements in recruitment, seem then to have been interpolated.

There were comments on Chu Te's report.[35]

## 29 January

### The Morning

There were further comments on Chu Te's report.

Chu Te made his concluding remarks in relation to the comments.

### The Afternoon

Because news had arrived that vast Kuomintang forces were closing in on the Central Soviet Area, Mao Tse-tung delivered a report on urgent mobilisation. Then he moved, on behalf of the presidium of the congress, that the congress be closed on February 1st, five days earlier than scheduled, so that the delegates could take part in the mobilisation. The motion was carried.

Lin Po-ch'ü delivered a report on economic construction. There was a discussion of the report.[36]

## 30 January

### The Morning

The discussion of the previous day was continued. Lin Po-ch'ü made his concluding remarks in relation to the discussion.

### Afternoon and Evening

Wu Liang-p'ing delivered a report on soviet construction, which was followed by a discussion.[37]

## 31 January

### The Morning

The discussion of the previous day was continued. Wu Liang-p'ing made his concluding remarks in relation to the discussion.[38]

### Afternoon and Evening

Hsiang Ying introduced the General Principles of the Constitution, as drafted by the party "centre".[39] The congress unanimously resolved to hand the draft over to the new Central Executive Committee, which was to be elected on the following day, for further elaboration and for promulgation.

Because of shortage of time the congress unanimously resolved that various propositions which delegates, or groups of delegates, had brought in, should be handed over to and be dealt with by the new Central Executive Committee.

The congress adopted some principles of a resolution on the report of the Central Executive Committee and the Council of People's Commissars. It unanimously resolved to charge the new Central Executive Committee with the task of working out the text of the resolution, and of issuing it in the name of the congress.

The congress unanimously adopted the draft resolutions on the Red Army, on economic construction, and on soviet construction. However, the new

Central Executive Committee was given the task of improving the style of the texts.

The congress unanimously adopted the draft resolution on the national emblem, the national flag and the army flag.

More red banners were awarded as an acknowledgement of extraordinary achievements in recruitment to the Red Army.

Groups of delegates discussed separately the list of candidates for the new Central Executive Committee.[40]

## 1 February

The congress decided to dispatch a telegram to protest against the Kuomintang terror, and another one to congratulate the Communist Party of the Soviet Union on the opening of its 17th congress. Possibly a third telegram was sent to protest against Fascism in Germany.[41]

The congress elected a new Central Executive Committee of 175 members and 36 alternates, and a 35-man strong central committee of the Workers' and Peasants' Inspectorate.

The Manifesto of the congress was issued.

The congress was closed with a speech by Mao Tse-tung.[42]

We have, then, some information on the Second National Soviet Congress. Although much of the inner workings of the congress must remain hidden, there is a basis for certain conclusions.

It can be said with certainty that the significance of the congress was not limited to the decisions it made. A large proportion of the delegates consisted of cadres from the soviet organisations of various levels[43] and from the Red Army.[44] These cadres were expected to learn a lot from the reports made by leading members of the Central Government, summing up positive and negative experience of the work of the past and laying down guiding lines for the work of the future. Especially instructive in this regard was the ten-hour long report by Mao on 24-25 January,[45] but those delivered by Chu Te, Lin Po-ch'ü amd Wu Liang-p'ing from January 28th onward served similar purposes.[46]

And these four reports were significant in an even wider sense. Each of them served as a basis for prolonged discussion and an important resolution. The reports were at the very centre of the activity of the congress.

Obviously Mao Tse-tung's report was by far the most important one among these four. It was very long and fairly detailed; in fact it covered all the three special fields reported on by Chu Te, Lin Po-ch'ü and Wu Liang-p'ing, and in addition to that it dealt with several other aspects. And Mao's role at the congress was by no means limited to his long report. His opening[47] and closing[48] speeches, his "concluding remarks"[49] and his improvised appeal for urgent mobilisation[50] were all significant. His name topped the list of the 75-man strong presidium of the congress, [51] and he must be the man once referred to as the congress's chairman. [52] Mao Tse-tung's contribution on this occasion was thus particularly conspicuous.

The role played by the top leaders of the party at the congress itself was far less noticeable. But their preparatory work was extremely important. At the Fifth Plenum of the party's Central Committee, held in Juichin in January 1934, Chang Wen-t'ien (Lo Fu) delivered a report which the plenum subsequently adopted as its instructions to the party corps at the Second National Soviet Congress. [53] As Hsiao Tso-liang has pointed out, these instructions laid down the guiding principles for the work of the congress, and to a large extent they provided a basis for the drafting of Mao's long report. [54] However, there was quite a long way to go from the party's guiding principles to the fully elaborated texts of Mao's reports and speeches. In this connection there may of course have been, between Mao and the party leaders, a good many communications which have not been brought to light; nevertheless the reading of the available documents gives a definite impression that Mao Tse-tung's contribution at the Second National Soviet Congress to a quite large extent was based on his own insight and on his personal prestige. He was certainly not at this time free to draw up the political line according to his own judgement, but his experience in the day to day leadership of the state machinery presumably gave him a considerable influence with regard to the working out of details. Moreover, he was well suited to the task of inspiring the delegates for their subsequent work.

What role did then the body of delegates play at the Second National Soviet Congress? Not all of them were well qualified for deciding on the policy of the Chinese Soviet Republic – some of them were illiterates. [55] They were given the opportunity to express their opinions, especially in the groups organised for the discussion of Mao's report on January 26th, and they were expected to talk.[56] Some delegates are reported to have chosen the easiest way; at the group discussion they merely repeated Mao's words, and they were criticised for it.[57] Yet, they were not allowed to deviate much from the line already laid down. In his concluding remarks on January 27th Mao Tse-tung did indeed speak authoritatively:

"In the course of these two days the comrades expressed many opinions, and they related the experience and the lessons of the various aspects of our work. In summing up one can say that they unanimously accepted my report. With regard to the present situation, the tasks which arise from this situation, the measures taken in soviet policy within the various fields during the last two years, and regarding the existing weaknesses in our work, the comrades in the discussions of yesterday and of today in general agreed with my report. What the comrades said was in general extremely correct, this should first be pointed out."[58]

In spite of this assertion of general agreement Mao then proceeded to point out erroneous viewpoints expressed by delegates in the discussions. Some of the errors, if they are reported correctly, evidently arose from a failure to comprehend the situation,[59] but in a couple of cases it seems fair to say that the dissidents might well have been entitled to hold their opinions. Mao tells us:

"One comrade said that the People's Revolutionary Government in Fukien had a certain revolutionary character, and was not entirely counter-revolutionary. This viewpoint is also erroneous. I have already pointed out in my report that the appearance of the People's Revolutionary Government represents a new mode of deceiving the people, applied by a part of the reactionary ruling class in order to save their destiny from death."[60]

Quite a few delegates were reported to have held that the minimum age required for entering a marriage in the Chinese Soviet Republic ought to be lowered. This proposal Mao Tse-tung dismissed with humour:

"This view I think is not sound (t'o-tang). In the interest of the races (chung-tsu) and of the classes the minimum age for marrying ought not to be lower than 20 years for men and 18 years for women. One ought to understand that early marriages have their very bad sides. Comrades! One ought to be a little patient! (The whole auditorium roars with laughter.) In the past, under the rule of the landlords and the capitalists, some of the poor workers and peasants were not able to marry even at the age of 45. How is it that now one cannot wait even for one or two years? (Renewed loud laughter from the whole of the auditorium.)"[61]

The cited document does not at all depict a parliamentary debate between equals. The scene has in fact more resemblance to that of a schoolmaster putting his pupils on the right track. And apparently it was not only Mao who had such an attitude; Lin Po-ch'ü seems to have shown a similar attitude in correcting delegates in his own concluding remarks on January 30th. [62] Although the accounts of the proceedings are very far from complete, it seems reasonable to conclude that the opinions of the ordinary delegates, expressed in the discussions, did not count very much – they were accepted only if they conformed to the framework of policy already laid down.

Unfortunately we are totally ignorant of the extent to which ordinary delegates could bring their influence to bear through work in committees. The six committees elected on January 22nd are enumerated above, but we do not know how the congress elected them, how they were composed or how they worked. It may be of little consolation that we can negatively infer that the Committee for the Resolution on the Work Report of the Central Executive Committee did not achieve very much, as the congress on January 31st resolved that the working out of the full text of the resolution should be left to the new CEC. On the other hand, drafts were ready on the same day for the resolutions on the Red Army, on economic construction and on soviet construction, but even in these cases we do not know the extent to which the texts were actually elaborated by the committees, or to what degree they had been prepared at a still earlier stage. [63]

One device supposed to bring the will of the electorate to bear upon the decisions of the congress were the written propositions which groups of delegates handed in on behalf of their localities or organisations. [64] Unfortunately we cannot tell how they had been worked out; but almost all of them conformed quite closely to the party line, an exception being the demand to lower the minimum age for marriages which also appeared in this form. [65] Hung-se Chung-hua observed that most of the issues raised in this way had already found their general solutions in the course of the discussions of the congress. [66] On January 31st Chang Wen-t'ien moved that, because of shortage of time, the propositions should not be further discussed by the congress, but handed over to the new Central Executive Committee. The motion was unanimously adopted. [67]

A characteristic feature of the congress was the unanimity of its decisions. With the exception of the election of the CEC, which will be dealt with below, no report has been found of any delegate voting against any motion. And a glance through the day to day proceedings, as sketched above, reveals that a number of decisions are explicitly stated to have been taken unanimously. We have here a strong indication of a controlling force standing above the delegates.

The election by the congress of the Central Executive Committee seems this time to have been well controlled by the party leadership. Leading members of the 28 Bolshevik group evidently made use of this opportunity radically to weaken Mao Tse-tung's position, in spite of the fact that Mao continued to be the head of the CEC. The organ seems to have been made more ineffective with regard to political decision-making, partly through the swelling of its membership from 63 to 175. Furthermore, among the 175 full members of the new CEC only 32 were re-elected from the old body. [68] The relative position of the Central Executive Committee will be discussed below, and only the proceedings of its election on February 1st 1934 by the Second National Soviet Congress will be dealt with here.

The following account of this election, found in Hung-se Chung-hua, may be interesting enough to deserve quotation:

"Subsequently the presidium of the congress submitted the list of candidates for the Second Central Executive Committee. [The names on] this list had been proposed beforehand to the chairman of the congress by the various corps of delegates. In all there were 175 full members and 35 alternates. With regard to the question of membership (jen-shu wen-t'i) the presidium, with the approval of the whole congress, appointed comrade Lo Mai to read [the names] one by one. [He] reported name, domicile, class status, sex, membership of the party or of the Communist Youth League, race (min-tsu)*, and the present occupation of each candidate. The candidates were first submitted one by one for approval by the whole body of delegates to the congress. There were five among the candidates who were accepted by the whole congress only after they had been questioned by certain delegates. But there was one candidate who failed to be elected because the history of his work was not clear. After a replacement for him had been found, the list as a whole was submitted for being voted upon, and thereupon the whole congress unanimously elected the following 175 persons as full members of the Central Executives Committee."[69]

---

* A proper translation of min-tsu in the present context has not been found. "Nationality" may be even more misleading than "race".

The alternate members of the new CEC were likewise elected after being approved of one by one, the congress having decided to raise their number from 35 to 36. We are not told whether or not a similar procedure was followed in the subsequent election of a 35-man strong central committee for the Workers' and Peasants' Inspectorate.[70]

The election by the Second National Soviet Congress of the new CEC cannot be said to have been rushed through. A considerable amount of time must have been spent on going through the procedure. Yet we can see that the election itself meant very little for the final result; what really mattered was the nomination of candidates. And the nomination is unfortunately largely hidden from view. We are told that the candidates had been proposed by the various corps of delegates, but we are not informed of what role the party played in these proposals. Against the background of our knowledge of the result of the election, and of the efforts which the party leadership at the time was making to obtain full control of the state machinery, it should be safe to conclude that the nomination was controlled by the 28 Bolsheviks and their associates.

What was, then, in essence the nature of the institution called the National Soviet Congress? Attempting to search into this problem we evidently have to focus our attention on the 1934 congress, as the available information on that of 1931 is too scarce to allow for an analysis.

Even with regard to the Second National Soviet Congress our information is of course very far from complete, but we may attempt a characterisation of it by using the concept of Democratic Centralism. The democratic aspect was not conspicuous, but it is probably incorrect to say that it was non-existent. The reports delivered at the congress – especially the long one produced by Mao Tse-tung – were evidently to a considerable extent based on an investigation of life at the roots of society; the opinions and sentiments of the common people must at least partly have been known, and must to some degree have been taken account of in political decision-making. Although the delegates to the congress were separated from the ordinary workers and peasants through several steps of election, they may nevertheless have taken part in the process of carrying the opinions and sentiments of the common people up to the top level. However, all this only provided a part of the basis for decision-making – it seems to be clear enough that the decision-making itself was done mainly or exclusively by organs or persons standing above the congress. The Second National Soviet Congress was not controlling – it was being controlled. The centralist aspect was the predominant one.

What was legally the competence of the National Soviet Congress ?
The General Principles of the Constitution, in its 1931 as well as its
1934 version, merely laid down that the congress held the supreme
political power of the state, while the CEC was the supreme political
organ when the congress was not in session.[71] The Organic Law of the
Central Soviet, promulgated on February 17th 1934, somewhat belatedly
went a step further. It enumerated a range of powers vested concurrently
in the National Soviet Congress and in the CEC - to these we will revert
below - but only one held exclusively by the former, namely the right to
promulgate and to alter the constitution.[72]

In retrospect the latter provision could not be said to conform to the
practice of the past. The earlier constitution of the Chinese Soviet Republic is somewhat of a mystery. We know that the First National Soviet
Congress adopted the General Principles of the Constitution.[73] A Chines
Communist source of December 1931 referred to a more complete constitution,[74] and the provisional electoral law promulgated by the CEC in
August 1933 implied some alterations in this.[75] At the Second National
Soviet Congress this more complete constitution was apparently treated
as non-existent, and a revised General Principles of the Constitution
was approved of, but only in principle - it was left to the Central Executive Committee to discuss its final form.[76]

### The Central Executive Committee, the Presidium and the Council of People's Commissars

From what is said above we should be justified in concluding that the
National Soviet Congress did not play a very significant role in forming
the policy of the Chinese Soviet Republic. More important in this respect
were the Central Executive Committee (CEC) and the Council of People's
Commissars. (See p. 67, fig. 4).

Being convened at long intervals and only for brief sessions, the congress was no equivalent of a modern western parliament. If we were to
make comparisons with western-style central state organs, we would do
best to compare the parliament to the CEC and the cabinet to the Council
of People's Commissars. However, even this comparison would be far
from adequate. A major reason is that Marx, and the Russian as well as
the Chinese Communists, sharply repudiated a political theory which,
after all, has retained a certain influence in the West - the theory of

separation of powers of Montesquieu.[77] The CEC and the Council of People's Commissars both held legislative as well as executive powers. There was no clear delimitation of their competence.

Potentially, such vagueness in defining competence could engender problems. It did in Russia after the October Revolution, but there the Council of People's Commissars soon became the dominant state organ, as it could show more efficiency than the CEC. [78] Something of the same sort happened in the Chinese Soviet Republic - the council was powerful because it was efficient.

In actual fact there seems in China never to have been any acute rivalry between the two organs. During the period November 1931 - February 1934 their activity was probably well coordinated, since both of them had Mao Tse-tung as their chairman and Hsiang Ying and Chang Kuo-t'ao as their vice-chairmen. [79] But from February 1934 onward the two organs had different heads - Mao continued as chairman of the CEC, while the "Bolshevik" Chang Wen-t'ien became head of the Council of People's Commissars. At the very least, personal relationships might now seem to have warranted rivalry between the two institutions, but it did not come. Although Mao formally still held the highest office in the state, he had by that time lost his real power in governmental affairs.

The first Central Executive Committee, consisting of 63 members, was elected by the First National Soviet Congress on November 18th 1931. [80] On November 27th the CEC elected Mao Tse-tung as chairman and Hsiang Ying and Chang Kuo-t'ao as vice-chairmen. [81]

When a new CEC was elected on February 1st 1934 by the Second National Soviet Congress, it swelled to 175 full members plus 36 alternates. [82] It was, however, laid down that the presence of a third of the members was sufficient for a quorum. [83] At its first meeting, on February 3rd, the second CEC re-elected Mao Tse-tung as chairman and Hsiang Ying and Chang Kuo-t'ao as vice-chairmen, and it also elected a 17-man presidium.[84]

It has earlier been assumed that the presidium was a completely new institution in February 1934. [85] This cannot be correct. A reference to a presidium of the first CEC is found already in a resolution adopted by the First National Soviet Congress in November 1931, [86] but we do not know its composition - the term may or may not at that time have been used for the chairman plus the two vice-chairmen.

It has also been assumed that the presidium of 17 persons, elected in

February 1934, was meant to keep Mao Tse-tung in check.[87] This may well be, although it should be noted that it had a rather mixed composition. No attempt will here be made to analyse the sympathies and antipathies of its various members, but it ought to be said that only two of them, Chang Wen-t'ien and Ch'in Pang-hsien, can be identified as belonging to the 28 Bolshevik group.[88] If the 28 Bolsheviks controlled the presidium, as one against the background of the general political situation of the time must assume they did, they must have relied more on supporters than on members of their own group. The composition of the 1934 presidium was as follows:[89]

Mao Tse-tung
Hsiang Ying
Chang Kuo-t'ao*
Chang Wen-t'ien
Chu Te
Ch'in Pang-hsien (Po Ku)
Chou En-lai
Ch'ü Ch'iu-pai
Liu Shao-ch'i

Ch'en Yün
Lin Po-ch'ü
Teng Chen-hsün
Chu Ti-yüan
Teng Fa
Fang Chih-min*
Li Wei-han (Lo Mai)
Chou Yüeh-lin

The problem of making distinctions is a very difficult one in the study of the top organs of the Chinese Soviet Republic. To distinguish between the CEC and the Council of People's Commissars is often very hard, as it is in many cases, to distinguish between the CEC plenum and the CEC's presidium. It seems to be clear that the term "Central Executive Committee", as used in our sources, can mean either the plenum or the presidium.

We are, however, able to differentiate the plenum and the presidium to a certain extent. The Organic Law for the Central Soviet, of February 1934 required that the CEC should normally have a plenary session every six months; there is a possibility that these sessions were actually held more frequently than that, but they may also have been held more rarely.[90] In our sources we find reports from only two ordinary plenary sessions, one immediately after the First[91] and one immediately after the Second National Soviet Congress,[92] and an extraordinary session is said to have been held in December 1931.[93]

Legally the CEC plenum had very great powers. The General Principles of the Constitution, in its 1931 as well as in its 1934 version, stated plain

---

* These persons were not in the Central Soviet Area.

ly that it was the "supreme political organ" of the state when the National Soviet Congress was not in session. [94] As the theory of separation of powers was rejected, it is clear that the supremacy of the CEC referred to its legislative as well as to its executive capacity. [95] This was confirmed in February 1934, through article 12 of the <u>Organic Law for the Central Societ,</u> which read:

> "The Central Executive Committee may promulgate (<u>pan-pu</u>) every kind of law and decree, and execute them within the whole territory of the Chinese Soviet Republic. "[96]

The cited Organic Law keeps the plenum and the presidium neatly apart - there is no doubt that the "Central Executive Committee" in the quoted passage refers to the plenum. The law also lists a range of more or less specific powers vested concurrently in the CEC plenum and in the National Soviet Congress. The list includes the general power of legislation, the right to conclude treaties with foreign states, to regulate the judicial system of the republic, to regulate the borderlines, to establish the powers of the local soviets, to declare war and negotiate peace, to take up internal and foreign loans, to investigate and to approve the budget, to establish the tax rates, to organise and to direct the military forces, to establish the principles of national schemes of education, to plan the development of industry, agriculture, trade and communications, to elect and dismiss the members of the Council of People's Commissars, etc. [97] It was found desirable to state these powers explicitly, perhaps in order to remind the two organs of their duties; but the list does not seem to be exhaustive - one should not see in it any limitation of the competence of the congress or of the CEC. [98]


What is, then, the information we have specifically on the CEC's presidium? We know that, through a resolution adopted by the First National Soviet Congress, the presidium was charged with the task of strengthening the Red Army, [99] and that prior to the Second National Soviet Congress it was active in dealing with the People's Revolutionary Government in Fukien. [100] With regard to its work after the Second National Soviet Congress we are informed that it was asked to work out the final text of the <u>Organic Law for the Central Soviet,</u> [101] and that on one occasion it discussed and gave instructions for the work of local judicial departments. [102] This is all our sources say explicitly about the activity of the presidium; we may, however, assume that the organ actually carried out much more work than that.

One of the grounds for making such an assumption is that legally the presidium was granted very wide powers. It is true that no regulation in this respect has been found for the time before the Second National Soviet Congress. However, a document dated February 5th 1934 said that the presidium was the supreme political organ of the state when the CEC was not in session, [103] and this was confirmed about two weeks later by the Organic Law for the Central Soviet. [104] Apparently the provision meant a lot, since, as we have already seen, the plenary sessions of the CEC were supposed to be held at rather long intervals. The Organic Law further stated that even the presidium had the power to "promulgate every kind of law and decree", that it had the right to suspend and to revise decisions taken by provincial soviets, and that it should supervise the execution of laws and resolutions adopted by the National Soviet Congress or by the CEC. [105] The presidium was given wide powers, and presumably it did, to a considerable extent, make use of them.

Up to this point we have been able to keep apart the plenary session and the presidium of the Central Executive Committee, but we cannot, unfortunately, do it further on. A number of edicts were reported to have been adopted by the CEC, but often we have to leave open the question as to whether they were passed by the plenum or by the presidium. *If not otherwise stated, we will henceforth use the term "Central Executive Committee" in this vague meaning.

Keeping this qualification in mind, we can note that the CEC displayed considerable activity. We learn that on December 15th 1933 the organ issued its instruction (hsün-ling) No. 26, but it is not clear how comprehensively the term "instruction" is used in this connection. [106] However, we know the texts of a number of laws and regulations issued in the name of the CEC. [107] Generally speaking, there is no doubt that the edicts of the CEC had a tremendous significance; further discussion of this point must, however, wait until we have dealt with the apparently most efficient state organ at the top level - the Council of People's Commissars.

The Council of People's Commissars, as elected by the CEC on November 27th 1931, had the following composition: [108]

---

* During the period February - October 1934 the Central Government did not always show much regard for legal formalities. There is, therefore, also the possibility that the men in power in this period arranged for some edicts to be issued in the name of the CEC, without even calling a full meeting of the 17-man strong presidium.

| | |
|---|---|
| Mao Tse-tung | Chairman |
| Hsiang Ying<br>Chang Kuo-t'ao | Vice-chairmen |
| Wang Chia-ch'iang | People's Commissar of Foreign Affairs |
| Teng Tzu-hui | People's Commissar of Finances |
| Chou I-li | People's Commissar of Internal Affairs (nei-wu) |
| Chu Te | People's Commissar of Military Affairs |
| Chang Ting-ch'eng | People's Commissar of Land |
| Chang Kuo-t'ao | People's Commissar of Justice |
| Hsiang Ying | People's Commissar of Labour |
| Ch'ü Ch'iu-pai | People's Commissar of Education |
| Ho Shu-heng | People's Commissar for the Workers' and Peasants' Inspection |

Gradually some important changes were made in this set-up. Hsü T'e-li was appointed Acting Commissar of Education as early as March 1932,[109] and in February 1933 Hu Hai was appointed Acting Commissar for Land.[110] From April 1933 onward Liang Po-t'ai was Vice-Commissar and presumably Acting Commissar of Justice.[111] In February of the same year it had been decided that a People's Commissariat of National Economy should be established, and the Finance Commissar, Teng Tzu-hui, was appointed to serve concurrently as its head.[112] However, Teng Tzu-hui's powerful position did not last long. Sometime in the spring or summer of 1933 Lin Po-ch'ü replaced him as People's Commissar of National Economy; in August Lin was made Finance Commissar as well, while Teng was degraded to Vice-Commissar of Finances.[113]

Slightly after the Second National Soviet Congress a People's Commissariat for Food was added to the list, and the new Council of People's Commissars which was elected by the CEC on February 3rd 1934 had the following members:[114]

| | |
|---|---|
| Chang Wen-t'ien | Chairman |
| Wang Chia-ch'iang | People's Commissar of Foreign Affairs |
| Kao Tzu-li | People's Commissar for Land |
| Ch'en T'an-ch'iu | People's Commissar for Food |
| Ch'ü Ch'iu-pai | People's Commissar of Education |
| Chu Te | People's Commissar of Military Affairs |
| Lin Po-ch'ü | People's Commissar of Finances |
| Liang Po-t'ai | People's Commissar of Justice |
| Hsiang Ying | People's Commissar for the Workers' and Peasants' Inspection |
| Teng Chen-hsün | People's Commissar of Labour |
| Wu Liang-p'ing | People's Commissar of National Economy |
| Tseng Shan | People's Commissar of Internal Affairs |

Numerically the 28 Bolsheviks were not at all strongly represented in the Council of People's Commissars. As far as can be seen there was only one of them in the 1931 council, namely the People's Commissar of Foreign Affairs, Wang Chia-ch'iang*. It was apparently not until February 1934 that the second one entered – but he was a figure to be reckoned with the new chairman Chang Wen-t'ien. However, one problem is who the 28 Bolsheviks were, another one who were the persons on whom they could fully rely. We can give a fairly satisfactory reply to the former question, [1] while it is much more difficult to answer the latter one. [116)

The fact that Chang Wen-t'ien in February 1934 replaced Mao Tse-tung as chairman of the Council of People's Commissars had of course tremendous significance. Chang was from now on the real head of the state apparatus while remaining one of the most powerful members of the Politburo of the Communist Party. [117)] From about this time onward we have evidence of a progressive merging of the soviet machinery and the party machinery – a matter which we will revert to below.


For the relatively early period of the republic we have a lot more information on the work of the Council of People's Commissars than for the other top state organs. We know that by September 10th 1933 the council had held 51 meetings, [118)] and for more than half the number brief but concise communiques are found in Hung-se Chung-hua. [119)]

Participation in the meetings of the council was not strictly limited to its members. The communique on a meeting held February 6th 1932 said that so many of the commissars had at this time gone to the front that it was not possible to obtain a quorum (while not informing us what the quorum was). It was decided that under such circumstances it was permissible to call on "the responsible comrades of the various commissariats" to attend the meetings in lieu of the commissars. [120)] Later on a commissariat would often have a vice-commissar, [121)] and he must then naturally be supposed to have taken his chief's place in such a situation. But even persons standing outside the apparatus of the Central Government might be asked to take part in the meetings of the Council of People's Commissars. On August 16th 1933, at a meeting where the soviet work in Fukien was discussed and heavily criticised, "more than ten" local cadres from that province were present. [122)] Of course presence at the meetings did not automatically mean power; it seems reasonable to assume that a vice-commissar taking the place of his chief might have some influence on the decision-making of the council, while the more than ten local cadres mentioned from Fukien were there in order to supply information and to be orientated.

---

* Also called Wang Chia-hsiang.

The Council of People's Commissars to a large extent dealt with soviet work at the local levels. It listened to reports from the various provinces and counties and issued directives to their soviets. [123] In some cases instructions are reported to have been given even to provincial soviets outside the Central Soviet Area. [124]

Naturally the council often discussed the work and the organisation of the various commissariats, and it gave far-reaching instructions on these matters. [125] It discussed different sorts of regulations drafted by the commissariats, and approved them or altered them. [126] Through the various commissariats it gave directives for the work of the corresponding departments in the local soviets. [127] It appointed members of the committees attached to the commissariats, and it appointed, or nominated for appointment by the CEC, new commissars and vice-commissars. [128]

Generally speaking the Council of People's Commissars was concerned with every problem of importance for the government of the republic. Examples of matters which it dealt with are finance, agriculture, forestry, food provisions, the social position of women, military mobilisation, privileges for Red Army men, education, training of cadres, struggle against corruption and counter-revolutionary activity, class struggle, elections, sanitation and postal service. [129] Formally the council in some cases merely made proposals to the CEC, but it also took many extremely important decisions on its own authority.

Some data are available on the quantity of work carried out. The Mao-led Council of People's Commissars issued its decree (ming-ling) No. 49 on October 10th 1933, [130] while its communication (t'ung-ling) No. 8[131] and its instruction (hsün-ling) No. 17[132] appeared the same year on May 11th and on September 15th respectively. When Chang Wen-t'ien became chairman, a new enumeration was started; and under his leadership the council issued its decree No. 16 on April 10th[133] and its instruction No. 2 on May 11th 1934. [134] A certain number of the texts are available. If the edicts of the CEC were of vital significance, so also were those issued by the Council of the People's Commissars.

What then was the relationship between the CEC and the Council of People's Commissars?

According to the legal provisions the latter was definitely subordinate to the former; but there seems never to have been any clear delimitation of the competence of the two organs. The General Principles of the Constitution, in the 1931 as well as in the 1934 version, had this to say on the matter:

"Under the Central Executive Committee a Council of People's Commissars shall be organised, which shall deal with current matters of government and issue all kinds (i-ch'ieh) of laws, decrees and resolutions."[135]

This paragraph implied a contradiction. The council was subordinate to the CEC, yet it was given an apparently unlimited power to issue "all kinds of laws, decrees and resolutions". The Organic Law for the Central Soviet of February 1934 gave much more detailed regulations on the matter, but it did not solve the contradiction.

Article 25 of the Organic Law,[136] stating that the Council of People's Commissars was the "administrative organ" (hsing-cheng chi-kuan) of the CEC, may at the first glance seem to rehabilitate the doctrine of separation of powers. The context, however, made it clear that this was not the intention. From arts. 12, 17, 24 and 28 we can see that the National Soviet Congress, the CEC, the CEC's presidium and the Council of People's Commissars were all given legislative as well as executive powers.

The law stated clearly that the council was subordinate to the Central Executive Committee as well as to the latter's presidium.[137] The council had the power to issue laws, decrees and regulations, but the sphere of its activity in this respect was to be laid down by the CEC.[138] The most informative article on the relationship between these organs is No. 30, which reads:

"If the decisions of the Council of People's Commissars concern the general political line (ta-cheng fang-chen), they shall be submitted to the Central Executive Committee or its presidium for examination and approval. But if the matters are urgent, the Council of People's Commissars shall decide them, and also report to the Central Executive Committee or its presidium."

The clause allowing the council to decide urgent matters on its own authority was extremely important. In times of war political matters tend to be urgent. According to E. H. Carr the Russian Council of People's Commissars made use to a very large extent of such a provision in the 1918 constitution for avoiding the control of the CEC,[139] and the same possibility existed in China.

It should be borne in mind that the Organic Law for the Central Soviet appeared as late as February 1934. If we attempt to investigate the relationship in practice between the Council of People's Commissars and the CEC, the available material will in the main direct our attention toward an earlier period.

To some extent the difference in rank of the two organs was observed. The communiques in <u>Hung-se Chung-hua</u> report quite a number of instances when the Council of People's Commissars in important matters made proposals to the CEC, or asked for the CEC's assent, rather than making decisions exclusively on its own authority. But the practice varied. For the time before January 1933 reports of such instances are few.[140] They are, however, frequently reported for the three months 11 January - 11 April 1933.[141] After that our sources do not mention such a procedure at all, while it should be noted that the last available communique on the council's activity concerns a meeting on September 10th 1933.[142]

It was the CEC which in early 1933, at the request of the Council of People's Commissars, appointed Hu Hai as Acting Commissar for Land[143] and Liu Shao-ch'i as Vice Commissar of Labour,[144] while such appointments at other times are reported to have been decided on by the council without any mention being made of the superior organ.[145] Of course we cannot tell how accurate the communiques are, but we do have sufficient evidence of a certain inconsistency in this regard.

As far as we can see, the council did not in practice issue any of the edicts which were given the status of "laws" (<u>fa</u>) - they were all passed by the National Soviet Congress or promulgated in the name of the CEC.[146] Moreover, the CEC issued the decrees and regulations which in actual fact, according to their content, made up the penal legislation.[147] Furthermore, it was probably no accident that it was the CEC that promulgated the <u>Matrimonial Regulations</u> (December 1931),[148] the <u>Detailed Regulations for Elections</u> (December 1931)[149] and some tax regulations[150] - they all belonged to the hard core of the legislation of the Chinese Soviet Republic. But in the latter cases we have reached a point where no sharp distinction can be made.

It was the Council of the People's Commissars that issued the resolution on the tree planting movement of March 16th 1932,[151] the decree on currency of June 21st 1932[152] and that on drafting rich peasants for hard labour brigades of November 25th the same year[153] - all very significant edicts. Of tremendous importance were the council's instructions on the Land Investigation Movement, dated June 1st 1933,[154] as were its <u>Decisions on Some Problems of the Land Struggle</u> of October 10th that year[155] and its instructions on the continuation of the Land Investigation Movement of March 15th 1934.[156] In quite a large number of cases it seems to be impossible to fit the edicts of the Council of People's Commissars and those of the Central Executive Committee into two separate categories, as far as content is concerned.[157)]

The Government was aware of the fact that the relationship between the council and the CEC was far from clear. At the Second National Soviet Congress it was pointed out - in Mao Tse-tung's long report[158)] as well as in the Resolution on Soviet Construction[159)] - that a suitable division of work between the two organs had to be established. At that juncture the lack of such a division of work was declared to have been a shortcoming in the past, when both organs were under the leadership of Mao; it would seem likely to be more intolerable in the period to come, when Mao was to continue as chairman of the CEC while Chang Went-t'ien was to be the head of the Council of People's Commissars. One would then naturally expect that clear regulations on the issue were to be embodied in the Organic Law for the Central Soviet, to be promulgated on February 17th 1934. We have, however, already seen that although the law did contain more detailed regulations in this regard, taken as a whole they were not clear.

We can then say for certain that at least by early 1934 a clear division of work between the two organs was still lacking. But important questions remain, to which satisfactory answers are not possible. We know that a number of important laws, decrees and regulations were promulgated in the name of the Central Executive Committee - but did this fact mean that the CEC or its presidium actually determined their content, or was it only a formality? The same question can be asked even with regard to the edicts of the Council of People's Commissars. We know that some of the edicts of the CEC had been proposed or suggested by the council, [160)] but how common was such a procedure? Did the fact that the council sometimes asked for the CEC's assent have a real or merely a formal significance? And how detailed were the directives of the top party organs?

On the basis of the available material it seems reasonable to conclude that the Council of People's Commissars was an efficient and quite powerful organ. It is probably no accident that the journal Hung-se Chung-hua gives a very much better accont of the council's meetings than of those of the CEC and its presidium. The Council of People's Commissars was a fairly small body - a very essential prerequisite for efficiency in the government of a state during times of crisis. It included the heads of the various commissariats, the men who at the very top level were responsible for the day to day leadership of the state machinery with its system of local branches. The people's commissars and the council's chairman would through their close contact with the administration gain an insight which must be taken account of in political decision-making. The political insight which the council possessed gave it power, not only in relation to the other top state organs, but presumably to some extent also to the party leadership.

When Chang Wen-t'ien in February 1934 took over the position of chairman of the Council of People's Commissars, he was probably on the whole able to coordinate party policy and state policy very well. But it was different in the earlier period, when the party leadership and the council more clearly constituted two separate bodies, and the latter was headed by so strong a personality as Mao Tse-tung. If the party leaders laid down the political line, it must have been largely left to the commissariats and the council to work out the details - and the details were many and important. The running of a state is too complicated a matter to allow every step to be decided by people standing outside the state apparatus.

In general the Central Executive Committee probably did not play a very significant role through its plenary sessions. It was too large a body for actually directing the affairs of the state in a critical situation, and at least during the late period of the republic it was convened only at long intervals. The election by the CEC, from its own members, of the presidium and of the Council of People's Commissars, [161] was of course important, but unfortunately our sources are silent on the question of how these elections were prepared.

Another question is which role the CEC played through its presidium. This may at times have been a significant role, but we know very little about it. For the period before February 1934 we do not even know how the presidium was composed. However, some institution must have been responsible for the promulgations made in the name of the CEC, and presumably it was often the presidium; but we cannot tell the extent to which this organ was the real decision-maker.

Finally there is the role of the chairmen. Before February 1934 Mao Tse-tung was concurrently chairman of the Council of People's Commissars, chairman of the CEC and head of the CEC's presidium. In these capacities he must have been able to effect an important coordination of work, and also to influence very significantly the decisions of these organs. However, party discipline was always there. The party leadership laid down the political line, and Mao's role concerned the details. But, as already said, the details were many and important.

When Chang Wen-t'ien was made the chairman of the Council of People's Commissars, the situation became radically different. Some particular attention must be given to power relations in the last period of the republic - from February 1934 onward.

A new factor of great significance in this last period was that party organs took charge of governmental affairs in a more direct way than before. This development seems to have started slightly before the Second National Soviet Congress, but it gained momentum after it. The election of Chang Wen-t'ien as chairman of the Council of People's Commissars was presumably of crucial importance in this regard. Combining a very strong influence in party affairs with control of the council Chang now held two sets of reins in his hands – the first leading to the party apparatus and the second to the soviet apparatus. He could pull on the one or the other – or both. Judging from the material studied so far the top leader of the Communist Party, Ch'in Pang-hsien, seems in this respect to have played a less conspicuous role, but an overall study of party documents may possibly change the picture.

The more direct party rule is partly evidenced by the fact that a certain number of important edicts were issued jointly by a leading party organ and the Council of People's Commissars. Two such cases can be documented already for January 1934, [162] indicating that the party leadership started the process of acquiring more complete control of the council while Mao was still its chairman. Further, we find one edict of this kind from February 1934, [163] one from April, [164] two from June [165] and one from July. [166] As a rule the party was in these cases represented by its Central Committee, with the interesting exception of a directive of June 27th issued jointly by the Party Organisation Bureau and the Council of People's Commissars. [167]

The jointly issued edicts contained orders to the local party organs as well as to the local soviet organs. There had of course always been a very close co-operation between the two sets of organisations; but the available material seems to show that the party organs now were in the process of also acquiring even tighter control of soviet work on the local levels. [168]

We have earlier assumed that the Mao-led Council of People's Commissars in general disposed of certain power even in relation to the party leadership. There was probably a change in this regard when Chang Wen-t'ien stepped into the role of coordinating the party policy and the state policy. It may be of interest to quote a sentence from one of Chang's articles, dated June 25th 1934, which reads:

"The party has again, in instruction No. 3 of the Council of People's Commissars, clearly pointed out that........" [169]

Perhaps we should not generalise too much on the basis of this single sentence, but it does reveal that the party centre might use the council merely as a medium for communicating its own decisions.

From February 1934 onward Chang Wen-t'ien's unique position as a prominent member of the party leadership and chairman of the Council of People's Commissars enabled him to speak with enormous personal authority. Through his articles he gave, evidently with great confidence, his instructions for the administration of justice and for the class struggle, [170] while at the same time mocking at those who wanted to work within the framework of official legislation. [171] It seems to be clear enough that his personal directives in these fields were sometimes meant to be even more binding than edicts issued by any one of the top state organs.

What about the CEC's position from February 1934 onward? From February and again from April of that year we do find some important laws and regulations promulgated in the name of the organ, [172] and we also find a last and lonely decree dated August 15th. [173] However, the importance of these documents is not the main issue in this regard. What we would like to know is the part played either by the CEC or by its presidium in actually determining their content, and our ignorance in this respect has been pointed out above. But we have indeed strong reasons to believe that - in face of the presumably very effective Council of People's Commissars, the joining together of the authority of the council and that of leading party organs, and the very strong personal position of Chang Wen-t'ien - it would be impossible to stage any sort of opposition through the CEC or its presidium.

What about the position during the same period of the CEC's chairman, Mao Tse-tung? His contribution to the revolutionary cause was not insignificant. His detailed instructions, dated April 10th 1934, for the work of the hsiang soviets were of great importance, [174] and his pronouncements against the Kuomintang and Japanese imperialism had a very strong appeal. [175] But he cannot at this time have had much influence on governmental affairs at the top level. We see quite clearly from our source material, and especially from the columns of the journals Hung-se Chung-hua and Tou-cheng, that from February 1934 onward the strong man within the state apparatus was Chang Wen-t'ien and not Mao Tse-tung. To Mao, his removal from the position as chairman of the Council of People's Commissars must have been a very severe blow. [176]

The building of the Chinese soviet regime was indeed a difficult task. The new organisational pattern of the society was so totally different from the old one that everything had to be built up from the ground. The lack of educated personnel was desperate. While fighting to overcome these difficulties the new republic had to face, not only an enormous military pressure from without, but also strong subversive activities within its territory. These subversive activities can largely be classified into two categories, counter-revolution and corruption.

## A.  Counter-Revolution

Our possibility of tracing counter-revolutionary activity carried on in the Central Soviet Area is of course very limited. Our material consists entirely of Communist sources, which may well exaggerate its extent. In general we are not in a position to judge how well the reports on the counter revolutionaries, or the charges made against them, are based on actual facts. Often the accused are reported to have admitted their guilt, or their guilt is said to have been fully proved. But many strange things may occur in the administration of justice of a revolutionary state, and a measure of scepticism is justifiable. Essentially, we are reduced to giving a summary of the reports and the charges.

### The AB League

We cannot, however, totally abstain from forming judgement in this respect. With regard to the AB (Anti-Bolshevik)* League, probably the most feared of all the counter-revolutionary organisations, we have to judge whether it did or did not in fact exist within the territory of the Central Soviet Area. Ex-Communists and KMT sources claim that in ac-

---

\* Some KMT sources deny the Communist claim that AB meant Anti-Bolshevik, saying that the two letters designated respectively the provincial and the county organs of an Anti-Communist league dissolved already in 1927. (See Tsao Po-i, 1969, pp. 420-21.)

tual fact it was not active there. [1] It is not contested that such an organisation was founded by anti-Communist Kuomintang-members in 1926 or 1927; what is disputed is how long it was in existence and how wide was its scope of activity. Chu Te claims to be able to prove that the league was active by 1930, [2] which contradicts Kung Ch'u's statement that it disintegrated less than half a year after it was born.

We may assume that the AB League did exist by the early 1930s, but it is quite clear that its activity was sometimes gravely exaggerated. In a letter from the party "centre" to the soviet areas, dated September 1st 1931, a warning was issued against a tendency to see the AB-ghost everywhere. [3] The Central Bureau of the Soviet Areas adopted the criticism, and in a letter to local party organs it wrote:

> "Our understanding of the AB League was in the past too general (lung-t'ung), and we overestimated it. The AB League is the organisation of the remaining landlords and of the rich peasants, and therefore [we] treated (k'an-tai) all the remaining landlords and rich peasants as members of the league. The AB League wants to make use of, and it also has made use of, the wrong line of the party, and therefore [we] connected those who executed the wrong line with the question of the AB League, [we] thought they possibly were all members of the league. Members of the AB League want deliberately to commit errors in order to wreck (p'o-huai) the revolutionary work, and therefore [we] immediately connected all (i-ch'ieh) party members and people among the masses who committed errors with the question of the AB League, [we] thought they were not reliable and that they possibly were all members of the league." [4]

This was the voice of the party authorities. In addition, we have an account from Mao Tse-tung, confirming the seriousness of the problem. Mao tells me following from an election in a local soviet apparatus in 1930:

> "On one occasion the chairman said that those who approved of a man should raise a hand, there were some people who did not raise their hands, the chairman then pointed to those who were not raising their hands and said they belonged to the AB League". [5]

In late 1931 and early 1932 serious efforts were made to correct erroneous methods of dealing with counter-revolutionaries, and henceforth the reports on counter-revolutionary activity may accordingly have become more sober. But the errors of the past could probably not be changed overnight. We have a general to stick to our principle of reproducing the reports on, and the charges against, the counter-revolutionaries, without judging how well they were based on actual facts.

99

Valuable information regarding the charges brought against members of the AB League is found in the records of some trials held during the first part of the year 1932. The charges concerned counter-revolutionary crime which in the main were committed before the beginning of our special period; nevertheless they deserve to be reported here.

The records claim that the AB League had a highly developed underground organisation. It was said to have its branches on the district level, on the county level, and a head section was reported to have existed for Southern Kiangsi. (This did not, however, imply that the league had its organisatio in every locality). Some branches of the AB League were also said to have been detected in the Red Army. [6]

The members of the AB League were reported to be highly effective doubl dealers; several of them held responsible positions in the Communist Par or in the soviet apparatus. [7] The record of a trial held in Kiangsi in April 1932 provides an illustrative example. One of the defendants, the 33 year old docker Hsiao Tzu-cheng, would seem to have been a rather successful Communist cadre - he had been head of the organisational department of t revolutionary committee of Hsingkuo county, head of the labour movement department of the county party committee, secretary of the county party committee and head of the organisational department of the Special (Party Committee of Southern Kiangsi. However, he was alleged simultaneously to have made a similar career in the AB League - he had served as its section leader for the town of Hsingkuo and for the county of Hsingkuo, an as a member of the league's committees for the Southern Route (Nan-lu) and for Southern Kiangsi. [8]

Clearly, such people could do a lot of harm to the Communist Party and to the soviet regime. Members of the league were reported in general to have acted as agents or spies for the enemy. Some of them were said to have perverted the execution of the land policy, or they had arranged for AB-members and other reactionaries to join the Red Army in order to carry on subversive activity there. There were also some who allegedly had perverted the work of liquidating the counter-revolutionaries; they ha caused the killing of revolutionaries, common people or wavering AB-members, whereas true AB-members were spared. [9] A female member of the AB League, who was supposed to serve the revolutionary cause as a political commissar at a hospital, was accused of having plotted to in-jure the health of faithful Red Army men - she had arranged for a reckles use of medicines for them, to prevent them from recovering or from re-covering quickly, while good medicines were given to patients belonging to the league. [10]

Some of the AB-members sentenced at the recorded trials of 1932, or

possibly all of them, had already been arrested in 1931; in fact the AB
League in the Central Soviet Area seems to a very large extent to have
been wound up during the years 1930-1931.[11] However, it was reported
to be still active in some localities in the spring of 1933.[12] And even a
year later, on May 21st 1934, it was announced that in Want'ai three employees of the soviet apparatus, including the head of the military department of the county soviet and the chairman of a district soviet, had recently been denounced as members of the league.[13]

An interesting notice is found in Hung-se Chung-hua of June 14th 1933.
It deals with the arrest of an AB-leader at the very top level in Kiangsi,
Tuan Ch'i-feng. (In sound the name is quite similar to that of Tuan Hsi-
p'eng, the founder of the AB League, but they must have been two different
persons). We cannot verify the allegations that Tuan Ch'i-feng had a bandit
background, or that he had secretly played a leading role in the Fut'ien
incident of December 1930. It seems reasonable to accept, however, that
he had for some time been hiding in the mountainous area on the border of
the soviet counties Yungfeng and Kunglüeh, from where he carried on
counter-revolutionary activity, before he was arrested in February 1933.
He was subsequently sentenced to death at a public trial (kung-shen) on
May 30th, and taken to Kunglüeh for execution.[14] The justification for
accepting the information on his trial, his arrest and his hiding in the
mountains before the arrest, is that these data must have been verifiable
by some of the readers of Hung-se Chung-hua. The journal would not tell
obvious lies.


## The Social Democrats

The Social Democratic Party was said to be as determinedly anti-commu-
nistic as the AB League. Both organisations are, however, rather obscure.

Like the members of the AB League the Social Democrats were reported
to have carried on effective double-dealing, and to have infiltrated the
soviet apparatus, the Red Army and the Communist Party. Some of them
were accused of having perverted the execution of the land policy and the
work of exterminating counter-revolutionaries, or they were said to have
planned large-scale killing of revolutionaries.[15]


## The Big Sword Society

The Big Sword Society (Ta-tao-hui) was one of the Chinese secret societies,

and it caused a lot of difficulties to the Communists in the Central
Soviet Area. It may to some extent have infiltrated the soviet apparatus.
In April 1934 it was reported that the chairman of the soviet - or possibly
of the revolutionary committee* - of a hsiang in the soviet province of
Minkan had been found to belong to the Big Sword Society. [16] Moreover,
in Shihch'eng in Kiangsi many landlords and rich peasants were reported
to have sought resort to the society in the summer or early autumn of
1933, under the first phase of the campaign known as the Land Investigation Movement. [17] However, the anti-communist struggle of the Big Sword
Society seems mainly to have been carried on as a kind of guerilla warfare.
Numerous clashes between the military units of the society on the one side
and units of the Red Army or of the local soviet militia on the other, are
reported in the years 1933-34. [18] And earlier, in July or August 1932, the
society had forcibly overthrown the soviet government of Ich'ien (probably
a district) in Kiangsi. [19]

The Big Sword Society claimed that its members were protected by magic
- they could not be killed. The journal Ch'ing-nien shih-hua of January
29th 1933 gives an example of how this claim in a gruesome way was
proved to be false. A master (shih-fu) of the society had been captured by
a Communist guerilla unit and brough down from his hiding place in the
mountains of what was later to become the soviet province of Minkan. He
was hated by the masses of workers and peasants, and they demanded
that he should undergo a test. Finally the executioner demonstrated to
every one who might have believed in magical protection that he had no
difficulty in parting the master's head from his body. [20]

There was reported to be a number of other counter-revolutionary groups.
In February 1932 the Supreme Court found that an extensive subversive
activity had been carried on in the Seventh Red Army by the so-called
Reorganisationists (Kai-tsu-p'ai), i.e. the Kuomintang-fraction led by
Wang Ching-wei. Allegedly they had intended to turn Red Army units into
white units. [21] In the spring of 1933 some secret Kuomintang groups were
reported to have been detected in Fukien and Minkan. [22] And there were
the followers of Trotsky and Ch'en Tu-hsiu, [23] the Third Party, [24] the
New Communist Party, [25] etc. Much trouble was caused by some military
units, not belonging to the KMT regular forces but still fighting to protect
or to reestablish the old order; they were the Pacification and Protection
Units (Ching-wei-t'uan), the Protection Units (Pao-wei-t'uan), the Young
Boys' Army (T'ung-tzu-chün), etc. [26]

---

\* The revolutionary committees were organs of provisional government
in localities where no regular soviet had been established.

There was, then, no lack of organs for channelling counter-revolutionary activity. Nevertheless, our sources report many anti-communist and anti-soviet acts without mentioning any counter-revolutionary organisation whatsoever. Sometimes, for instance when counter-revolutionary slogans were pasted up in various localities, [27] the case may well have been that the activity had been organised but the organisation had not been detected. Other counter-revolutionary acts were caused by loyalty to the family or to the clan. This was the case of a soviet employee who misused his position in an attempt to help his brother to escape when the government wanted to arrest him, [28] and of the head of the judicial department of a district soviet who led some armed men in an attempt to free his arrested uncle, who was a landlord. [29] Moreover, the landlords and the rich peasants could, in an organised or in an unorganised way, try to counteract soviet and party policy, and think out methods of regaining their own influence. [30]

Some crimes which in another society would not be characterised as political were nevertheless in the Central Soviet Area branded as counter-revolutionary. Such were the trespasses of some private traders who damaged the soviet economy by violating various economic regulations, [31] and of the persons who made or imported forged banknotes. [32]

A bandit from Juichin, who had spent part of his time in the soviet service, was among other things accused of having "illegally struggled against a local tyrant and shared the spoils; in the premises of the [soviet] government he raped the local tyrant's wife, and thus he damaged the prestige (hsin-yang) of the soviets." [33] The damage done to the soviet reputation was probably deemed to be the most grave aspect of these charges.

It is not strange that religion and superstition should to some extent constitute obstacles to the revolutionary cause. Our sources provide one conspicuous example. In November 1933 a rock rolled down from a mountain in a place called Ts'aohsiehp'ing in the county of Juichin, and a woman explained the phenomenon as a manifestation of the goddess Kuan Yin. This happened at a time when various epidemics in Juichin had prepared the ground for a religious revival. There was a wave of worship, in which even the chairman of a district soviet, the chairman of a hsiang soviet and a couple of other cadres took part. Landlords and rich peasants were said to have made use of the opportunity to spread religious propaganda, in a deliberate attempt to damage the cause of the revolution. People from various counties made pilgrimages to Ts'aohsiehp'ing. In actual fact special passports were required for people travelling from one locality to another; but a false rumour was spread that no passport was needed for making a pilgrimage. A collection was started in order to build a temple, and a sale of articles to be used for divination was organised. Most serious of all: it was said that Kuan Yin, other Bodhisatvas and hidden soldiers and hidden generals (yin-ping yin-chiang) were capable of protecting the people and assuring victories, and that there was accordingly no need for expanding the Red Army. In March 1934 the movement was relentlessly suppressed. [34]

## B. Corruption

For thousands of years corruption was deeply embedded in the Chinese civil service. The Communist regime has obtained outstanding results in fighting this pervasive evil, but the results were not obtained overnight. It was only natural that corruption should to some extent find its way into the administration of the Chinese Soviet Republic, and be overcome only gradually.

The corrupt elements could probably operate most easily during the relatively early period of the republic, up to the end of 1932. The soviet state was then only in the process of building up a unified financial system, and there must have been an acute lack of supervision of accounts. However, the corruption of this period may to a large extent have been carried on undetected - in any case we have not many reports on it. But several cases of corruption were disclosed in 1933, and a lot were reported in 1934. Even in this respect we can only reproduce the evidence presented in our sources and are in no position to judge how well the charges in each case were based on actual facts.

One kind of corruption was connected with expropriation from the landlords and other reactionary elements. Some of the expropriated money and valuables which should have been handed in to the treasury failed to reach their destination, and not all the other expropriated goods were distributed among the masses of the people as they were supposed to be. [35] The Communists tried hard to make expropriation a major source of income for the state, so corruption in this respect could seriously damage the finances. The situation was further aggravated when part of the collected taxes failed to reach the treasury, [36] and some of the grain collected to support the Red Army failed to reach the granaries. [37]

Quite a large number of employees in the soviets and in other public institutions were found guilty of embezzlement of funds. The amounts involved were often relatively small, in many cases less than a hundred yüan. But in January 1934 the head of an accountancy office in Juichin was reported to have secured for himself more than two thousand yüan, [38] and a little earlier a soviet employee in Huich'ang had, according to a preliminary report, embezzled more than four thousand yüan. [39] The book-keeping was sometimes very bad - the main charge made against the head of the financial department of the Central Committee for Mutual Aid (Chungyang hu-chi tsung-hui) in February 1934 was that he was responsible for accounts where no receipts were found for expenditures amounting to 2, 858. 81 yüan. [40] An accountant, probably employed by the Commissariat of Labour, was in the same month accused of having embezzled somewhat more than 24 yüan, but he said: "I do not understand the affairs of accounting."[41] This remark probably did not improve his position.

The corruption scandal which received most attention was that revealed in the county of Yütu in early 1934. It appears that the amounts of money involved in no case exceeded five hundred yüan, and if they reached this proportion, more than one person had probably taken part in the embezzlement. In some cases the amount was only "some (chi) yüan", which would probably mean less than ten. But there were said to be "more than twenty-three" cases of embezzlement of funds in the county. Most of the culprits were persons in responsible positions in the soviet apparatus, and some of them held important posts in the party or in the Communist Youth League. [42]

The embezzlement of funds was only one aspect of the Yütu scandal. Another was that more than sixty cadres in the soviet apparatus, the party and other revolutionary organisations were reported to have engaged in private trade. They were in the first place making good money by exporting rice to white areas and importing salt. In eight cases embezzled money was found to have been used as capital in the trade. Very often the trade had formally been carried on by co-operatives, but in actual fact these were mainly joint-stock companies through which the cadres acted as capitalists in pursuit of profits. The misuse of co-operatives also meant tax evasion, since only private traders had to pay commercial tax. In any case it was regarded as quite impermissible that cadres should degenerate into profit-seeking traders, especially as it was found that this had meant serious neglect of their duties in the service of the revolution. [43]

# CHAPTER V. ADMINISTRATION OF JUSTICE

A study of the administration of justice of the Central Soviet Area is interesting for its own sake. It is also interesting because it exemplifies a general trend in the policies of the Chinese Soviet Republic in the period under discussion - namely a gradual swing toward the left.

We can trace a swing toward the left in judicial policy prior to the Second National Soviet Congress, in the period when members of the 28 Bolshevik group and their associates were in control of the party machinery, while Mao apparently staged a gradually yielding opposition as head of the Council of People's Commissars. The same radicalisation process continued with accelerated force after the congress, when the 28 Bolsheviks and their supporters were in full control of the party machinery as well as of the state apparatus, and nobody was in a position to stage an effective opposition.

The swing toward the left in the judicial policy of the Chinese Soviet Republic ought to be thrown in relief, while at the same time care should be taken not to miss any information which might disturb the general pattern. These considerations make the organising of the material somewhat problematic. The present chapter is, then, sub-divided into two sections - the first dealing with the apparatus, and the second dealing mainly with the swing toward the left. But the two fields are of course very much interdependent, and therefore no strict separation can be maintained.

## A. The Apparatus

### The People's Commissariat of Justice

The People's Commissariat of Justice (Jen-min szu-fa wei-yüan-pu) was one of the nine commissariats whose chiefs were elected in November 1931 shortly after the First National Soviet Congress. Chang Kuo-t'ao was the first People's Commissar of Justice[1], and he may have continued in that position right up to the time of the Second National Soviet Congress. However, he must be assumed to have held this post, as well as those of Vice

Chairman of the Central Executive Committee and Vice-Chairman of the Council of People's Commissars, only formally, as he appears never to have set his foot within the territory of the Central Soviet Area[2]. In April 1933 Liang Po-t'ai was appointed Vice-Commissar of Justice[3], and presumably he was henceforth the real leader of the commissariat. Liang Po-t'ai was formally elected People's Commissar of Justice immediately after the Second National Soviet Congress.[4]

It appears that for quite a long time the Commissariat of Justice functioned rather poorly. A document of July 30th 1933 says that it employed "some ten or more" (shih-chi) persons; this tiny staff had by that time not finished its training period, and the commissariat had not established any specialised department. The commissariat wanted to raise the number of its employees to 150 before the end of the year, but it seems clear that this figure can never have been reached.[5] The commissariat planned to establish, during the last five months of 1933, one department for criminal affairs (hsing-shih), one for civil affairs (min-shih), one for labour camps and prisons, as well as a department of general affairs and a central judicial committee.[6] Unfortunately no report has been found on the actual development of these organs.


## The Supreme Court

Whereas the People's Commissariat of Justice was the central organ of judicial administration, the (Provisional) Supreme Court could be said to have a similar position with respect to trial and adjudication. The status of the court was, however, rather ambiguous – an edict of April 1934 said it was the last instance of appeal[7], whereas a law of February the same year stated that it was subordinate to the Central Executive Committee.[8] A basic problem is: How supreme was the Supreme Court? In early 1932 it was evidently not regarded as supreme – the CEC simply revised four of the court's sentences.[9] In general the Chinese Soviet Republic did not pretend to observe the principle of independence of the judiciary.

Ho Shu-heng was the first chairman of the Supreme Court,[10] and he probably continued as such up to the time of the Second National Soviet Congress, when Tung Pi-wu was appointed to the position.[11]

The first trials before the Provisional Supreme Court were held in February 1932. At that time the court, at least as it appeared at the trials, was composed of a chairman (chu-hsi), who presumably acted as a head judge, two "commissioners" (wei-yüan), who may have been secondary judges, and the court employed two secretaries (shu-chi). Moreover, a state prosecutor (kuo-chia yüan-kao-jen) took part in the legal proceedings.[12]

In our sources there is no mention of any counsel for the defence.

The Organic Law for the Central Soviet, of February 17th 1934, envisaged a far more complicated organisation. It provided for a Supreme Court with one chief (yüan-chang), two deputy chiefs, one chief procurator (chien-ch'a-chang), one deputy chief procurator and some other procurators. The court was, moreover, to have one chamber for criminal affairs (hsing-shih), one for civil affairs (min-shih) and one for military affairs. Furthermore, there was to be a committee for discussing and deciding upon principal questions in connection with the court's activity. [13]

These regulations were evidently not complete. The Organic Law for the Central Soviet also stipulated that the detailed organisation of the Supreme Court should be laid down in a separate act[14]; but we do not know whether or not such an act ever appeared. The general trend after the promulgation of the law was certainly not to expand public institutions, but, on the contrary, to cut down on expenses and personnel. It is therefore uncertain whether even the structure of the court as sketched did or did not materialise.

## Local Judicial Departments, Judicial Committees and Courts

In December 1931 and January 1932 the soviets at the provincial, county and district levels received instructions to establish judicial departments.[15] However, because qualified personnel were extremely scarce, or perhaps nearly non-existent, the instructions could naturally not be carried out overnight. The actual work of establishing judicial departments started in general in March 1932; by June it had been carried through at the provincial and county levels, but the departments were still lacking in many districts. [16] Even almost a year later, in a pamphlet dated May 30th 1933, the Commissariat of Justice complained that up to then the judicial department of the district existed in most cases only in name, while the provincial and county departments were badly understaffed. [17]

Regulations for the staffing of the judicial departments are found in the draft bill for local soviets of December 1933. Again remembering the 1934 campaign for cutting down administrative costs, it is not possible to establish the extent to which these regulations were carried through, but nevertheless some figures will be reproduced here. The bill provides for the following staff:[18]

| | Head of dept. | Deputy head(s) of dept. | Judges (ts'ai-p'an-yüan) | Inspectors (hsün-shih-yüan) | Procurators (chien-ch'a-yüan) | Secretary (mi-shu) | Clerks (wen-shu) |
|---|---|---|---|---|---|---|---|
| Judicial dept. of the province | 1 | 1-2 | 1-2 | 2-5 | 2-5 | 1 | 1-3 |
| Judicial dept. of the county | 1 | 1 | 1-2 | 2-3 | 2-3 | 1 | 1-2 |
| Judicial dept. of the district | 1 | 1 | | | | 1 | |
| Judicial depts. of towns and cities | 1 | 1 | 1-3 | | 1-3 | | 1-2 |

As this programmed composition of the staff indicates, the power of the judicial departments was supposed to be twofold - both strictly judicial and administrative. The fact that the two powers were vested in one organ, and in an organ which was a part of the general administrative apparatus, is further evidence that the principle of independence of the judiciary was not accepted. It was, however, recognised that there were two different tasks to be performed, and at the central level an organic differentiation was made - the judicial department of the province was in strictly judicial matters subordinated to the Supreme Court, and in administrative matters to the Commissariat of Justice. [19]

The judicial departments of the various levels were supposed to organise courts for taking charge of the legal proceedings. These courts seem normally to have been composed of one head judge (chu-shen or chu-hsi) and two secondary judges (p'ei-shen). Moreover, one or two state prosecutors took part in the proceedings, and the court employed one or two secretaries. [20] No mention is found in our sources of any counsel for the defence. A source of October 1932 says that the head of the judicial department, or one of the judges attached to it, used to serve as head judge of the court, whereas representatives from the various mass organisations were secondary judges. [21] In trials of counter-revolutionaries the prosecutor was usually a representative of the State Political Security Bureau.

This organisational pattern applies in the first place to the <u>criminal courts</u> - the only ones with which we are fairly well acquainted through our sources. In principle the judicial departments were also supposed to establish <u>civil (min-shih) courts,</u> which according to an October 1932 report from the Commissariat of Justice conformed to the pattern as far as the judges were concerned. [22] It is uncertain whether the civil courts played any significant role in practice; a report from Fukien implies that they did, but one may suspect that the authors had a rather confused conception of the terms criminal and civil. [23] Moreover, the <u>ambulant courts (hsün-hui fa-t'ing),</u> to which we shall revert in the second section of this chapter, were said to constitute a third category; and it was within their competence to deal with criminal as well as with civil cases. [24]

Finally there were the <u>labour courts,</u> the earliest reference to which has been found in a source of May 1933. [25] They were established only in the judicial departments of town and city soviets, [26] and their task was to try employers and managers who had violated laws and regulations on labour or collective labour agreements. [27]

The various courts constituted one type of institution attached to the judicial department, another type was the judicial committee. A May 1933 directive from the Commissariat of Justice ordered every judicial department at the provincial, county and district levels to establish such a committee*, and it also assigned to the committee a very important role - before a trial it should discuss every case and lay down the general lines (<u>piao-chun</u>) for the adjudication. [28] The draft bill for local soviets of December 1933 stated that the judicial committee should discuss and advise on questions concerning judicial administration, investigation and adjudication. [29] Unfortunately we do not know how these instructions were carried out in practice.

In dealing with the judicial departments, the judicial committees and the courts we encounter difficulties with respect to terminology. The terminology in our sources is rather confused. Sometimes it is reported that criminal cases have been dealt with by judicial departments without any mention being made of the courts, [30] or the same departments are designated as the "provisional judicial organs" (<u>lin-shih szu-fa chi-kuan</u>) of the local soviet government. [31] The term "judicial department" is evidently often used in a wide sense, as comprising the committee and the court. Or the term may sometimes be used synonymously for the court. In fact the men of the apparatus could themselves be confused on this issue. In

---

\* Judicial committees had by that time already been established in some places.

one or two soviet documents of April 1932 the term "Revolutionary Court of Kiangsi" was used, but the Supreme Court corrected it to "Judicial Department of the Soviet Government of Kiangsi Province". [32]

It is probably not possible to clear up the issue completely. We shall below occasionally have to make use of the term "judicial organs" to comprise the judicial departments, the judicial committees and the courts.

In its May 1933 directive the Commissariat of Justice pointed out as a serious fault that the courts were sometimes ignored. In some places criminal cases were not being brought up before the courts, but punishment was decided upon secretly in the office of the head of the judicial department. The commissariat said that such a procedure was permissible when dealing with cases of a secret nature, but as a general practice it was very bad. An essential task to be performed by the courts was to educate the masses of the people in the soviet laws and in the fight against counter-revolutionaries; trials should therefore normally be held before the courts and be open for attendance by the masses of the people. [33]

In the same directive the Commissariat of Justice voiced several other complaints. It ciritcised the sentences of the local judicial organs as being often too light, but yet occasionally too severe. The liaison between superior and subordinate judicial departments was in general highly unsatisfactory, and in some cases extremely bad. The departments often ignored or disobeyed instructions and regulations from the Central Government. Sometimes there was no proper collecting of material on alleged crimes, and if the material had been collected, it happened that the judges ignored it. Although, according to the instructions, a case should normally have been adjudicated within a fortnight of it being handed over to the judicial organs, it happened that the accused was kept in custody for more than half a year before sentence was passed. [34]

Two passages from this criticism made by the commissariat deserve to be quoted verbatim:

> "In records of sentences there are often many general and abstract terms, such as 'reactionary local tyrant', 'reactionary rich peasant', 'exploited the blood and sweat of toiling (lao-k' u) workers and peasants', 'killed revolutionary comrades', etc.; but the concrete realities, the time and place, who the killed persons were, are not pointed out. Moreover, the records of sentences are all alike (t' ien-pien i-lü), they could be used for A and they could be used for B. (Juichin, Hsünwu and Huich' ang)." [35]

> "Moreover, when lower [judicial departments] send criminals to

111

higher judicial departments, they only write a name; they do not write out any facts on the crimes, and they do not at the same time send the material. Sometimes there is even no name, but they write only the number of criminals. (The Tut'ou district in Juichin and various districts in Ch'angt'ing)."[36]

It seems reasonable to assume a certain amount of exaggeration in these criticisms, but nevertheless we must conclude that the judicial departments and their courts were by May 1933 functioning very unsatisfactorily.

The main reason for this bad state of affairs was obviously the low qualifications of the personnel. However, some efforts were made to raise the standard. One method of training the personnel was for a judicial department on a lower level to send cadres to work for a time in the judicial department of a superior soviet, after which they returned to the organ they came from.[37] Another method was training through short theoretical courses.

In June 1933 the judicial department of Kiangsi province held such a course for cadres working at lower levels, and it planned to hold a second one, for county personnel, in July.[38] The rather ambitious plan of the Commissariat of Justice for the last five months of 1933 included a project for a training course, to be arranged by the Central Government, for 200 cadres; while at the provincial level, according to this plan, three courses were to be held in Kiangsi, three in Fukien, one in Minkan and one in Yüehkan. It is uncertain whether this scheme was fully carried out; if it was, the total number of cadres thus trained for work in judicial departments must have been quite large. However, the training can by no means have been thorough. The commissariat said that the course to be arranged by the Central Government was to last for two weeks, while those to be held at the provincial level were scheduled to have a duration of only 10 days.[39]

The training courses, together with the scheme of local cadres practising in organs at a higher level, may have had a considerable effect, but they probably did not work wonders. Presumably the low qualifications of the personnel of judicial organs continued to be a serious problem.

The Commissariat of Justice informs us that about 70 per cent of the cases included in table 11 refer to political crimes.[40] Against this background it is rather puzzling to read a 1932 report from the soviet of Fukien province, stating that only a relatively small proportion of the cases dealt with by judicial organs concerned political crimes or the activity of "local tyrants".[41] There may have been a considerable difference between Kiang and Fukien in this respect, and there may also have been differences con-

Tabel 11

Numbers of persons sentenced by the judicial departments and their courts
at the provincial, county and district levels within the Central Soviet Area
during the months of July, August and September 1932.

| | | |
|---|---|---|
| Sentenced to death by shooting | 271 | persons |
| Sentenced to hard labour (k'u-kung) | 399 | " |
| Sentenced to imprisonment | 349 | " |
| Fined (fa-k'uan) | 141 | " |
| Acquitted and released | 481 | " |
| Total | 1, 641 | persons |

Source: Doc. 39.


Note

The figure on fined persons does not include the so-called "local tyrants"
(t'u-hao) which had been fined or expropriated by organs not coming under
the judicial departments. Moreover, the Commissariat of Justice, in
commenting on the figures, assumed that a certain number of adjudicated
cases had not been reported.

A report of the soviet government of Kiangsi province suggests much
higher figures for persons acquitted and for those sentenced to hard
labour, but it seems impossible to establish the exact period which it
covers. (Doc. 43, pp. 46-47).

cerning definition of terms. According to the official view the main task of the judicial organs certainly was of a political nature - it was to protect the soviet power and to fight against counter-revolution and reaction.[42]


## Jails, Labour Camps, Forced Labour Brigades

Right from the outset the judicial departments needed custodial jails (k'an-shou-so) where criminals, or suspected criminals, were kept before trial. These institutions developed, and in December 1933 the draft bill for local soviets laid down that there should be such jails under the judicial departments at all levels. [43]

A reproachful passage on the custodial jails is found in the May 1933 directive of the Commissariat of Justice:

"The general situation with regard to the work of the custodial jails is that the warders lack a sense of responsibility, they do not have common sense (ch'ang-shih) as warders, the buildings of the custodial jails are not solid (chien-ku), so that it often happens that criminals run away. (The province of Fukien and the counties of Yütu, Anyüan and Hsünwu). In Huich'ang there is no head warder (k'an-shou-chang), and the custodial jail has no register of criminals, so that the judicial department does not know what criminals there actually are. Attention is not paid to hygiene, and therefore it occurs that criminals die. (Fukien, Huich'ang and Shihch'eng)."[44]

The available reports on the labour reform camps (lao-tung kan-hua-yüan), where long-term convicts were placed, are on the whole far less negative. We know that by October 1932 there was one such camp for the province of Kiangsi, one for Fukien and one for the county of Juichin. [45] According to the draft bill for local soviets of December 1933 there should be one labour reform camp attached to the judicial department in each province, and to the extent that it was found necessary camps should also be established at the county level. [46]

One of the professed aims of these institutions was to transform the prisoner into law-abiding persons. Some political and cultural education was arranged for in the camps, and books and newspapers were made available. However, this educational work was found to be highly insufficient by the Commissariat of Justice, as can be seen from its report of October 1932 as well as from its directive of May 1933. But taken together the two documents give a more positive estimate of the economic achievements of the camps. The cost of living of the prisoners was reported to be covered by the income from their production. The 1932 report says that there was also a surplus, and that a number of highly important articles were produced in the labour reform camps. Such articles were printing ink (yu-mo), letter-paper, straw sandals, etc. The commissariat's directive of May 1933 informs us that "more than twenty" different articles had been produced in the camps, but nevertheless this highly critical document says that the achievements even in the field of production were far from being satisfactory. [47]

Relatively short-term convicts were placed in the hard labour brigades (k'u-kung-tui), and dispatched to the front areas to be engaged in military transport. Admitting that it was not well-informed in this regard, the Commissariat of Justice estimated that in all "more than 900" criminals had been sent to the front by October 1932. [48] Later the hard labour brigades were to contain not only criminals, but ordinary landlords and rich peasants as well.

## The State Political Security Bureau

The State Political Security Bureau (Kuo-chia cheng-chih pao-wei-chü) was an extremely important instrument in the fight against counter-revolution. It was modelled on the Russian GPU, and Ch'en Shao-yü (Wang Ming) as well as some western writers simply refer to is as the GPU of the Chinese soviet areas. [49] The State Political Security Bureau was primarily a police organisation; but it could also, under certain circumstances, deal with counter-revolutionaries independently, without going through the judical organs. In late 1931, shortly after the First National Soviet Congress, Teng Fa was appointed head of this organisation, [50] and he is reported to have continued in that capacity at the time of the evacuation of the Central Soviet Area and afterwards. [51]

The relative competence of the State Political Security Bureau on the one hand, and the judicial organs on the other, is a matter which will be dealt with below. Here it will suffice to point out that the former was more experienced than the latter, which was important with regard to what might be called a rivalry between the two. After the First National Soviet Congress the judicial organs had to be built up from the ground, and the building-up process naturally took some time. The State Political Security Bureau seems to have had a much easier start. It was established as a state organ shortly after the congress, but it had its forerunner. Teng Fa and his machinery had already for some time been engaged in the fight against real or imagined counter-revolutionaries. [52]

The central organ of the State Political Security Bureau was subordinated to the Council of People's Commissars. [53] The bureau also had its local organs attached to the soviets at the provincial and the county levels, and its commissioners at the district level. In a similar way it was represent in the Red Army and in various other institutions. Further, the bureau's central organ, as well as each of the local ones, were supposed to have o intelligence section (chen-ch'a-pu or chen-ch'a-k'o) and one executive section. The intelligence sections had their network of information agents and the executive sections had their own armed units. The principle that subordinate organs owed absolute obedience to the superior ones was ever more strongly emphasised for organs in the hierarchy of the State Politic Security Bureau than for the various soviet departments. [54]

## Other Police Forces

The State Political Security Bureau was not the only organisation charged with police functions. The local militia organisations, the Red Guards (Ch'ih-wei-chün) and the Young Vanguard (Shao-nien hsien-feng-tui), kep watch at certain points on the roads, and it was probably in the main thes forces the judicial departments relied upon when making arrests indepen of the Security Bureau. [55] Some efforts were made to build up a People' Police (Min-ching), attached to the departments of internal affairs in tow and cities, but this work did apparently not proceed very far. [56] The dr bill for local soviets of December 1933 said that the judicial departments should establish a Fa-ching, [57] which apparently meant a police force of a conventional type, but we are ignorant of its actual development.

## The Handling of Criminal Cases

Having so far been concerned with the establishment and the organisation structure of the judicial organs and the police, we proceed to deal with the functional aspect. This is a rather complicated topic, and in an attem to clear it up a description of some standard procedures will initially be given here – a description which in part shall have to be modified in the second section of the chapter.

In spite of a desire to treat administration of justice in general we shall have to deal in particular with counter-revolutionary cases, or cases characterised as counter-revolutionary. The material determines the content of the discussion.

First, then, some words on a serious problem which the republic inherited from the practice of the past. A document issued by the Central Executive Committee in December 1931 says that previously torture had been widely used in the interrogation of suspected counter-revolutionaries. It also says that the investigation of alleged crimes had at the same time been badly neglected. In this way the fight against counter-revolution could of course easily be led astray; under heavy torture a man will normally confess what he is asked to confess. The Central Executive Committee therefore laid down that torture should be absolutely eliminated, and that it should be replaced by thorough investigation. [58] It was, however, much easier to issue orders than to change a deeprooted practice. The May 1933 directive of the Commissariat of Justice tells us that the use of torture had even up to that time been common in some places, while there continued to be serious neglect with regard to investigation. [59]

The first action against a suspected counter-revolutionary individual or group was supposed normally to be taken by one of the local organs of the State Political Security Bureau. The Security Bureau was the special political police; as already said, it had its intelligence agencies for detecting activity carried on against the regime, and it possessed the physical power required to make arrests. It also undertook the preliminary interrogation of suspects before handling them over - if it did hand them over - to a judicial department. For the ensuing legal proceedings the bureau normally also assigned one or two representatives to act as prosecutors.[60]

It is not clear what then was left to do for the procurators employed by the judicial departments of the province, the county and the city. [61] There is, in fact, a possibility that these procurators existed only on paper, and that the problem thus never arose. If they really existed, they probably contributed to the investigation and the prosecution of counter-revolutionary cases, as well as of cases of a different nature.

The role played by the committees attached to the judicial departments is also obscure. As mentioned above, the judicial committee was supposed to discuss every case before a trial, and to lay down the general lines for the adjudication, but we cannot tell the extent to which it fulfilled these tasks.

We now come to the functions of the courts. The general proceedings of a trial in 1932, and at least during part of 1933, seem to have been quite simple. The prosecutor(s) brought forward the charges against the accused, and the judges examined and sentenced him. Sometimes, but not always, in the brief and certainly incomplete records of the trials, witnesses are reported to have been heard; while no mention is made of any counsel for the defence. The defendant might himself plead his cause as best he could;

but if he failed to convince the court of his innocence or of extenuating circumstances, then he should not have tried. Attempts to evade the guilt could result in additional punishment. [62]

No general rules have been found to determine which cases should be dea with a which level. Legal proceedings were by no means always initiated the bottom of the hierarchy. They might begin at the level of the district, the county, the province, or in the Supreme Court.

In the relatively early period of the republic the judicial organs of the district were supposed to deal only with minor cases, [63] but, as we shal soon see, their competence was later highly increased. Very little is known on the division of work between the judicial organs of the county an those of the province. The main reason why a certain number of cases w directly to the Supreme Court in early 1932 may well have been that the system of lower judicial organs had not yet been built up. [64] But the sam might also happen at later dates. [65] The Organic Law for the Central Sov of February 1934, stated that one of the tasks of the Supreme Court was "examine" (shen-ch'a) cases involving violation of the laws by staff mem bers of "high-ranking organs" (kao-chi chi-kuan). [66] Presumably the cov was then also supposed to adjudicate such cases, and in the first instance

However, the Organic Law for the Central Soviet made one exception. Th were some persons who were not subject to the jurisdiction of even the Supreme Court. In a parenthesis the law stated that "cases of violation o laws by members of the Central Executive Committee shall be dealt with separately by the Central Executive Committee or the Presidium."[67] What here seems to be suggested is a court of impeachment, and in this case it is in accordance with general practice that the legal proceedings were initiated at the top level.

We then come to the right of appeal. In December 1931 the Central Exe- cutive Committee laid down that a person condemned to death by the judicial organs of the province - the lowest level at which death sentence at that time could normally be passed - should be allowed 14 days to appe to the Supreme Court. [68] However, on April 3rd 1932 a court under the judicial department of Kiangsi province passed some sentences simply ignoring this provision[69] - an error which the Supreme Court later poin ed out. [70] The judicial department of Kiangsi province seems also to be responsible for an unsigned article published in July 1933, stating that th right of appeal was only for workers and peasants, and not for "local tyrants", gentry or landlords. [71] The Judicial Procedure of the Chinese Soviet Republic, promulgated by the CEC in April 1934, was in some wa more moderate than that - it said that counter-revolutionaries and peopl from the most reactionary social groups were to be deprived of the right only under certain circumstances, for example in border areas and in areas under attack by enemy forces. Otherwise, said the Judicial Procedure, there was to be a general right for a convicted person to appeal the sentence, but only once and within a maximum period of seven days. If the legal proceedings had been initiated at the district level, the sentence could be appealed to the county, but not further. If the proceedings had been initiated at the county level, an appeal could be made to the province; and if they had been initiated at the provincial level, an appeal could be made to the Supreme Court. A third trial of a case could only be arranged if a procurator demanded it. [72]

Different from the right of appeal were the provisions that sentences passed by judicial organs at a lower level under certain conditions required the approval of judicial organs at a higher level. The known regulations requiring such approval of death sentences will be dealt with in the second section of this chapter.

With regard to actual practice we know that the Supreme Court in 1932 approved some and and also revised some sentences passed at the provincial and the county levels. As mentioned earlier we even have an example from the same year of the Central Executive Committee revising four sentences passed by the Supreme Court. What was at stake with these reported approvals and revisions was not always capital punishment. Our sources do not mention any appeal having been made, and no new trial was staged. The approval or the revision of the sentences was based on the records of the courts which had originally passed them, and possibly also on other written material. [73] The Judicial Procedure of April 1934 abolished this "system of approval from above", while at the same time laying down in some detail the right of appeal. [74]


B. The Gradual Swing Toward the Left

It is not at all surprising to find that the apparatus built up for the administration of justice and for the exercise of police power had many shortcomings. The transition from the traditional Chinese system of justice to soviet justice was indeed a radical one. The building up of an entirely new machinery, under the extremely difficult circumstances, may have seemed to be an almost impossible task. The efforts made to overcome the shortcomings are quite impressive.

A judgement on how good the system was depends on what standards we use. Shall it be judged from a revolutionary or from a legal point of view?

Was the purpose solely to kill or to send to the labour camps as many counter-revolutionaries as possible? Or ought there also to be certain safeguards against doing injustice to individuals? If we base our judgement on the presumption that such safeguards are of vital significance, then we are very likely to come to the conclusion that the system started to deteriorate before it had been fully built up. As time went on the revolutionary motives took complete command over the legal motives. While aware that the use of terms may be disputed, I think it is justifiable to call this a swing toward the left.

The judicial policy was probably a major issue in the struggle between the leftist radicalism of the party leadership and the relative moderation of Mao Tse-tung. Liang Po-t'ai, who apparently was the real head of the Commissariat of Justice from April 1933 onwards, had of course a very important position in this regard, yet he seems to have merely been an instrument for carrying out policies decided upon at still higher levels. If he was responsible for the commissariat's directive of May 30th 1933, [75] then he was relatively moderate at this time, when Mao Tse-tung was still in a quite strong position. Later, after Ch'in Pang-hsien and Chang Wen-t'ien had gained full control, Liang Po-t'ai became extremely radical. [76]

## Relative Competence of the State Political Security Bureau and of the Judicial Organs

One important aspect of the swing toward the left in judicial policy is the development of the relative competence of the State Political Security Bureau - the most significant police organisation - on the one hand, and of the judicial organs on the other. It seems to be clear that the standard procedure which the Central Government wanted to introduce in the early period of the republic was that the Security Bureau should arrest counter-revolutionaries and carry on preliminary interrogation, whereas the judicial organs should arrange for trial and adjudication. If a society has a police and a judiciary, the normal division of work between the two will be along such lines. However, in the Central Chinese Soviet Area the division was never absolute, and in the later period it was almost completely obscured. There were two trends in the development - the judicial departments were further authorised to make arrests, and the State Political Security Bureau was further authorised to punish counter-revolutionaries independently, without legal proceedings. The latter trend marked a swing toward the left, while the former by no means meant a tendency in the opposite direction.

The principle that normally only the State Political Security Bureau had the right to arrest counter-revolutionaries was laid down by the CEC in late 1931. There were important exceptions to the rule - other organs were allowed to make arrests under certain circumstances, especially in new soviet areas - but the rule was nevertheless there. [77]

In April 1934 the rule was completely abolished. The judicial departments and several other organs were generally given the power to arrange for arrests. [78] The purpose was by no means to curb the activity of the State Political Security Bureau - at this very critical time the Central Government undoubtedly wanted to expand it. All available forces were to be mobilised for a total war against the counter-revolutionaries; the full capacity of the Security Bureau was to be made use of, but it was no longer sufficient.

As for the right to try and to adjudicate counter-revolutionary cases, the CEC's instructions of December 13th 1931 stated plainly that it belonged to the judicial organs. [79] However, the General Principles for the Organisation of the State Political Security Bureau, issued by the CEC at about the same time as the instructions, said something rather different. It did confirm that the right in general belonged to the judicial organs, but continued:

> "Only at the time of internal war and of outward expansion (hsiang-wai fa-chan) of the soviet movement, the State Political Security Bureau has the right, within the sphere allowed by its committee* and in accordance with the laws, to sentence and to carry out the punishment for some categories (mou-chung) of counter-revolutionary criminals. "[80]

The quoted passage did indeed open wide possibilities for the intrusion of the Security Bureau - this police organisation - into the judicial field. One obvious reason for making such a provision was that the judicial organs simply did not exist at the time. The actual work of establishing judicial departments started in general only in March 1932, while the Supreme Court passed its first sentences in February of the same year. Somebody had to fill the vacuum, and this was mainly left to the Security Bureau.

And even somewhat later, when there was not such a complete vacuum, the Security Bureau was probably supposed to deal with counter-revolutionaries independently in very urgent cases, especially in war zones and in border areas. Nevertheless, the CEC's instructions of December 13th 1931, together with the efforts made to build up a judicial apparatus, seem

---

* This was the committee attached to the central organ of the State Political Security Bureau.

to show that the Central Government in the relatively early period aimed at allotting judicial business to the largest possible extent to the judicial organs.

In the late period of the republic the Central Government's policy in this regard changed quite radically. It is true that the short and scattered reports found in Hung-se Chung-hua from the spring of 1933 onward, informing us that the Security Bureau had executed criminals without any mention being made of a trial, [81] do not provide a basis sufficiently solid to define a trend in the development. Somewhat more informative is a decree issued by the Council of People's Commissars on February 9th 1934, soon after the 28 Bolsheviks and their supporters had gained full control and Chang Wen-t'ien had become the real head of the state apparatus. The decree, citing the critical military situation of the time, regulated the competence of the Security Bureau to arrest and to execute counter-revolutionaries in the following way:

"1. For the suppression (ya-p'o) of enemy spies, Fascists of the border areas, reactionary local tyrants and gentry, landlords, and people plotting to rebel, the local organs of the Security Bureau in the border areas and the organs of the Security Bureau in Red Army units at the front have the right to undertake the punishment (ch'u-chih) of such counter-revolutionaries directly, without going through the courts. But after they have been punished a report must be sent to [the central organ of] the State Political Security Bureau for recording and control.

2. In areas where the activity of the Big Sword bandits has not yet been liquidated, the State Political Security Bureau, its local organs and its organs in the Red Army shall, without going through the courts, directly undertake to punish leaders of the Big Sword bandits, and stubbornly counter-revolutionary Big Sword bandits with a landlord or a rich peasant background, whom they have captured in the course of their work. But after the punishment a report must be sent to [the central organ of] the State Political Security Bureau for recording and control.

3. In relation to serious (chung-ta) and urgent (chin-chi) counter-revolutionary cases, the State Political Security Bureau, its local organs and its organs in the Red Army and in the military district have the right to undertake urgent (chin-chi) punishment. If, after urgent punishment has been undertaken, a dispute arises with the local government or other organs, or with military or political chiefs (chün cheng shou-chang), the right to determine whether the punishment was right or wrong belongs to the Council of People's Commissars." [82]

Even this decree does not remove every doubt about the correctness of concluding that a change in policy had taken place. The vague decree did provide a very wide competence for the Security Bureau, at the cost of the judicial organs, but something of the same sort might be implied by the still vaguer passage quoted from the "General Principles" of late 1931. It is extremely difficult to make any concrete comparison. Fortunately we have an article by Chang Wen-t'ien, dated February 17th 1934, which can help us to clear up the problem.

Chang Wen-t'ien's article shows clearly enough that there were two conflicting views on the issue: on the one hand was the impact of an old policy of division of functions between the Security Bureau and the judicial organs, on the other was a new policy of enhancing the position of the former. He wrote:

> "Sometimes the Security Bureau blames the judicial organs for not carrying out its advice, but in actual fact the Security Bureau has itself the right to carry out its own will. Sometimes the judicial organs blame the Security Bureau for having meddled with their independence, but actually the judicial organs ought to co-operate with the Security Bureau, so as to deal jointly with counter-revolution. Of course the judicial organs and the Security Bureau have clearly different tasks, .... But under the conditions of the present internal war such a clear division of work is still in actual life extremely difficult; nor is it necessary. This is especially true in new soviet areas, where the establishment of political power is in its beginning; there we have no division at all between judicial departments and Security Bureau, we have only the committees for suppression of counter-revolutionaries. .... It is quite clear that the Security Bureau and the judicial organs can only in the course of gradual consolidation of the soviet power further manifest (piao-hsien ch'u) the clear division of work between them. The reason why it is often necessary for the Security Bureau, after having arrested and undertaken a preliminary interrogation of criminals, to send these fellows (chia-huo) to the courts for judgement, by no means is that this is a question of formality or procedure, nor is it that the judicial organs are better suited to judge criminals, but it is in the main that only in this way is it possible to make the masses clearly understand the counter-revolutionary plots, to teach them how to struggle against counter-revolution, and thus to increase the enthusiasm of the masses' support of the soviet power."[83]

Chang Wen-t'ien, as the new head of the Council of People's Commissars, would let all legal considerations in this respect go by the board. The quoted passage gives one example of his contempt for "formality" and "procedure", and a clear sign that he was pushing the judicial policy toward the left. We shall soon bring forward more.


## Relative Competence of Judicial Organs at Different Levels

In the early period of the republic there was a certain gradation of the competence of judicial organs at the different levels. There was a special reason for this in the Chinese Soviet Republic. The shortage of qualified personnel was desperate, and in allocating the personnel which could be found preference was naturally given to the higher organs. The higher judicial organs had a more qualified personnel at their disposal, and they were supposed to carry a higher responsibility. The competence of the lower organs was then correspondingly circumscribed. However, as time went on a very significant change was made in this respect.

The CEC's instructions of December 13th 1931 said that even the county judicial organs had no right to pass death sentences, although exceptions to the rule could be made under certain circumstances, [84] and presumably the power of the district organs was then meant to be still more limited. The Provisional Organic and Judicial Regulations for the Judicial Departments, promulgated by the CEC on June 9th 1932, gave the county judicial organs a somewhat freer hand, while those of the district were held firmly in check. As this important document unfortunately is not available, I shall quote some of its provisions as reproduced, or possibly copied, [85] by Chang Wen-t'ien:

> "The district judicial departments shall deal with general and not important cases. If they pass sentences of punishment, the period of forced labour or of imprisonment must not exceed half a year. The county judicial departments have the power to pass death sentences, but they can be carried into effect only after having been approved by the provincial soviet. The judicial departments of the provinces have the power to pass death sentences, but they must be handed over to and approved by the Provisional Supreme Court before they are carried into effect." [86]

First of all we see from this passage that the Central Executive Committee' circumscription of the power of the district judicial departments was a a very narrow one. It was not, however, always observed. In May 1933 the Commissariat of Justice complained that there even were some district departments that passed and executed death sentences, in ignorance or in defiance of the regulations. [87]

The second point to be noted from the quoted passage is that death sentences passed at the county level, or even at the provincial level, must, according to the 1932 regulations, be approved before execution by higher instances. Writing in February 1934 Chang Wen-t'ien bitterly criticised this system:

"Many counter-revolutionaries who ought swiftly to have been executed have had their lives saved through our many "approvals", thus letting the enthusiastic demands of the masses be cooled off by the many "approvals", and causing the effect of the executions of counter-revolutionaries in inciting the struggle of the masses, and in educating the masses, to be very badly weakened."[88]

Neither did Chang Wen-t'ien like the narrow circumscription of the power of the district judicial departments. He noted as a step forward an instruction issued by the Commissariat of Justice on July 5th 1933, saying that "whenever the judicial departments at the district level during the Land Investigation Movement encounter landlords and rich peasants whose crimes are evident (tsui-o chao-chu), and who are bitterly hated by the local masses, they can, if a majority among the masses has demanded it and the judicial department of the county soviet has approved it, carry out capital punishment."[89]

But by February 1934 even this provision did not satisfy Chang Wen-t'ien. He thought the clause requiring the approval of the county soviet was unnecessary, and wrote:

"I think that, with regard to the counter-revolutionaries among the local tyrants, gentry, landlords and rich peasants who are bitterly hated by the masses, the district judicial departments can, if the broad masses ask for it, first carry out capital punishment and afterwards report to the county soviet for recording. Last year, at a conference on the Land Investigation Movement, comrade Mao Tse-tung also pointed out that such a thing was necessary. Because the counter-revolutionary activity of the local landlords, the local tyrants and the gentry, and the demands of the masses, are what the head of the district judicial department knows most clearly, it is not absolutely necessary to have so much knowledge of the laws. If he just has a firm class standpoint, then he can correctly give the criminals the punishment they ought to get."[90]

Unfortunately I have not been able to check the reference which Chang makes to a pronouncement by Mao. If the reference should be found to be correct, we would still be left with the almost impossible task of establishing whether Mao on this occasion had expressed his own view, or whether he had spoken under pressure. The relative radicalism of Mao Tse-tung

125

during the Land Investigation Movement will be dealt with in the next chapter.

Chang Wen-t'ien's standpoint is clear. He evidently wanted to allow the head of the district judicial department to take the real decision on death sentences for counter-revolutionaries from reactionary classes. This meant the opening of another channel for large-scale killing, and it signified another aspect of the swing toward the left in judicial policy. Considering the contempt for laws and regulations expressed by Chang Wen-t'ien and Liang Po-t'ai, to which we will revert below, we may well assume that the Central Government expected Chang's words to be observed even before they were legally sanctioned.

The legal sanction came, however, with the Judicial Procedure of the Chinese Soviet Republic, of April 8th 1934. This edict laid down the circumstances under which the judicial organs of the district could pass and execute death sentences for counter-revolutionaries exclusively on their own authority - in fact these circumstances comprised the general situation of the time. [91]

## The Influence of Mass Sentiments

The development of the role played by agitated mass sentiments in judicial matters signifies still another aspect of the swing toward the left. It is true that the demands of agitated masses could play a significant part in this regard in the time before the First National Soviet Congress. [92] After the republic had been established, the soviet authorities were apparently in a dilemma as to whether the judgement of criminals should be governed by mass sentiments or by judicial regulations. It was not always possible to serve two masters. In the relatively early period of the republic the Central Government seems as a whole to have attached more importance to the observance of the official regulations than to the listening to mass sentiments. After the Second National Soviet Congress, when Chang Wen-t'ien had become the real head of the state apparatus, it was definitely the other way round.

One of the documents from the early days of the republic, the CEC's instructions of December 13th 1931, did imply that the demands of the masses on judicial matters might by decisive in new soviet areas, but at the same time the need to establish "revolutionary order" (ko-ming chih-hsü) was stressed in general. [93] The first annual report of the Commissariat of Justice, dated October 24th 1932, did not mention that sentences should be influenced by demands directly expressed by the masses (although it claimed that the masses controlled the soviet courts indirectly), but it firmly demanded that the laws and regulations should be observed. [94] The judicial organs were again seriously warned against breaking laws and regulations by the May 1933 directive of the Commissariat of Justice, which, however, also told them to pay attention to the opinions of the masses when judging criminals. [95] The role played by agitated mass sentiments in judicial matters became very conspicuous during the Land Investigation Movement, which started full operation in June 1933; [96] and at the end of the same month the judicial department of Kiangsi province issued a warning to the district judicial departments against following the "procedure" (shou-hsü) mechanically. [97] In February 1934 Chang Wen-t'ien plainly told the judicial organs to pay more attention to revolutionary necessity and the demands of the masses than to laws and procedure. [98]

The development of the ambulant courts is essential in this connection. Such courts are mentioned already in the October 1932 report of the Commissariat of Justice, [99] but they did not play a very significant role before the Land Investigation Movement was fully launched in the summer of 1933. [100] We know that in September and October the same year they were quite active in some of the counties of Kiangsi; [101] and apparently it was also during this summer and autumn that their role changed to some extent.

The general idea in organising ambulant courts was all the time to enable the people of the same locality as the accused to attend the legal proceedings; the trial was therefore held where the accused lived or where the crime had been committed. [102] But the purpose of providing this sort of contact with the local masses does not seem to have been quite the same during the whole period under study. In the relatively early part of the period the purpose was said to be that of educating the masses, and of unmasking counter-revolutionary plots before the masses. [103] This educational aspect was even at later dates considered to be of great importance; however, our sources from June 1933 onward tell that there were additional aims to be attained – the ambulant court was now also regarded as one of the instruments to be used for enabling the masses to express their opinions on judicial questions, and for arousing, or for releasing, mass sentiments at the trial. [104]

Another instrument enabling mass sentiments to play an increasing role was the "public trial" (kung-shen). The term is very difficult to evaluate. Probably it was sometimes simply used for trials held by a court and open to the public. In May 1933 the Commissariat of Justice said that legal proceedings should normally be counducted in this way. [105] When the term is used merely in such a sense, the public trial is indistinguishable from the ordinary one. Nevertheless, there is reason to have a closer look at the available reports on the trials which were explicitly designated as public, because they seem to have developed into a special institution. As time went on there were apparently two trends in their development. The role of legal procedure in the public trials seems to have been diminishing, while the role of mass sentiment was increasing.

At least four of the "public trials" in 1932 and 1933 were explicitly said to be conducted, or organised, by a court. [106] In two instances we are also told that there were a head judge, secondary judges and prosecutors. [1] The numerous reports found on public trials from 1934 are as a rule very short, and none of them says that a court took part in the proceedings. [108] Yet it is possible, or one might say it is probable, that there was even at this time a court of some kind organising the action, but in any case this was ignored by the reporters. By 1934 the emphasis was definitely laid on the opinions and the sentiments expressed by the masses.

As already mentioned, the mass influence on judicial matters was not a new thing in 1934. It is reported to have had some impact in the single trial found to be designated as public in 1932. [109] It is more conspicuous in the reports on public trials in 1933, [110] while the only thing that is revealed of the whole procedure in most of the short reports from 1934 is that the culprit was executed after public trial, and according to the demands of the masses. [111]

Mass sentiments could not be left uncontrolled. And the problem of control might under certain circumstances be a very difficult one. A resolution adopted in June 1933 by a conference of local soviet personnel warned against staging public trials of treacherous cadres in areas where clan struggles, or struggles between localities, were going on. [112] The implication is obvious - the development of the people's sentiments might take a wrong course.

Documents from the summer and the autumn of 1933 also tell about the local masses being prepared by propagandists and agitators before public trials were staged, [113] and the agitation carried on at the trial itself may have been still more important. One report, from T'aching district in Huich'ang, informs us that a team dispatched by the Commissariat of the Workers' and Peasants' Inspection organised the participation of the local activists (chi-chi fen-tzu) in public trials of bad cadres - one person was given the task of persuading those among the local population who were opposed to the trials being held, one was to get people among the masses to express their opinions on the accused at the trial, one was to struggle against people defending him, etc. [114] Knowing that such things were practised in 1933, we may well be justified in using our imagination to supplement the brief accounts from 1934, assuming that the frequently reported demands of the masses that the culprit should die were to a large extent the results of propaganda and agitation.

At some public trials in 1932 and 1933, and perhaps even in early 1934, mass sentiments may well have been held in check after first having been aroused by agitation, since there was a difference with regard to the punishment given to the convicted. [115] But no suggestion of such an effective check has been found in reports on public trials held from about mid-March 1934 onward; the punishment was then uniform - it was death. [116] An agitated crowd can indeed be a cruel judge.


Development of the Penal Legislation

The penal legislation of the Chinese Soviet Republic probably did not come to play a very significant role. In the relatively early period of the republic it may have been virtually non-existent; no penal act has been found previous to October 1933. [117] To some extent such legislation was developed in late 1933 and early 1934; but already from February 1934 onward the Central Government showed a very strong contempt for laws and regulations, warning the local cadres not to allow the fight against counter-revolution to be restrained by legal considerations.

Before examining the penal acts which are available, we should note that the Chinese Soviet Republic did not fully adopt the principle of equality before the law. The constitutional outlines of 1931 and 1934, adopted respectively by the First and by the Second National Soviet Congresses, did state that there was equality before the law for the "citizens" (kung-min), but this concept applied only to workers, ordinary peasants, red soldiers and other toiling people (lao-k'u min-chung) with their families. [118] Such an equality was not offered to people from reactionary classes. Already in late 1931 it was clearly laid down that landlords, rich peasants, capitalists, etc. should be punished much more severely than for instance workers and ordinary peasant would be, for the same counter-revolutionary offence. [119]

It is very difficult to say whether the development of the penal legislation did or did not represent another aspect of the general swing toward the left. There may have been statutes which are not available, and some of those which are available are extremely vague.

The least informative of them all is the Regulations of Punishment for Violation of Laws and Ordinances on Labour, promulgated by the Central Executive Committee on October 15th 1933. [120] This statute merely pre-

scribes minimum penalties, mainly for employers and managers violating
the rights of their workers. With regard to the very smallest enterprises
these minimum penalties were very light - three days' forced labour or
imprisonment, or a fine of three yüan, for such offences committed by
employers with less than three employees. However, they rose rapidly -
minimum three months' imprisonment, or a fine of 100 yüan, for employers of seven or more workers, provided that the offence had affected
a majority of the employees. [121] This differentiated treatment is in itself interesting; but we would have to know something about the gravity
of the offences, and much more about the scale of penalties, to be able
to say what tendency the statute represented.

Secondly we have the CEC's decree of December 15th 1933 concerning
the problem of flight from the Red Army. The following treatment which
it prescribed for individual deserters who, not carrying a gun, had fled
home "because their political consciousness (chüeh-wu) was insufficient",
may astonish many a werstern observer:

> " ... the government of each locality must strengthen its propaganda
> and agitation toward them, organise the work of preferential treatment
> (yu-tai) for their families*, and make them voluntarily return to their
> units. Such measures as arrest and confinement must absolutely not
> be taken against them, ...."[122]

One reason for this almost idyllic provision must have been a desire not
to contradict the principle of the voluntary nature of Red Army service.
Another reason - the government was more concerned with making useful
soldiers out of the apparently large number of deserters than with punishing
them. The decree as a whole was not so idyllic. It said that a man who fled
from his unit carrying a gun with him should be shot, and the same fate was
to befall those who organised the running away of soldiers on a larger
scale. [123] Compared with earlier, more informal instructions on this
issue, [124] the decree seems to have represented a stricter and not a more
lenient line.

Another decree issued by the CEC on December 15th 1933 dealt in the
main with the punishment of employees of soviet organs, state enterprises
and public bodies who were found guilty of embezzlement of funds. The
penalties which it prescribed for such crimes, in addition to a partial or
a total confiscation of the convict's property, were as follows:[125]

---

* What is meant here is the same sort of "preferential treatment" which
should be given to the families of Red Army men in general.

| Amounts of money embezzled | Penalties |
| --- | --- |
| More than 500.00 yüan | Death penalty |
| 300.00 - 500.00  " | Imprisonment of from two to five years |
| 100.00 - 300.00  " | Imprisonment of from half a year to two years |
| Less than 100.00  " | Forced labour of less than half a year |

Unfortunately our knowledge of punishment for corruption prior to the issuing of this decree is too scanty to make a comparison.

The penal legislation of late 1933 is on the whole quite difficult to evaluate, but it does not seem to be very rigorous. There is no reason, however, to believe that it was more lenient than earlier practice; it may rather have been the other way round. Nevertheless, against the background of the general radicalisation of judicial policy we might well have expected these acts to have prescribed a harder line. On the other hand, it must be borne in mind that they were issued at a time when Mao Tse-tung's power in the state apparatus was not yet done away with. He may still have had a moderating influence on the legislation.

On April 8th 1934, a little more than two months after Mao had definitely been removed from power, the CEC promulgated the Regulations for Punishment of Counter-Revolutionaries.* Even this statute, dealing with a large number of political, military and economic crimes, is rather difficult to evaluate - it is too vague. The offences defined by its various articles could be grave indeed, but some of them were not necessarily so. For almost all of them capital punishment was ordained in principle, but very often the penalty could be reduced under extenuating circumstances, in some cases right down to six months' imprisonment. The following articles are quoted by way of demonstration:

"Art. 6. Those who organise or incite the people to refuse to pay taxes, or not to carry out other obligations, [thereby] trying to threaten and damage (wei-hai) the soviets, shall be punished by death. Under relatively extenuating circumstances (ch'ing-hsing chiao ch'ing) they shall be punished by imprisonment of from one year and upward."

"Art. 7. Those who for counter-revolutionary purposes deliberately

---

* A draft had, however, been worked out already by December 1933. (See doc. 62, p.1.)

oppose or violate the various kinds of soviet laws and regulations, or the various sorts of undertakings carried on by the soviets, shall be punished by death. Under relatively extenuating circumstances they shall be punished by imprisonment of from one year and upward.

"Art. 25. Those who for the purpose of damaging the economy of the Chinese Soviet Republic manufacture or import forged soviet money, forged government bonds or forged credit letters, those who incite the people to refuse to use the various sorts of soviet currency or who depress the rate of the various sorts of soviet currency and bring about a crisis in the market, those who incite the people to make a run on the soviet banks, and those who conceal or secretly export large amounts of silver cash and deliberately disturb the soviet money market, shall be punished by death. Under relatively extenuating circumstances they shall be punished by imprisonment of from six months and upward."[126]

This statute seems in the main to be very radical, but nevertheless it allowed for the possibility of a moderate application. Everything depended on its interpretation. It must be evaluated against the background of what we otherwise know about the judicial policy at the time of its promulgation. And against this background, which will be further clarified below, it should be safe to assume that the act was intended to be used as a radical and not as a moderate, weapon against crimes which might threaten the security or the economy of the republic.

## Examples of Individual Cases

A comparative study of reports on criminal cases can, far better than a study of the penal legislation, show the swing toward the left in judicial policy. Such reports from the early period of the republic are markedly different from those of the late period, which can best be demonstrated through rather extensive quotations. First, then, some examples from the first half of the year 1932.

Case 1. From the record of a trial before the Provisional Supreme Court on February 25th 1932

## Ground of Judgement

"Ts'ao Shu-hsiang, age 22, female, unmarried, from Linying in Honan,

132

family background middle peasant, has studied at a normal school, has studied for three years in the Soviet Union, originally a member of the Communist Party, later expelled, has been political commissar at the Fourth Branch Hospital, arrested on October 5th 1931. In August 1931 she joined the AB League in Shihwochung in Hsingkuo, introduced by Tai Chi-min. After she had joined the AB League she secretly led the league's work and developed its organisation in the Fourth Branch Hospital. Ts'ao Shu-hsiang was the political commissar of the Fourth Branch Hospital, she held a commission from the Communist Party and the Soviet Government. She not only did not energetically carry out the tasks given her by the Communist Party and the Soviet Government, on the contrary she ran over to the counter-revolutionary camp, and served as a tool of the counter-revolutionaries for attacking the soviet area. This is her crime of counter-revolutionary activity and of gross negligence of duty. At the hospital she actively carried on the counter-revolutionary work of the AB League. Together with other league members she on the one hand dispatched a man to go and search out a flight route, making preparations for running away; on the other hand they jointly conspired with the white army and served as a fifth column (nei-ying) of the enemy. In her work at the hospital she used good medicines to cure all who were members of the AB League, while using medicines recklessly (luan yung yao) on those who were not members of the league, so that they could not recover quickly. Or she plotted to injure (mou-hai) them to make them unable to serve again in the Red Army. This is using another method for damaging the Red Army. She embezzled public funds and used them to pay for the activity of the AB League. She had vacillating members of the AB League killed immediately. Ts'ao Shu-hsiang is a counter-revolutionary who has directly damaged the revolution, the Red Army and the soviet area, and who has caused panic."


Sentence

"Ts'ao Shu-hsiang shall be imprisoned for two years, to be reckoned from October 5th 1931. After the end of the period of imprisonment she shall be deprived of the right to vote for five years."[127)

This was one of the sentences of the Supreme Court which the Central Executive Committee revised. Adding to the charges that Ts'ao Shu-hsiang's political attitude while studying in the Soviet Union had been bad, the CEC prolonged the period of imprisonment to three years and three months.[128)

Case 2. From the record of a trial before a court under the judicial department of Kiangsi province on April 3rd 1932

## Grounds of Judgement

"Lü Chi-pin, age 28, male, from the town of Hsingkuo, carpenter. Introduced by Hsiao Tzu-cheng he joined the AB League in June 1930. He was responsible for the propaganda of the league's branch in the town of Hsingkuo, and was a member of the committee of the league's county branch. On the revolutionary side he has been chairman of the soviet government of the town of Hsingkuo. He used the title of chairman to carr on counter-revolutionary activity. Later, when he was head of the committee for suppression of counter-revolutionaries of Hsingkuo county, he systematically injured (hsien-hai) revolutionary comrades and killed people among the masses. Up to this day there is nobody among the mass of Hsingkuo who does not talk about the tiger and change colour (mo pu t'an-hu pien-se). Because this criminal is a worker, the former provinc soviet allowed him to reform himself (tzu-hsin). Contrary to expectation this criminal recently again, on purpose or not on purpose (yu-i wu-i chi carried on reactionary agitation (shan-tung), thereby violating the regula tions for those who give themselves up and reform themselves (tzu-shou tzu-hsin t'iao-lieh). Moreover, the masses of Hsingkuo have accused this criminal of counter-revolutionary activity, and officially requested that he be severely punished. "

## Sentence

"Lü Chi-pin. After the former provincial soviet, because he was a worke allowed him to reform himself, he again, on purpose or not on purpose, carried on counter-revolutionary agitation, thereby violating the regulati for self-reformation. Moreover, the masses have accused him of counte revolutionary activity. From the beginning to the end he has not been rou ed to consciousness. He is a counter-revolutionary who with a light hear (kan-hsin) betrays his class. He shall be imprisoned for three years, to be reckoned from August 27th 1931. Furthermore, he shall be deprived of the right to vote for five years from the day he was imprisoned. "[129]

There may well be reason for a certain suspicion with regard to these records. There seems to be a too big discrepancy between the grounds of judgement on the one hand and the sentences on the other. One questio is whether the charges conformed to the reality, another whether the cov really took them seriously. It may be recalled that the May 1933 directive of the Commissariat of Justice seems to imply that some local judicial organs wantonly included such phrases as "killed revolutionary comrades" among the charges against counter-revolutionaries. Could similar things be done even by the Supreme Court or by a court under the judicial department of Kiangsi province? However, even if we should allow ourselves to suggest some reduction of the guilt, the fact would remain that the charges were grave and the sentences were mild.

But it is important to note that the class background of these two culprits was sound or relatively sound - the first came from a middle peasant family and the second was a handicraft worker. People from reactionary classes were normally dealt with more severely. Some more examples are needed.

Case 3. From the record of the trial (the same one referred to under case 1) before the Supreme Court on February 25th 1932

## Grounds of Judgement

"Ch'en Tsung-chün, age 22, male, from T'aoyüan in Hunan, family background landlord, student of a normal school, not a member of the Communist Party, married. He has been the head of the administrative office (tsung-wu-k'o) of the Red Army's Sixth Branch Hospital. On November 8th last year he joined the AB League. After that he was responsible for the organisation of the branch of the league. According to his confession he has worked for the development of the AB League among the cooking team and the laundry team, and has together with other league members sabotaged (p'o-huai) the work in the hospital. He is an activist (huo-tung fen-tzu) of the AB League. Moreover, his background is that of a landlord family, and thus there are subjective conditions (chu-kuan t'iao-chien) for his entering the counter-revolutionary organisation."

## Sentence

"Ch'en Tsung-chün. Because his background is that of a small landlord family he shall be imprisoned for three years, to be reckoned from October 15th 1931. * Moreover, he shall for ever be deprived of the right to vote."[130)

---

* An error seems to have been made with regard to dates - cf. the date given for Ch'en Tsung-chün's joining the AB League.

135

Case 4. From the record of a trial before a court under the judicial department of Western Fukien\* 12-13 February 1932

## Grounds of Judgement

"Liu Fan-chang, male, age 22, from the second district of Hangwu, from a rich peasant family. He has elementary and middle education. He is a Reorganisationist. He has been secretary (mi-shu) of the soviet of the second district of Hangwu. Liu Fan-chang was a special agent of the Reorganisationists. In Amoy he received the directives of the Reorganisationists, and having returned to Western Fukien he made contact with the rehabilitation (shan-hou) committee of the local tyrants, the gentry and the landlords. He tried to develop the organisation of the Reorganisationists within the soviet area. His plan was to prepare the establishment of a school to unite the children (tzu-ti) of the local tyrants, the gentry and the landlords, and to carry on activity against the soviets."

## Sentence

"Liu Fan-chang. Imprisonment for five years, to be reckoned from November\*\* 1931."[131]

Although the charges recorded for the two latter cases are not very informative, we have nevertheless quite clear examples of the class policy in judicial matters. In case 3 it is explicitly stated that the class background was an aggravating factor, while the relative severity of the sentence in case 4 stands out in its proper relief only when compared with other sentences passed on the same occasion.[132] Yet, even with regard to counter-revolutionaries from reactionary classes there was a great difference between the penalties inflicted in 1932 and those allotted one or two years later. Had Ch'en Tsung-chün and Liu Fan-chang been tried in 1934, they would almost certainly have been executed soon after the trial.

---

\*   The western part of the traditional province of Fukien is in later sources designated as the soviet province of Fukien.
\*\*  The date is missing.

The material from 1933 and 1934 most suitable for a comparison consists of some short notices in Hung-se Chung-hua. Although the cases reported from these years do not correspond well with those referred to from 1932, we are nevertheless able to illustrate quite clearly the hardening of the climate. This is not to say, however, that we can draw a neat dividing line between the earlier period of a relatively lenient judicial policy, and the later period when the policy became much harder. The borderline is rather diffuse.

At least one group of the population - the traders - might already in the spring of 1933 be punished with extreme severity for crimes which do not seem to be too grave. It seems evident that the following report, printed in Hung-se Chung-hua of April 2nd 1933, tries to make the culprit blacker than he was:

"Recently the Security Bureau of Shihch'eng county discovered and arrested a counter-revolutionary. He systematically plotted to sabotage the economic policy of the soviets. In buying and selling commodities on the street he refused to use the cheques (chih-p'iao)* of the State Bank, and he deliberately raised the rate of silver dollars in cash. In this way he would incite the masses to make a run on the exchange (chi-tui). According to his confession he has under the Kuomintang regime of the past served as a small bureaucrat, collecting likin and miscellaneous taxes, and therefore he even dared to carry on counter-revolutionary activity openly on the street, and deliberately to damage the economic system of the soviets. Now this criminal has already, on the 25th, ** been shot."[133]

As for the landlords and the rich peasants, in general they had a much harder time after the full launching of the Land Investigation Movement in the summer of 1933. The core of this movement was a class war, which will be described in the next chapter. It is true that it is difficult to find a borderline between the class war and the administration of justice, but we may well try. The general class struggle will therefore be left out for the moment, and we shall here only give some examples, all from early 1934, of punishment of landlords and rich peasants charged with special offences.

Hung-se Chung-hua of February 16th 1934 relates:

"There was for instance in Kuanch'ien district in T'ingtung a rich peasant called K'ang Ch'ing-li, who sabotaged [the sale of] government bonds for economic construction. He spread a rumour that: "The soviets are cheating people." Thereafter, as the masses demand-

---
* The meaning is probably "banknotes".
** The month is evidently March 1933.

137

ed it, the soviet had him shot."[134]

On March 1st 1934 the same journal reported:

"In Telien district the masses demanded that a rich peasant woman
called Ts'ao ta-sao should be executed, because this rich peasant
woman was sabotaging the Rice Collection Movement. However, the
judicial department of the district soviet was extremely slow in deciding on this case. It was not until the masses for the third time
urged it that a meeting of the court was held to try the case, and this
rich peasant woman was shot."[135]

And on March 22nd 1934:

"The masses of Panyüan hsiang in Ch'iaoyang rose up to take part
actively in the land struggle; there was a landlord who impeded the
Land Investigation, the masses then caught him, held a mass meeting,
and shot him."[136]

It is rather difficult to obtain a picture of how offenders among the workers
and ordinary peasants were dealt with in the late period of the republic.[13?]
It is clear however, that the judicial policy was becoming more rigorous
also in this regard, as we shall soon see from Chang Wen-t'ien's
general instructions on the fight against counter-revolutionaries.

While regretting the lack of examples from these classes, we may record
the fate of a man whose class status was not very sound, not because his
position was above that of the workers and peasants, but rather because
it was below. Hung-se Chung-hua of July 17th 1934 reports the following
from Hsinch'üan county in Fukien:

"There was for instance in Nanyang hsiang a man called Kao Li-shan
who openly spread rumours and thus frightened the masses. He also
acted in secret, telling the masses not to save [rice] and not to lend
rice. * Later, after he had been denounced (chü-fa) by the masses,
he was detained. As a result of the investigation he was found to be a
vagabond (liu-mang), who often expressed his dissatisfaction with the
revolution to the masses. Thereafter a mass meeting for public trial
was organised, and in accordance with the unanimous demand of the
masses he was shot. Because of this there was a still greater upsurge
of the activism of the masses."[138]

---

* The campaign for persuading people to save rice, and to lend it to the
Red Army, will be dealt with in a later chapter.

The general picture emerging from a study of penal cases is clear. From 1932 to 1934 there was a tremendous radicalisation in the judicial policy toward people branded as counter-revolutionaries. Some modifications of this general picture should, however, be allowed for.

There seems to have been a considerable inconsistency in the judicial practice of the earlier as well as of the later period. The Commissariat of Justice complained of such inconsistency in May 1933, at a time which can not have been far from the vague border between the moderate and the radical period. We do not know how far back in time the commissariat on that occasion went to fetch examples from Juichin, where a "local tyrant" who had been leader of a reactionary local militia was sentenced to only three years imprisonment, whereas "a 70 year old poor peasant, who gossiped that the white army had reached Ch'ingliu and Kuihua, was sentenced to death."[139] There was also inconsistency later, as not all judicial organs were prepared to follow suit in the radicalisation. In February and March 1934 a couple of cases were reported in which local judicial organs continued to be rather moderate, for which they were severely rebuked.[140] At about the same time even the Supreme Court passed some relatively light sentences on corrupt cadres,[141] and in an article dated February 17th Chang Wen-t'ien criticised the Supreme Court as well as local judicial organs for being too moderate.[142]

However, the inconsistency of practice does not change the general pattern at all. An overall study of the reported penal cases clearly shows a tremendous swing toward the left in judicial policy.


From Justice to Red Terror

A study of the reported penal cases is useful, but nevertheless such material is quite limited. It merely gives us a taste of the red terror instigated by the party and the Central Government in the late period of the republic. More will be revealed in the next chapter, on rural class policy. And a lot is to be inferred from general instructions on the fight against counter-revolution, given by Chang Wen-t'ien and Liang Po-t'ai from February 1934 onward.

A central point in these instructions is the relation between legality and red terror. It is not at all strange that the judicial and the legislative organs of the Chinese Soviet Republic should have a rather free view on legality. There was a serious lack of laws and regulations, especially in the early period of the republic, but even the later penal legislation was far from sufficient to fill the gap. It is not surprising, then, that the government should allow for a thing which a society with a well developed penal legislation normally tries to avoid - to base sentences not directly on existing laws, but on analogy. Article 38 of the Regulations for Punishment of Counter-Revolutionaries, of April 8th 1934, reads:

> "Every counter-revolutionary crime not covered by these regulations shall be punished according to analogous articles in these regulations."[143]

If the lack of penal legislation was so bad that not even an analogy could be found, then a judicial organ simply had to pass sentences on its own discretion. This was an act of necessity. Allowing for all this, one may yet be astonished by the cynicism by which Chang Wen-t'ien and Liang Po-t'ai in 1934 viewed the concept of law.

Chang Wen-t'ien was anxious to point out that no legal consideration should prevent judicial organs from condemning counter-revolutionaries to death, if revolutionary considerations so warranted. In his article of February 17th 1934, he wrote:

> "We must get our comrades in the judicial organs to understand profoundly that the soviet laws are produced to meet the demands of the struggle against counter-revolution, and that they are not made in order to serve as a basis for extenuating the crimes of the counter-revolutionaries..... It is only those foreign class elements intentionally distorting the soviet laws, or those bookworms (shu-tai-tzu) or prisoners of war adoring (ch'ung-pai) the "sacredness of legality" (szu-fa shen-sheng) of the capitalist class, who can use the soviet laws for defending the counter-revolutionaries, or for extenuating their crimes."[144]

Stronger words still were used by Liang Po-t'ai, now a full-fledged Commissar of Justice, in his article in Hung-se Chung-hua of March 1 st 1934. He complained of responsible cadres in many judicial organs not understading that "the laws are developing in accordance with the demands (hsü-yao) of the revolution," and continued:

> "What is to the advantage of the revolution, that is the law. Whenever it is to the advantage of the revolution the legal procedure (fa-lü ti shou-hsü) can at any time be adapted. One ought not to hinder the interests of the revolution because of legal procedure."[145]

Such an extent of contempt for law and legal procedure, expressed by top leaders of the state apparatus, meant in fact a farewell to justice. Under the existing circumstances it meant a transition from justice to terror.

In his March 1st article Liang Po-t'ai mentioned the necessity of red terror in border areas and in new soviet areas; and in an editorial in the same journal, dated May 22nd 1934, Chang Wen-t'ien went more into detail on that point. Chang claimed that the counter-revolutionary activity from within was highly intensified at this time, accompanying the ferocious enemy attacks from without, and wrote:

"Red terror ought to be our reply to these counter-revolutionaries. We must, especially in the war zones and the border areas, deal immediately and with extreme swiftness with every sort of counter-revolutionary activity. Every one among the local tyrants and the gentry, every landlord, rich peasant, trader, capitalist, shop proprietor (lao-pan) or vagabond who carries on counter-revolutionary activity must immediately be caught. There are exceptions for certain most important persons for whom a thorough investigation is necessary to see if they have accomplices; for the rest of them it is not necessary to undertake any careful interrogation, it is not necessary to escort them to the county [capital], they shall all be shot on the spot. Even those among them who are under suspicion of being counter-revolutionaries ought immediately to be caught; in grave cases they shall be shot at the place, in light cases they shall be sent in custody to the rear for imprisonment. With regard to those with background among the workers, the peasants or the poor people (p'in-min) who have taken part in counter-revolutionary activity, they shall likewise be shot on the spot if they are leaders; if they are followers (fu-ho ti fen-tzu) or suspicious persons they must be sent in custody to the rear for punishment or investigation."[146]

This was indeed a dangerous passage - not only for the reactionaries, but for the soviet regime as well. It must have been part of the cause for the later running amuck of local cadres in their fight against real or imagined counter-revolutionaries. It is true that Chang Wen-t'ien in the same editoral warned against "arresting and killing indiscriminately" (luan-cho luan-sha); yet, he had allowed for the shooting of people from reactionary or unreliable classes merely on suspicion, and that was not a very different thing. Under the existing extremely tense conditions the local cadres could not be expected to make fine distinctions. Chang Wen-t'ien's instructions applied especially to war zones and border areas, but only "especially" so. Moreover, some cadres, not unnaturally, soon came to regard all the soviet counties of Kiangsi as war zones.[147]

Chang Wen-t'ien's instructions were after all put forward in very general terms, and they were radical indeed. At an earlier stage some of the local cadres might have tried to tone down directives of this kind, but during the spring of 1934 that became increasingly dangerous - such cadres would run the risk of being vigorously denounced themselves. And other men within the apparatus of the State Political Security Bureau and in the judicial organs would interpret the radical instructions very radically. By late June even Chang Wen-t'ien had apparently become more worried about the radicals than about the moderates. While having previously bitterly attacked what he branded as a too moderate judicial practice, he now as vigorously attacked what he called the "ultraleftism" (chi-tso chu-i), and at the same time he revealed that there had been too much killing. In an article in Tou-cheng, dated June 24th 1934, Chang wrote:

> "In some places the red terror has changed into arresting and killing indiscriminately (luan-cho luan-sha), and there is no more talk about the "class line" and the "mass line". Among some comrades there are now developing such theories (li-lun) as "if one or two are killed erroneously there is no reason to worry (pu-yao chin)" or, "the more who are killed the better. ""[148]

In the same article Chang Wen-t'ien also expressed his concern over the too strong position which was being given to the State Political Security Bureau, at the cost of the judicial organs. [149]


In spite of Chang Wen-t'ien's rebuke to the leftist extremists in the summer of 1934, the general tendency is clear enough – there was indeed a radical swing toward the left in the judicial policy of the Chinese Soviet Republic. However, when it comes to interpreting this development in terms of personal power relations we encounter certain difficulties. If we could confine our study strictly to the time of the republic, we might find little reason to doubt that the trend was a result of a struggle between the moderation of Mao Tse-tung and his men on the one hand, and the radicalism of the 28 Bolsheviks and their supporters on the other. Such a view would be in harmony with the official Chinese historiography.

The difficulties arise when we take a glance at the time before the establishment of the republic, i. e. before November 1931. Although a study of that period is not within the scope of our discussion, we may note that the treatment of real or alleged counter-revolutionaries can by no means be said to have been moderate at that time. A Chinese Communist document from late 1931 makes it clear that Communist organs were misled by false confessions which they had themselves extracted by the use of torture;[150] and Kung Ch'u says that such a procedure led to very large-scale killing. Kung Ch'u also says that the bloody purges of cadres in the period before the establishment of the republic were executed by Teng Fa, but that the man directing these affairs from behind the screen was Mao Tse-tung. [151]

It is not necessary to go further on this topic; the exploration of the extent to which the purges of the time reflected intra-party struggle rather than a fight against counter-revolutionaries, must be left to others.

Kung Ch'u says that about the time of the establishment of the republic the party purges, and the work of suppressing counter-revolutionaries, were "somewhat moderated". Our study of Communist documents seems to make it clear that this was a very significant moderation. Who, then, stood behind it? Kung Ch'u apparently believes it was the party leader-ship.[152] Such an assumption may be sustained by the reading of the Directive Letter of the [Party] Centre to the Soviet Areas, dated September 1st 1931, which severely criticised the way in which the fight against counter-re-volutionaries had been carried on in the Central Soviet Area.[153] In fact we here come quite close to the turning upside down of our pattern for the later period - Mao seems to have been responsible for a certain terror, while the party leadership, consisting of members of the 28 Bolshevik group and their associates, appears to have been a significantly moderat-ing factor.

Our interpretation of the apparent shift in the pattern of policies must be rather speculative. It was presumably not only a question a persons in leadership, but to a large extent also a matter of machinery. Before the establishment of the republic the machinery for dealing with counter-revolutionaries must have been of a very rudimentary type. As we have seen, there was nothing bearing the name of judicial organs. The then existing machinery seems mainly to have consisted of local committees for suppression of counter-revolutionaries and of the apparatus headed by Teng Fa - an apparatus which was the predecessor of the State Political Security Bureau. The machinery was rudimentary and the situation was utterly confused. Mao Tse-tung and Chu Te may well have been haunted by the fear that the enemy might manage to infiltrate the Red Army, the party and the soviets as effectively as the Communists in some cases managed to infiltrate Kuomintang organs. Lacking a machinery experienc-ed in thorough investigation, it was rather natural to hit hard, ruthlessly and haphazardly, especially if we add to the situation a bitter intra-party struggle.

The party leadership's bitter criticism of the methods used in the fight against counter-revolution in the Central Soviet Area, embodied in the Directive Letter of September 1931, was undoubtedly, as Hsiao Tso-liang has shown, part of a personal attack on Mao Tse-tung.[154] Mao must have felt deeply hurt by this personal attack, and he must have feared the threat to his position, but nevertheless he can not have been wholly opposed to the changes demanded. He was still for some time to play a very signifi-cant role in directing the politics of the Central Soviet Area, and he must have been aware of the dangers represented by the degeneration of the fight against counter-revolutionaries into a witch hunt. An improvement of the methods of investigating counter-revolutionary cases was after all the only sensible way to take.

Such an improvement of investigative methods required a development of the machinery. This was just at the time when a more regular state apparatus was about to be built up, and the judicial organs and the State Political Security Bureau became significant parts of it. We have seen that it took time to build up the machinery, but it was developing; accordingly the regime could feel more confident than before, and afford to be more moderate in its judicial policy.

The moderate period came at a time when Mao Tse-tung not only formally, but also in reality, had a very strong position in the republic. The subsequent new radicalisation of the judicial policy may to a considerable extent be explained by a new insecurity, caused by the massing of vast Kuomintang forces against the Central Soviet Area; but it also seems to have coincided with the process of Mao being squeezed out of power by the party leadership. This radicalisation gained a tremendous momentum when Mao, immediately after the Second National Soviet Congress, had been removed from his position as chairman of the Council of People's Commissars; and it was then in the first place voiced by Chang Wen-t'ien, who presumably was backed by his close associate in the 28 Bolshevik group, the party chief Ch'in Pang-hsien.

It seems to be relatively safe then, to conclude that after the First National Soviet Congress in November 1931 Mao Tse-tung stood for a relatively moderate judicial policy, and that the party leadership gradually pushed it toward the left. The issue can be further explored through the study of a field closely related to the administration of justice - the rural class policy.

# CHAPTER VI.   RURAL CLASS POLICY AND THE LAND INVESTIGATION MOVEMENT

During the period of the Chinese Soviet Republic the rural class policy followed a zigzag course, but its general tendency was toward the left. The insufficiency of material presents certain obstacles to our attempt to investigate this extremely important matter, but a number of interesting things can nevertheless be pointed out.

## General Class Characteristics

First of all we have to know something about the rules for class differentiation. However, these rules were not static - their development formed an essential part of the trends of the policy. Anyhow, we need some general principles to start with, and we will then turn our attention to the document How to Differentiate Classes, [1] composed by Mao Tse-tung, adopted by a conference of soviet cadres in June 1933[2] and given the status of a Central Government edict in October of the same year. It will here be referred to as the "June regulations". The criteria given below are in the first instance based on this document. However, the characteristics of landlords and rich peasants are also basically described in a June 1932 statement of the Commissariat for Land. [3]

The Landlords are persons in possession of land who exclusively or mainly make their living by exploitation of others. Their main mode of exploitation is the collection of land rent, but they may also have subsidiary revenue from money lending, commerce and industry, or they may exploit hired agricultural labour. Some of them have income from communal land under their control. The landlords either do not engage in productive work at all, or they only carry out supplementary labour (fu-tai lao-tung).

The Rich Peasants are normally in possession of land, although a few of them rent a part or the whole of the land they use. As a rule they are better equipped with instruments of production and with liquid capital than the average. They regularly practise exploitation, and many of them derive most of their income from this source. Their main form of exploitation is the hiring of labour, but they may also have income from renting out part of their land, from communal land under their control, from money lending or from engaging in industry or trade. Apart from being exploiters they also engage in labour themselves.

The Middle Peasants often own land, but some of them rent a part or the whole of the land they use. They are fairly well equipped with farm implements. They wholly or mainly derive their income from own labour. As a rule they do not exploit others - some of them do practise exploitation to a certain extent, but this is not their regular or their main source of income. Many middle peasants suffer themselves from exploitation by having to pay land rent or interest on loans, but generally they do not sell their labour power.

Some of the Poor Peasants own part of the land they use, while others have to rent all their land. The poor peasants are insufficiently equipped with farm implements. As a rule they suffer from exploitation by having to pay land rent and interest on loans, and to hire themselves out to some extent. *

The Workers - among them the Farm Labourers - as a rule own no land or farm implements, although some of them do own a very small amount of land and a very few farm implements. The workers make their living wholly or mainly by selling their labour power.

These are the main categories defined by the "June regulations", but the document also mentions some additional small groups of the extreme reactionary wing. One of them is the usurers. The document further says that "warlords, officials (kuan-liao), local tyrants (t'u-hao) and evil gentry are political representatives and especially ruthless members of the landlord class." The version included in the official edition of Mao Tse-tung's selected works qualifies this statement, declaring that "minor local tyrants and evil gentry are also often to be found among the rich peasants."[4] A much more exact definition of the latter two categories would obviously be desirable.

The Chinese term for "local tyrants"[5] is t'u-hao, which has also been translated as "local bullies"[6] and as "village bosses".[7] The expression is a rather diffuse one; it seems to refer to persons having for one reason or another - usually through possession of land - attained very strong social positions in their localities, which they used for the oppression or the exploitation of the common people.

---

* According to the version of the "June regulations" which is included in the official edition of Mao Tse-tung's selected works, the principal criterion for distinguishing between a middle and a poor peasant is that in general the former does not need to sell his labour power, while the latter has to sell part of his labour power. (Mao Tse-tung hsüan-chi, Peking 1958, vol. 1 p. 123; SW, Peking 1964, vol. 1 p. 139).

A proper definition of the Chinese "gentry" might require several pages. Under the Manchu dynasty the group included officials, persons who had attained the academic qualifications for being appointed officials and persons who had purchased official or academic titles. Landed property was not a necessary prerequisite for gentry status, but was nevertheless very often linked up with it. In the present context, however, the term would probably mean people who, normally by virtue of their wealth, had a special influence on local government before the Communist insurrection. [8]

## Class Exploitation Before the Revolution

Table 12 indicates, with many reservations, the proportions of the population and of land property in the old society. Mao tells us that in Yung-feng the exploiting classes, constituting only a tiny portion of the population, owned 70 per cent of the total amount of arable land, and were in control of a further 10 per cent representing the communal land. He also informs us that in the same district the land rent was 50 and in some cases 60 per cent of the harvest. [9] These data help us to understand that the Communist redistribution of land - along lines which will be explained below - meant a revolution of tremendous magnitude.

## Class Fluctuations After the Revolution

Social fluctuations after the Communist take-over complicate the study of classes and class policy to a considerable extent. We cannot expect to clear up this aspect of the topic completely. There was confusion among the Communist leaders themselves on the issue, which in the summer of 1933 caused a polemic between Chang Wen-t'ien and a certain "comrade Li" in the soviet province of Fukien. No attempt will here be made to reconstruct comrade Li's view, as we know only fragments of it as brought to light by Chang for polemical purposes. Chang's standpoint on the issue, as found in various articles in Tou-cheng, presumably represents the view of the party leadership by the summer of 1933; and it is therefore worth reviewing.

Chang Wen-t'ien claimed that after the revolution there was a massive movement of poor peasants, and even a certain movement of farm labourers, into the middle peasant category, so that by 1933 the middle peasants constituted the largest group among the population of the soviet areas. [10] This statement is plausible enough - it is quite logical that poor families which thanks to the agrarian revolution had been allotted additional land and more

Table 12

Data, supplied by Mao Tse-tung, on proportions of the population and of the land property in Yungfeng district in Hsingkuo before the Communist take-over. (Mao obtained the information from interviews with eight Red Army men from Yungfeng in late 1930).

## A. Proportions of the Population

(The family, and not the person, is used as a unit)

|  | Approximate Percentages of the Population |
| --- | --- |
| Landlords | 1 |
| Rich peasants | 5 |
| Middle peasants | 20 |
| Poor peasants | 60 |
| Farm labourers | 1 |
| Handicraft workers | 7 |
| Small traders | 3 |
| Eléments déclassés (yu-min)* | 2 |

## B. Proportions of Land Property

|  | Percentages of the Arable Land (t'ien-ti) of the District in Possession of the Various Classes |
| --- | --- |
| Landlords | 40 |
| Communal land (kung-t'ang) | 10 |
| Rich peasants | 30 |
| Middle peasants | 15 |
| Poor peasants | 5 |

Source: Doc. 139A pp. 21-22.

## Notes to table 12

1. Since the data were collected as early as 1930, we cannot take for

* For the composition of the group of éléments déclassés see doc. 139A pp. 45-46.

granted that the class criteria applied were exactly the same as those described on pp. 145-47 of this thesis.

2.  Mao explains that only families making their living exclusively by hiring out their labour power were placed in the category of farm labourers. Such restrictive criteria were also applied to the groups of small traders and éléments déclassés.

3.  We are informed that if the absentee landlords had been included in the statistics of section A, the percentage of landlords among the population would probably have risen to 2 or 3.

4.  The family, and not the person, is used as a unit in the statistics of the table. The larger families were probably as a rule to be found among the landlords and the rich peasants, and especially among those of them who could afford to have concubines.

5.  The percentages are obviously rounded off, and in connection with section A we are explicitly informed that the data are approximate ones. Section A accounts for 99, and not for 100, per cent of the population.

6.  The statistics of the table concern only one single district. An overall survey of the districts which were to make up the Central Soviet Area would presumably have disclosed considerable differences between the localities.

---

farm implements would move up into the more prosperous group. Further Chang made a distinction between these new middle peasants and the old ones; the former still retained the right to membership in the revolutionar organisations of the classes which they had previously belonged to, the poor peasant unions or the farm labourer unions. [11] Although it was not stated by Chang, we can infer from other sources that farm labourers who moved upward would also retain the most tangible of their privileges - the exemption from paying land tax. [12]

Another aspect of the class fluctuation after the agrarian revolution was, according to Chang Wen-t'ien, the movement of a certain number of form ly non-exploiting families into the rich peasant category. It may well seen paradoxical that a Communist-sponsored revolution should create new ex-ploiters, but Chang, who in this respect was in line with the Comintern directives, regarded it as a natural thing. It was part of the dialectical process that capitalism should to some extent be promoted by the revoluti in the Chinese soviet areas, a revolution which first of all was of an anti-feudalist nature. The possibilities of exploitation were still there - the purchase and lease of land and the hiring of labour were not prohibited in principle. The movement of ordinary peasants into the rich peasant cate-gory, said Chang Wen-t'ien, was going on only on a very small scale, but it was going on. [13]

This latter aspect of the class fluctuation brings a confusion into the "rich peasant" concept, which is rather difficult to clear up. Chang recognised that there were new members of this class, who had appeared only after the revolution, but he made it clear that they should be treated very much more leniently than the old ones. Such a radical measure as the deprivati of all the good land, which we will revert to below, was to be taken only against the latter and not against the former. [14] A few months after these articles of Chang Wen-t'ien were written, on October 10th 1933, the Cour cil of People's Commissars passed a resolution in which the term rich peasants quite clearly is used in a restricted sense, leaving out altogethe those who had appeared only after the revolution. [15] Later we shall be dealing with various documents prescribing a quite hard policy toward the rich peasants without any explanation of the term, and it then seems reasonable to assume that it is used in a similarly restricted sense, re-ferring to the rich peasants left over from the old society only.

A natural question to pose would be whether or not the social fluctuations after the revolution could imply movements in the opposite direction, i. e. from the exploiting to the non-exploiting classes. The regime's own an-swer would in general be no. The case of the party and soviet cadres with background in reactionary classes may to some extent be regarded as an exception, and this matter we will revert to below. Further, the Council of People's Commissars in its resolution of October 10th 1933 recognised the possibility of landlords and rich peasants moving into one of the non-exploiting classes before the revolution. [16) After the revolution the long-term aim was certainly to reform the reactionary class elements – or those of them who had survived and not fled – but in general it was not acknowledged that their change of class status could be effected in the short period of the Chinese soviet regime. As we shall see later, the Land Investigation Movement from the summer of 1933 onward was in the first instance a struggle against landlords and rich peasants who after the revolution had managed to disguise themselves as belonging to the middle or the poor peasantry – the change in their way of life did not in the long run save them from attack.

### Rural Class Policy November 1931 – May 1933

For a study of the rural class policy in the early period of the republic we must in the first instance turn our attention to the land law adopted by the First National Soviet Congress in November 1931. [17) Hsiao Tso-liang describes it as "the most Moscow-oriented of all land laws enacted by Chinese Communists" during the period 1930 – 1934. [18) One of the features distinguishing it from a Mao-sponsored land law, probably of 1930, [19) as well as from the one sponsored by the Li Li-san leadership, of May the same year, [20) is a harsher anti-rich peasant line; and this was presumably to a large extent a reflection of Stalin's anti-kulak policy from 1928 onward. [21)

However, the very sternest measures were naturally reserved for the landlords, and for class elements whose animosity toward the regime was supposed to be equal to that of the landlords. Article 1 of the 1931 land law read:

> "All the land belonging to feudal landlords, local tyrants, gentry, warlords, officials and other big private landowners, shall be subject to confiscation without any compensation whatsoever, irrespective of whether they administer (ching-ying) their land themselves or rent it out on lease .... The former owners of the confiscated land shall not be entitled to receive any land allotment."

And art. 8:

> "All movable and immovable property, houses, granaries, cattle and farm implements belonging to feudal lords (feng-chien-chu), warlords, landlords, local tyrants and the gentry shall be confiscated."

We can say with certainty that the policy was to annihilate the landlords as a class, [22] but this did not necessarily imply that they were to be extinguished physically. However, how could they survive physically - or how could they subsist materially - if the quoted provisions were carried into effect? It is true that landlords or their families under certain circumstances might be allowed to open, for their own use, such waste land as nobody else was interested in; [23] but it would be extremely hard for them to subsist on that, especially if all their farm implements had been confiscated. Their survival would seem to depend very much on the non-fulfilment of the provisions quoted from the 1931 land law; and from the time of the Land Investigation Movement we have many reports saying that these provisions were very far from having been fully carried into effect.

For the rich peasants the 1931 land law did in general provide the means of subsistence, although their living was designed to be a very hard one. Their land was to be confiscated, and at the redistribution they were to be allotted only relatively poor land and land which was hard to work. [24] Apart from this the law did not regulate definitely the allotment of land, but it did suggest a system of redistribution which meant a still further discrimination against the rich peasants. * Moreover, it was laid down that members of this class who had taken active part in counter-revolutionary work were not entitled to hold any land whatsoever. [25] And rich peasants were not allowed to rent their land out on lease or to hire labourers to work on it, [26] both of which were still permissible for others. [27] Finally, the rich peasants were to be deprived of their surplus (to-yü) houses, farm implements, cattle, etc. [28]

Having dealt with the class enemies, we proceed to the beneficiaries of the revolution. The land law laid down that the middle and poor peasants, the farm labourers and the coolies of the countryside were all in principle entitled to hold equal shares of land - taking account of quality as well as of quantity -[29] and they were also to benefit, individually or collectively,

---

* One of the principles for land redistribution suggested by the law was as follows:
1. Each person among the farm labourers and the poor and middle peasants would be entitled to hold land plots of equal value.
2. In rich peasant families only persons capable of labour should receive plots of poor land in the first instance, and these plots were apparently meant to correspond in acreage to those referred to in point 1. Members of rich peasant families who were not capable of labour should only be given smaller plots of poor land in a supplementary allotment. (Doc. 71 art. 7. In order to get the meaning of this article one ought to read doc. 90 A as well).

from the redistribution of confiscated houses, cattle and farm implements. [30] The debts which they had contracted under the old usury
system were generally cancelled. [31] Two alternative methods of land
redistribution were suggested as far as these classes were concerned,
and both of them were apparently regarded as conforming to the egalitarian
principle: The land could either be redistributed according to a mixed
system, taking account of the total number of persons as well as the labour
power of each family; or according to the number of family members
alone. [32] Precautions were to be taken not to antagonise the middle
peasants – if the majority among this class in a given locality so wanted,
they could be kept completely out of the process of land redistribution. [33]

We do not have much information on the actual implementation of the land
law in the early period of the republic. A November 1932 report says that
the principles for land redistribution had by that time to a large extent
been carried into effect in Kiangsi, but it also makes clear that a good
many mistakes had been committed. [34]

A number of instructions for the implementation of the class policy prescribed by the law were circulated from late 1931 to early 1933. [35] The
party leadership and the Central Government did certainly show some
activity on the issue; nevertheless, they were evidently much less vigorous
in their pursuit of the class struggle in this period than they were during
the later Land Investigation Movement.

A few regulations bearing no direct relation to the land law are of significance with regard to rural class policy in the early period of the republic.

The former farm labourers and other workers who had been allotted land
were exempted from paying land tax. [36] These were of course the people
of the countryside from whom the Communists expected the most determined support, but nevertheless it seems rather strange that they should
have this material privilege. In this connection we may also deviate from
the chronology of our narrative and note an interesting occurrence from
the summer of 1934 – a period characterised by tremendous efforts to
mobilise all resources for combatting the enemy. Attempts were then
made, and with at least some success, to persuade the farm labourers
and other workers to ask for cancellation of their exemption from paying
land tax. [37]

Various regulations, enacted in 1931, 1932 and 1933, provided for a further discrimination against rich peasants by requiring them to pay land tax at a higher rate than the middle and the poor peasantry. [*38] Then there were the special money levies (chüan-k'uan) imposed on the rich peasants - a practice which became very conspicuous during the Land Investigation Movement. It is difficult to say how common these levies were in the relatively early period of the republic, but we may note that they are mentioned in a resolution adopted by the Posheng county soviet, published in March 1933. [39]

A very serious measure was of course the drafting of people from the reactionary classes for hard labour brigades. On November 25th 1932 the Council of People's Commissars issued a general instruction to the local soviets, ordering them to organise physically fit rich peasants in such units. The brigades were to be supervised by members of the militia organisation, the Red Guards (Ch'ih-wei-chün), and they were to be charged with the destruction of surrendered enemy fortifications, the building and repair of roads and bridges, and with transport services. [40] No corresponding regulations have been found from this period for the drafting of landlords, but they were certainly not supposed to be spared - that members of this class should be made use of for hard labour is mentioned as early as September 1931, in a letter from the party centre to the soviet areas. [41] However, actual practice did not necessarily fully conform to regulations and intentions. Judging from sources of slightly later dates it seems to be clear that in the relatively early period of the republic the drafting of landlords and rich peasants for hard labour brigades was carried on only to some extent. [42]

Even in this relatively early period the regulations for treatment of the rural reactionary classes were on the whole harsh. But these regulations seem by no means to have been thoroughly carried into effect at the time - at least this was so if we are to believe the reports from the later Land Investigation Movement.

The Land Investigation Movement - Its Nature and Its Programme

The date for the launching of the Land Investigation Movement (Ch'a-t'ien

---

* This principle is to be distinguished from the general progressiveness of the land tax rates. (See this thesis pp. 192-99)

yün-tung) may be disputed. In some districts there was a movement
called by this name going on as early as the winter of 1932-33. [43] But
the large-scale campaign, which meant a tremendous intensification of
rural class struggle in the Central Soviet Area, began in June 1933, and
for practical purposes we can date the launching of the movement to that
month.

Kung Ch'u's book, The Red Army and I, contains an interesting passage
on the preparations for the campaign. It is true that this source should
be used with a certain scepticism, as the author writes out of memory[44]
- in the present case about 20 years after the event; but on the other hand
we may miss some valuable information if we ignore it. Kung Ch'u re-
calls that in late May 1933 he was called to Juichin to take part in a conference for higher party cadres. At the meeting Chou En-lai introduced
the new guide-lines for an intensification of the rural class struggle.
Kung Ch'u opposed, and he was supported by some of the cadres present.
However, Chou spoke again, saying that the new instructions were laid
down in accordance with the Comintern directives, and thereby silenced
all opposition. [45]

Although no direct Comintern authorisation for the launching of the Land
Investigation Movement has been found, there are very good reasons to
believe that the Russian impact was significant. The movement can to a
large extent be seen as a campaign for a more thorough implementation
of the Moscow-inspired land law of November 1931. But there was by no
means a mere transplantation of Russian policy into China. The movement
must also have been deeply rooted in the conditions of the Central Chinese
Soviet Area. Directives from Moscow could hardly alone have stirred up
the activity of the Chinese party and soviet apparatus to such an extent
as was seen during the Land Investigation Movement.

We will now see how Mao Tse-tung based his arguments for launching the
campaign on the state of affairs in Kiangsi and Fukien. Unfortunately we
are in no position to check Mao's argumentation - we cannot tell how
correctly it represented the situation of the Central Soviet Area. Nevertheless, we can learn a great deal from it. This argumentation did form an
essential part of the mechanism of the Land Investigation Movement.

The arguments are put forward in a systematic way in Mao's article in
Hung-se Chung-hua of June 17th 1933. According to his analysis the districts under Communist control could be grouped into the following three
categories:

1. Areas where the revolutionary struggle had reached an advanced stage.
2. Areas where the revolutionary struggle was lagging behind.

3. Areas recently conquered by the revolutionary forces.

Mao was mainly concerned with category No. 2. It included districts where a revolutionary regime had been established for some time - the provisional political organs had been replaced by regular ones. But the revolutionary struggle had been badly corrupted. Although the landlords and the rich peasants had already been defeated in their open counter-revolutionary struggle, many of them continued to work for their own class interests, only in a different way. They "take off their own counter-revolutionary masks and put on revolutionary masks. They approve of the revolution as well as of the land redistribution, call themselves poor and miserable peasants, and [claim that] they are entitled to land allotments as a matter of course. They are very active (chi-chi ti huo-tung), and they make use of their traditional (li-shih ti) advantages. "When it comes to talking it is they who know how to talk, when it comes to writing it is they who know how to write."" 46)

Accordingly, said Mao Tse-tung, these reactionary elements had to a considerable extent managed to grab the fruit of the land revolution. In many places the landlords and the rich peasants had at an early stage been able to control the organs of the revolution, to penetrate the local militia and to obtain more and better land at the redistribution than had the poor and toiling peasants. The true revolutionaries had fought back; some of the reactionary cadres had been purged, and part of the land illegally appropriated by landlords and rich peasants had been recovered. But the abnormalities had by no means been thoroughly corrected. In the soviets, in the mass organisations and in the local militia there were still many "foreign class elements" (chieh-chi i-chi fen-tzu) carrying on subversive activities. The landlords and the rich peasants made use of every means in an attempt to suppress the struggling revolutionary masses, to "preserve their privileges (ch'üan-li) with regard to political power, land and property, and to keep their remnant feudal power." As a result the revolutionary work within various fields was seriously impeded.

Such was, according to Mao Tse-tung, the situation of the areas where the revolutionary struggle was lagging behind, and these were by no means rare exceptions. Relatively backward were the thirteen counties Huich'ang, Hsünwu, Anyüan, Hsinfeng, Loan, Ihuang, Kuangch'ang, Shihch'eng, Chienning, Lich'uan, Ninghua, Ch'angt'ing and Wup'ing; * so were parts of Juichin, Yütu, Posheng, Shengli, Yungfeng, Kunglüeh, Want'ai, Kanhsien, Shanghang, Yungting and Hsinch'üan, and even two districts in the model county of Hsingkuo. In space the backward districts made up about 80

---

* In an article in Hung-se Chung-hua of June 23rd 1933 Mao to some extent qualified the statement, saying that even in these counties one might exceptionally find relatively progressive districts. (Doc. 95).

# ！實果的命革地土喫偷想你！咄

<u>Cartoon in Hung-se Chung-hua of June 29th 1933</u>

The landlords and the rich peasants are stretching out a hand to grab
the fruit of the land revolution, but the hand is cut off by the farm
labourers and the poor and middle peasants by means of a sickle which
symbolises the Land Investigation Movement.

per cent of the Central Soviet Area, and the people inhabiting them counted more than two million. [47]

How would the party and the government remedy this situation? Various
available instructions for the Land Investigation Movement give the answer. The first aim of the campaign was naturally to search out the disguised landlords and rich peasants. Then a large-scale confiscation would
follow. The landlords were to lose all their land and all their property,
while the rich peasants would be deprived of the part of their property
and of their land which did not legally belong to them. The republic as
such would benefit from the confiscation - large amounts of money were
to be raised in this way and used for the defence of the soviet state. And
the local revolutionary masses would benefit - they were to be allotted
confiscated land* and confiscated articles. This was a class struggle, and
the enthusiasm of the revolutionary people would be aroused. At the same
time the soviets and other revolutionary organisations were to be purged
of reactionary elements; the obstructive activities carried on by landlords and rich peasants through these channels would be eliminated. The
rousing of the mass enthusiasm and the elimination of the reactionary
obstruction would, taken together, create very favourable conditions for
revolutionary and constructive work in various fields. [48] Thus, the Land
Investigation Movement was comprehensive indeed. It was much more
than a land investigation and a class investigation; we may also make
use of an anachronism and describe it as an attempted "great leap forward".

If so, we have to view the Land Investigation Movement in its very
broadest sense. It is true that the term can also be given a more restrictive meaning, and our sources are vacillating on the point. The movement
can be considered to be dealing with land policy and class policy alone,
and as being only closely related to a number of other drives. This is,
however, an "academic question". It may be useful to view the whole process as a unity, and to consider the Land Investigation Movement in its
broadest sense.

What we will mainly be concerned with here is the class policy of the Land
Investigation Movement - the detection and exploitation of disguised landlords and rich peasants. But we cannot ignore the "great leap forward"
aspect, and some quotations from a resolution adopted in June 1933 by a
conference of soviet cadres from eight counties may help to clarify this
matter.

   "If we can launch a widespread and thoroughgoing Land Investigation

---

* A part of the confiscated acreage was to be made communal land, to
  be used for the benefit of Red Army men and for other purposes.
  (Doc. 60 A p.4).

Movement in July, August and September, and stir up all the broad masses in the eight counties, it is entirely possible for us to mobilise within six to ten months 80, 000 new fighters in the eight counties to be sent to the front. Therefore, this task has to depend upon the development of a thoroughgoing Land Investigation Movement."

"In the midst of the success of the Land Investigation Movement the eight counties should set up co-operatives as far as possible. The principal co-operatives should be those for consumer goods, those for the regulation of food [supply], those for the necessary tools of production (chiefly farm implements), and those for making loans to the poor and miserable masses. .... To prosecute the war on the economic front quickly and on a large scale requires the great organisational strength of the soviets and the masses as well as large amounts of capital. Therefore, the Central Government is hereby requested to issue three million yüan of economic reconstruction bonds to be paid in grain in order that the work can be done quickly. The accomplishment of this task also depends upon the successful outcome of the Land Investigation Movement. If we do not exert great efforts in the sphere of the Land Investigation Movement so as to mobilise the majority of the masses to participate in economic reconstruction, it will be impossible to expect the complete success of this task."

"The autumn harvesting and the autumn plowing are two big events which are confronting us today. They are crucial to the livelihood of the masses and to the revolutionary war. Therefore, we must struggle to win complete success in the autumn harvesting and the autumn plowing this year during the Land Investigation Movement."

"The widespread development of the cultural and educational campaign can also be realised only in the midst of the success of the Land Investigation Movement. With the positive support of the great majority of the masses, for instance, it would not be difficult to accomplish such cultural and educational reconstruction projects as the establishment of a club for every 1, 000 people, a primary school for every 500 people, a night school for every 100 people, and classes in which most people over 16 years old will be taught Chinese characters."[49]

According to an edict of the Central Government, issued on September 1st 1933, the Land Investigation Movement had wider implications still. It was also to be linked with the expansion of the militia organisations, the Red Guards and the Young Vanguard, with the development of industrial production, the development of external trade, the work for full implementation of the provisions of the Labour Law, the construction and repair of roads and bridges and the election campaign.[50] The soviet areas had no

heavy industry; but nevertheless the optimistic atmosphere inevitably re-
minds one of the great upsurge in the whole of the country in 1958. Another
similarity – the events of 1933 as well as those of 1958 were connected with
the struggle against "reactionaries". The 1958 Great Leap Forward followed shortly after the antirightist rectification campaign, while the attempted
"great leap forward" of 1933 coincided with the struggle against disguised
landlords and rich peasants.

Considering the broad scope of the Land Investigation Movement – including class struggle, partial land redistribution, raising of funds, economic
and cultural reconstruction and military mobilisation – it was quite natural
that a large apparatus should be set in motion to carry it out. We know this
apparatus partly from the party's and the government's instructions for
the campaign, and partly from later reports on what had actually been done
in the various localities. Let us first exploit the material found in the instructions, and later revert to the reports.

According to the instructions the party branches at the different levels
were engaged, [51] and so were various mass organisations. [52] The poor
peasant unions* (p'in-nung-t'uan) were supposed to play a very essential
role in organising the rural masses for the class struggle. [53] Here it is
natural to deal in particular with the role played by the soviet apparatus
at the local and the central levels.

In an article published on June 20th 1933 Mao Tse-tung stated that there
was not a single component of a soviet organisation which was allowed to
disassociate itself from the tasks of the Land Investigation Movement.
The same article, and also an instruction of June 1st from the Council of
People's Commissars, assigned specific duties to some of the governmental branches, activating the whole hierarchies from the top to the
bottom. The land departments, the judicial departments and the departments of the State Political Security Bureau and the Worker's and
Peasants' Inspectorate at the district, county and provincial levels,
headed by the corresponding organs in the Central Government, were to
join forces to carry out the prescribed confiscation and redistribution of
land, to purge local soviets of reactionary elements and to eradicate
counter-revolutionary activity. The Commissariat of Finances was
charged with directing the local finance departments in raising funds
for the central treasury through money confiscation from landlords and the
imposition of special levies on rich peasants. The Commissariat for Mili-

---

* It is important to note that the poor peasant unions were also open for
membership of farm labourers and other workers in the countryside.
(Doc. 60 C p. 15 and doc. 60 F p. 36).

160

tary Affairs was ordered to direct the local military departments in improving and expanding the local militia, and in recruitment to the Red Army. The Commissariat of National Economy and the corresponding local departments were to make efforts to recover and to expand the production of agriculture and handicraft industry, and to develop the co-operatives; while the commissariat and the departments of education were to supply the cadres and the masses with simple and clear guidebooks for the Land Investigation Movement. At the various local levels all these activities should be co-ordinated by the soviet presidium. [54] The Land Investigation Movement was indeed in the centre of the soviet activities in the summer and early autumn of 1933.

The soviets at the provincial and the county levels were instructed to organise short-term training courses for cadres to be engaged in directing the movement. Land investigation committees were to be set up at the county, district and hsiang levels; and under the hsiang soviets there should also be established special committees for confiscation and re-distribution. The soviets of the county and the district were told to work out local plans for the campaign. Extremely important was the mobilisation of the broad masses for participation in the Land Investigation Movement. Various mass organisations were to play an essential part, and much importance was attached to the mass meetings at the village level. [55] A mighty apparatus was set in motion, and a most significant movement was launched.

From what is said above it will be realised that the Land Investigation Movement was an extremely complicated affair. The party leadership and the Central Government were naturally much concerned with making it work properly, and to secure this they deemed extraordinary measures to be necessary, in addition to the usual instructions dispatched downward through the party machinery and the soviet apparatus. In order to prepare the campaign a series of conferences for local cadres were arranged by the party, the Central Government and the soviet of Kiangsi province.

One of these conferences seems to have been of special significance. It was convened through an order of the Council of People's Commissars, and held in Juichin 17-21 June 1933. Participants were soviet cadres at the district and the county levels from the eight counties of Juichin, Huich'ang, Yütu, Shengli, Posheng, Shihch'eng, Ninghua and Ch'angt'ing, plus some persons in responsible positions in provincial soviets - presumably those of Kiangsi and Fukien. More than four hundred cadres were present, and they were all persons to be charged with especially important tasks in the

Land Investigation Movement. * The central figure at the conference was Mao Tse-tung - on the two days 18-19 June he made a report on various aspects of the movement, a report which altogether lasted for about nine and a half hours. There were other speakers too, there were group discussions and there were performances by two different troupes of actors - all aimed at rousing the cadres for active participation in the Land Investigation Movement. A few of the cadres were reported to have expressed "erroneous" views on the problems concerned, and there was one serious case of dissidence - the head of the land department of a district soviet in Ninghua refused to change his negative attitude to the campaign. But what after all mattered most was that a large number of local soviet cadres returned to the eight counties determined to carry the movement through in their own localities. [56]

Soon after this conference had closed the Central Government arranged another one, this time for representatives from the poor peasant unions of the same eight counties. [57] And in late July the soviet of Kiangsi province held one conference for soviet cadres and one for representatives of the poor peasant unions from nine different counties. **[58] Moreover, according to Kung Ch'u's account high-ranking party cadres had been called for a meeting in Juichin already in late May. All this confirms that the Land Investigation Movement was considered to be much more than an ordinary campaign.


The Land Investigation Movement had very wide implications, but the hard core of it was a class war. As has been pointed out above, the objects of this struggle were the disguised landlords and rich peasants. Some words should be added on the classes that composed the revolutionary forces.

According to the party and government directives the farm labourers and other workers in the countryside were to make up the vanguard, and the struggle would also depend very heavily on the poor peasants. The middle peasants were to be regarded as allies, and great care was to be taken not violate their interests. [59] As we shall see, one of the main problems about the movement turned out to be that of making a clear distinction

---

* They were the soviet chairmen (for the provincial soviets the vice-chairmen), the heads of the land departments, the heads of the departments of the Workers' and Peasants' Inspection and the heads of the local offices of the State Political Security Bureau (for the district soviets the special commissioners of the Security Bureau).

** In actual fact only seven counties sent delegates to the conference of the poor peasant unions.

between the middle peasants, who were among the friends, on the one hand, and the rich peasants, who belonged to the foes, on the other. In practice it was shown to be extremely difficult.


## The Land Investigation Movement – Its First Phase

We have so far been dealing with the programme and the instructions for the organisation of the Land Investigation Movement. How did it work in practice? According to the reports the movement to a considerable extent brought the desired results, but it also led to serious repercussions.

To a large extent the outcome depended upon the quality of the local cadres. Among them were undoubtedly many ardent revolutionaries and people dedicated to their work. Nevertheless, the average standard of the local cadres was probably not too high. Educationally they were obviously on the whole very poorly prepared, and this must have meant a serious lack of the sophisticated minds required for dealing with the extremely complicated matters of Chinese class relations.

The movement also depended very much on the masses of the people. And among them there should be a very solid basis for a class struggle. It is true that our material does not include any detailed accounts of individual sufferings under the old regime, such as those recorded from other parts of China by Jan Myrdal and William Hinton. But there is no reason to doubt that the common people in the Central Soviet Area had previously suffered badly – Mao Tse-tung has made a systematic case study of the exploitation through land rent and usury which had been practised in Yungfeng district in Hsingkuo. [60] The masses had seen a class struggle already, many of the exploiters had been punished very severely. Now the party and the government called for a more profound class struggle, and this could still release vast resources of emotional energy among the masses. There were strong impediments to such a release of sentiments, there were the bonds of tradition and of family and clan feelings. But these impediments could be overcome, so that the sentiments and the struggling spirit of the masses would break through with a tremendous force. Then there was another problem – the mass sentiments were blind, they had to be guided into certain channels. But had the local cadres the qualifications required for guiding them? There were indeed grave problems about the implementation of the Land Investigation Movement.


The most detailed account available on the experiences of the first phase

of the Land Investigation Movement is given by Mao Tse-tung in an article
published in Tou-cheng on August 29th 1933. The article contains many
complaints about errors committed, and these we will refer to later. Her
we will deal with what Mao represented as positive examples. The best
results in the movement so far, he stated, had been obtained in the two
counties of Juichin and Posheng; and the model to be studied by the cadre
was above all the work done in Jent'ien district in Juichin during 55 days
of the campaign.

The Land Investigation Movement in this district benefitted from the guidance of a special team dispatched by the Central Government. Presumab
this team joined forces with the local party and soviet cadres at the distr
level, to form an organisational nucleus for the campaign - in any case s
a nucleus existed, and Mao refers to it as "the comrades of Jent'ien
district". In the first place the campaign concentrated on seven relativel
backward hsiang in Jent'ien. Within each of these seven hsiang "the
comrades" mobilised the party organisation, the Communist Youth Leagu
the hsiang soviet, the trade union, the poor peasant union and other mass
organisations, and making use of all these they mobilised the broad mass
Mass meetings were held at the very roots of the society, at the village
and the wu-tzu* levels. Efforts were made to explain the class differentiation to the workers and the poor and middle peasants, and to assure the
that the Land Investigation Movement was in their own interest. A large
number of people were engaged in collecting information on persons suspected of belonging to one of the reactionary classes. The issue as to
whether or not a man should be branded as a rich peasant or as a landlord was first dealt with by the land investigation committee and the poor
peasant union of the hsiang, and decisions taken at these instances were
then submitted to the district soviet for approval. Furthermore, before
any action was taken against a class enemy, the matter was explained at
a mass meeting to the population of the village where he lived. Only afte
the masses had approved of it, the prescribed confiscation was effected;
and the confiscated land and the confiscated articles were then promptly
distributed among the local population.

Sometimes "the comrades of Jent'ien district" met special difficulties.
They encountered one problem which Mao has described more in detail
elsewhere[61] - large villages were often backward and hard to reform.
In Jent'ien the obstacles were as a rule overcome through patient propaganda work, but "the comrades" might also use terror:

> "In Pok'eng hsiang there was a village where they could not break
> through. There turned out to be two notorious "big tigers" lording it
> over there. Then they applied a different method. They first caught

---

* Wu-tzu here means a group of houses within a village.

these two bad things, at the place they called a meeting of an ambulant court to try them, and after the masses had enthusiastically approved of it they had them shot. The struggle of the local masses then started to burn like a fierce fire."[62]

A number of mass trials were staged to deal with especially bad class enemies, and they were attended by people from all the different hsiang of the district. During the 55 days altogehter 12 counter-revolutionaries were executed in Jent'ien, while more than 300 families were labelled as belonging to the landlord or the rich peasant class.

In Jent'ien the Land Investigation Movement did, according to Mao's account, lead to great improvements of revolutionary work within various fields. Soviet cadres who had committed grave errors were denounced in the presence of the masses, and the soviet apparatus was purged of some reactionary class elements. Apart from the expropriated land and articles which had been distributed among the masses, a cash amount of 7,500 yüan had so far been secured for the state treasury through confiscation from landlords and special levies imposed on rich peasants; the district had pledged to raise another 10,000 yüan in these ways, and additionally 40,000 yüan from the sale of government bonds. More than 700 persons from Jent'ien had joined the Red Army, the commercial co-operatives had developed rapidly, and advances had also been made in cultural and educational work. [63] If this article is true, there was during the 55 days somewhat of a "great leap forward" in the district of Jent'ien, not only in planning but even in practice.

So much for Mao's report on the work carried out in Jent'ien district. There are also reports of similar procedures in other localities, but on the whole no uniform pattern can be drawn up for the implementation of the Land Investigation Movement. Where the movement worked as it should, the local party leadership and the local soviet leadership guided the whole process, sometimes under the supervision of a team dispatched by the Central Government. [64] At the county or the district level arrangements were made for special conferences of local soviet personnel, and there were training courses for cadres to be engaged in the campaign. [65] Purges of reactionary cadres were staged. [66] Various mass organisations - above all the poor peasant unions - were activated, [67] and the soviets organised land investigation committees, propaganda teams and "surprise attack teams" (t'u-chi-tui). [68] Through meetings in the village or in the wu-tzu the very broadest masses were aroused; the masses helped in searching out disguised class enemies, and their spirit naturally rose to still higher levels when they were allotted confiscated land and confiscated articles. [69] This is a much generalised sketch of the implementation of the movement when it worked as it was intended to - we will later deal with cases when it was reported to work very poorly.

Table 13

Results of the Land Investigation Movement obtained during the two month of June and July 1933, according to the incomplete statistics of various counties.

| County | Number of disguised landlord families detected | Number of disguised rich peasant families detected | Land confiscated, reckoned in piculs[*] of grain which it yielded per annum | Money confiscated from landlords, in yüan | Special levies imposed on rich peasants, in yüan |
|---|---|---|---|---|---|
| Kunglüeh | 41 | 32 | | | |
| Yungfeng | 64 | 81 | | | |
| Posheng | 406 | 326 | 20,000.- | | |
| Shihch'eng | 262 | 179 | | 4,829.- | 4,670.- |
| Loan | 216 | 115 | | | |
| Yütu | 66 | 149 | 7,155.- | | |
| Hsinfeng | 9 | 38 | | | |
| Hsingkuo[**] | 7 | 32 | | | |
| Want'ai | 88 | 81 | 850.3 | 6,015.85 | 36,737.- |
| Shengli | 122 | 188 | | | |
| Juichin | 608 | 669 | 60,591.5[***] | | |
| Kuangch'ang | 68 | 37 | | | |
| Total | 1,957 | 1,927 | 88,596.8 | | |

Source: Doc. 31, p. 4.

---

[*]  1 picul = 133 1/3 lb.
[**] The reason for the low figures for the model county of Hsingkuo is obviously that the revolutionary struggle had there advanced very far before the Land Investigation Movement started.
[***] The source gives this figures as 605,915.-, but it can be seen from the total figure for the column that the point has been misplaced.

Table 14

Results of the Land Investigation Movement in Kanhsien during the two months of August and September 1933.

| | |
|---|---|
| Disguised landlords detected | 236 families |
| Disguised rich peasants detected | 283 " |
| Land confiscated, and good land taken from rich peasants in exchange of poor land, reckoned in annual grain yields | 6, 536 piculs |
| Money confiscated from landlords and special levies imposed on rich peasants | 1, 339. - yüan |

Source: Hung-se Chung-hua November 2nd 1933, p. 3.


Notes

1. According to the same source the Land Investigation Movement worked rather poorly in Kanhsien up to August 1933.

2. Kanhsien was a medium-sized county as far as the population is concerned. (See this thesis p. 55).

Table 15

Results of the Land Investigation Movement in the Central Soviet Area,
with exception of the province of Minkan, during the three months July,
August and September 1933.

| Province | Number of disguised landlord families detected | Number of disguised rich peasant families detected | Land confiscated, reckoned in piculs of annual grain yields* |
|----------|------|------|------|
| Kiangsi | 5,114 | 4,830 | 254,429.9 |
| Fukien | 879 | 838 | 52,633.– |
| Yüehkan | 995 | 970 | 27,123.– |
| Total | 6,988 | 6,638 | 334,185.9** |

Source: Tou-cheng No. 72 p. 16 (from Doc. 100).

---

* It is not clear whether or not the figures in this column include the
  good land taken from rich peasants in exchange of poor land.

** Mao Tse-tung has given the figure 307,539.– piculs. (Doc. 5C p. 76).

Table 16. Data from Shengli

| A. | | B. | |
|---|---|---|---|
| Numbers of families registered as belonging to the landlord and rich peasant classes before the Land Investigation Movement. | | Disguised landlords and rich peasants detected during the Land Investigation Movement, presumably up to October 1933 (see this thesis pp. 172 and 176). | |
| Landlords | 810 families | Landlords | 196 families |
| Rich peasants | 766    " | Rich peasants | 340    " |
| Total | 1, 576 families* | Total | 536 families** |

Source: Doc. 96

---

\*     In <u>Hung-se Chung-hua</u> of April 14th 1934 (p. 3) the figure is given as 1, 581 families.

\*\*   In <u>Hung-se Chung-hua</u> of May 7th 1934 (p. 3) the figure is given as 530 families.

Some data on local results of the first phase of the Land Investigation Movement, based on the obviously not too exact statistics of various local soviets, are given in tables 13-16. The tables will show that the campaign developed very unevenly.

There is reason to pay attention to the data recorded in table 16. In the county of Shengli nearly three times as many families had been registered as landlords or as rich peasants before the movement started, as those added during the first phase of the campaign. This proportion suggests that, although the Land Investigation Movement was very important, we should still take care not to over-estimate its relative significance in the class struggle. One may easily fall into the error of over-estimating it. The Land Investigation Movement can be studied, since we have the material, while the earlier class struggle is largely hidden from view. But what is hidden from view is not necessarily less significant.

The hard labour brigade was obviously an institution of much significance in relation to the Land Investigation Movement, but unfortunately we know very little about it. We know definitely that the policy was to force all able-bodied men (chuang-ting) among the landlords into such units. [70] An October 1933 resolution of the Council of People's Commissars seems to suggest that the brigades among other things provided for the male landlords' physical survival - or for their material subsistence - saying that in the course of labour their class character should be transformed. [7] On the other hand we have a very harsh notice in Hung-se Chung-hua of December 5th 1933, criticising a cadre in Posheng for paying 0.25 yüan per day to members of a hard labour brigade composed of "local tyrants" and "evil gentry". This was wrong, the notice said, first because it was waste and second because it saved the local tyrants and evil gentry from "dying and disappearing" (szu-wang). [72]

From October 1933 we have evidence of a policy to treat the rich peasants much more leniently than the landlords as far as labour obligations are concerned. This matter will be further discussed below.

In the eyes of the party leadership and the Central Government the Land Investigation Movement produced many positive results during the summer and autumn of 1933, but it was by no means wholly successful. Our source report quite a range of shortcomings and errors at the local levels.

In spite of all efforts spent on mobilising the party, the soviets and the various mass organisations, and in spite of the urgent instructions dispatched by the top leadership, many local cadres reportedly neglected the campaign. For example, the party committee of Huich'ang county discussed the Land Investigation Movement for the first time in late July, · after having ignored the instructions from the Central Bureau for nearly two months. [73] The cadres in the county of Anyüan reported that they were unable to launch the movement, pointing to the immediate danger of enemy attacks. [74] The Land Investigation Movement developed very unevenly - it produced the desired results in some places, while other districts lagged behind. [75]

Clan loyalty and feelings of localism were major obstacles to the movement, and in certain cases they proved stronger than the revolutionary spirit. The class struggle had to cut across these traditional bonds, but quite often it was difficult to get poor and middle peasants to struggle against rich peasants and landlords of the same clan or of the same village. [76] Special difficulties might be met in villages where the whole population belonged to the same clan and had the same family name. [77] Clan considerations sometimes also produced second thoughts with soviet cadres when it came to struggle against class enemies, and made them vacillate in the execution of their revolutionary duties. [78] And landlords and rich peasants were sometimes reported to have made use of the clan bonds to mobilise the local population to withstand the revolutionary upheaval collectively, or they organised mass flights to white areas. [79] The revolutionary incentives were strong, but so were the traditions of the old society.

Even if the revolutionary spirit prevailed, many errors might be made. The policy was to mobilise the exploited for struggle against the exploiters, but many local cadres failed to grasp the exploitation criteria for class differentiation. In some cases they apparently wholly ignored the class distinctions, and proceeded to undertake a new overall redistribution of land.[80] If attempts were made to apply the class criteria, they were often applied wrongly. There were cases of "right deviation" in this respect, when landlords and rich peasants were not recognised as such. [81] The frequent occurrences of "left deviation" were probably on the whole regarded as even more serious matters - the cases when rich peasants were classified as landlords and middle or even poor peasants were placed in one of the exploiter categories. In some localities there were general assaults on the middle peasant class. In a number of cases the middle peasants were antagonised or panic-stricken, and sometimes landlords or rich peasants would make use of the leftist mistakes to frighten them still more. [82] A quotation from Mao Tse-tung's article of August 29th may be illuminating:

"At the beginning of the land investigation in the town area of Juichin [they] investigated family for family and mu* for mu; [they] investigated so that the middle peasants were panic-stricken. There were even some middle peasants who went to the soviet and begged to have their class status changed. They begged to be made poor peasants. They said: "It is very dangerous to be middle peasants; just one step higher and we shall become rich peasants. Let us be made poor peasants, then we will be a bit further removed from the rich peasants. """ [83]

When local cadres attacked the middle peasants, they did so in violation of the party and government directives [84] - whether they were aware of it or not. There was, however, in the Land Investigation Movement another leftist practice which apparently conformed well to the early instructions from the top organs. On June 1st 1933 the Council of People's Commissars ordered that the local soviets be purged of "all foreign class elements (chieh-chi i-chi fen-tzu) and other bad elements." [85] The council failed to define the term "foreign class elements", and this must be regarded as a grave mistake. Quite naturally many local soviet organs interpreted the instruction to mean they were to evict all cadres with background in one of the reactionary classes. [86] We may in this connection note that if a purge of that kind was to be carried out at the central level, then perhaps most of the top leaders would have to go. [87] In his article of August 29th Mao Tse-tung made a badly needed distinction between "foreign class elements" on the one hand, and cadres with background in reactionary classes, who had proved to be loyal in soviet work, on the other. The latter were not to be purged. [88]

The "October Resolution" and the Interlude

As far as class struggle is concerned, the first phase of the Land Investigation Movement was followed by an interlude. It is somewhat problematic to fix the time of the transition. In some areas the first phase seems to have extended right into January 1934. [89] However, the most significant turning point came in October 1933.

In the autumn of 1933 the Council of People's Commissars made a general review of the effects of the movement. [90] It found that the campaign had brought positive as well as negative results. The local soviets had partly been strengthened through the eviction of really unreliable elements, and partly they had been weakened through the purge of cadres who in actual fact could be very useful. The mass support for the regime had partly been

---

* 6. 6 mu equal one acre.

reinforced as the common people had benefitted materially from the upheaval, partly it had been reduced thanks to the left deviations violating
the rights of middle and sometimes even of poor peasants. In some places
the negative side was particularly conspicuous, as large portions of the
population had fled to the mountains or to white areas.[91]

Mao Tse-tung had played a very prominent role in launching and guiding
the movement. He had done so in his capacity of chairman of the Council
of People's Commissars as well as of the CEC, as author of various
articles, as the leading figure at the very important conference of soviet
cadres from eight counties held in June, and as the author of the principles
for class differentiation here referred to as the "June regulations". His
standpoint in the campaign may seem quite radical, yet it was moderate
in relation to the practice of many local cadres, and at least in some respects also in relation to later pronouncements by Chang Wen-t'ien. Mao
might advocate the use of terror in this connection, but it was a terror to
be kept within limits. On the whole he wanted the class struggle to conform to certain rules.

Mao was highly alarmed by the leftist tendencies shown by many local
cadres in carrying out the campaign. He had expressed such worries in
his article of August 29th, and in October he started the process of a
general correction of the errors which had been committed.

On October 10th 1933 the Council of People's Commissars adopted two
very important sets of instructions. The first one was How to Differentiate
the Classes, which only now was given the status of a Central Government
edict, although it had been written by Mao much earlier and had already in
June been adopted by the conference of soviet cadres of eight counties.[92]
It is this document which is here referred to as the "June regulations".

The second set of instructions adopted on October 10th has been less known,
although it is perhaps even more interesting. It is called Decisions of the
Central Government on Some Problems of the Land Struggle.[93] This latter
document is reported to have been drafted by Mao Tse-tung as well, and
it was later strongly criticised by Mao's opponents in the party leadership.[94]

A summary of some portions of the latter document, which will hereafter
be referred to as the "October resolution", will be of interest. It will de-
monstrate Mao's search for detailed rules in the class struggle, as con-
trasted to the sweeping revolutionary statements later made by Chang Wen-
t'ien. We will also see how the October resolution was related to the June
regulations.

The June regulations had laid down that the rich peasants were to be distinguished from the landlords mainly through the extent to which they engaged in labour - whereas the former engaged in "labour" themselves, apart from being exploiters, the latter did not work at all, or they carried out only "supplementary labour" (fu-tai lao-tung). [95] In the October resolution the borderline between "labour" and "supplementary labour" was drawn. If a person's activity was to be recognised as "labour", he had to engage in major productive labour* for at least four months of the year. However, the main issue was not a distinction between individuals but a distinction between families; and for a family to be recognised as engaging in "labour", and thus to avoid the landlord category, it was sufficient that one of its members carried out the said quantity of work. Let us attempt to embrace the whole point: If a family to a large extent practised agrarian exploitation but yet had one member who engaged in major productive labour for at least four months of the year, it was to be placed in the rich peasant category; while a family that made its living through agrarian exploitation and did not fulfil the minimum labour requirement should - provided that this had been the state of affairs for three consecutive years immediately preceding the Communist take-over - be placed in the landlord group. Such was the main rule, but exceptions were allowed for in both directions. If exploitation was carried on on a very large scale, the landlord label should be applied even if the minimum labour requirement was fulfilled. On the other hand, a family was not to be treated as landlords as a result of impoverishment - if it had lost its labour power through death or diseases and the only means of subsistence left to it was renting out the land on lease. The exceptions were not fully defined; there was still some room left for judgement by local cadres, but nevertheless the borderline between landlords and rich peasants was made much clearer than before. [96]

The same happened to the distinction between the rich and the middle peasants - this crucial borderline between foes and friends of the regime. The June regulations said that while the former regularly relied on exploitation for a part of their income, the latter normally did not practise exploitation, or at least they did not do so regularly or to a large extent. [97] Again the boundary had been suggested only very vaguely, and in actual fact there was found to be a great number of border cases. The October resolution laid down proportions even in this respect, saying that a middle peasant family might rely on exploitation for up to 15 per cent, or in special cases, for example if there were many mouths to feed and few hands able to work, for up to 30 per cent of its income. It then belonged to the group of "well-to-do middle peasants" (fu-yü chung-nung), but yet it was entitled to the same treatment as the ordinary middle peasants who did

---

* Relatively light tasks, such as looking after draught animals and helping in weeding or in growing vegetables, did not count.

not practise exploitation at all. If the percentages were exceeded, and if this had been the state of affairs for three consecutive years immediately preceding the Communist take-over, the family had passed the fatal border and stepped into the rich peasant category. The special cases, when the boundary was set at 30 per cent exploitation, were left to be decided upon by the local cadres, but in doing so they had to listen very carefully to the opinions of the masses of the people. [98]

To protect the middle peasants – to prevent their being treated as class enemies – was obviously one of the main purposes of the October resolution. Related to this issue was the problem of preventing a too hard policy toward the rich peasants. If too severe blows were dealt to the latter, it might frighten even the former, who would be aware that they were rather close to the crucial borderline between the friends and the foes. Moreover, it was considered to be important in itself that there was a gradation of the foes, the rich peasants and the landlords were to be dealt with differently. In principle this was nothing new, but in some respects the difference in treatment had so far not been properly defined.

So far the rule had been that the landlord families were subject to confiscation of all their money, whereas rich peasants had to discharge special levies. Some local cadres had committed the error of making the amounts of the special levies equal to the cash holdings of the rich peasants, which would normally obliterate the difference of treatment between the two classes in this regard. The October resolution laid down that a special levy was not to exceed 40 per cent of the "circulating capital" (huo-tung k'uan-hsiang)* in possession of a rich peasant family. A repetition of the levy for the same family was not precluded, but it was warned against repeating it many times. [99]

Moreover, the resolution said that there was to be a very marked difference in the burden of forced labour. All ablebodied men (chuang-ting) from the landlord class were to be placed in hard labour brigades, where their class nature was to be transformed through physical work. On the other hand, the drafting of rich peasants for obligatory labour should be more selective – they should be drafted only to the extent to which their families had a surplus of man-power, or otherwise were able to replenish the man-power lost. As far as members of the latter class were concerned, the drafting was not to be carried so far as to interfere with productive work on their own fields of land. First of all the policy seems to have been to charge rich peasants with short-term labour service, avoiding the busy farming seasons. The difference in treatment of the two classes in this respect was indeed a significant one. [100]

---

* The translation of this term is taken from Hsiao Tso-liang, 1969, p. 270.

There are several points in the October resolution which need not be discussed here. In order to avoid misrepresenting the document it should be noted that formally it is on the whole fairly well balanced, warning against rightist as well as against leftist tendencies. Nevertheless, its main purposes were evidently to have a moderating effect on the class struggle and to replace the haphazard practices of the local cadres by more definite rules. Further, there seems to be no doubt that the re-solution to a large extent represented Mao Tse-tung's views in October 1933, and the contrast to Chang Wen-t'ien's standpoint in March 1934 is indeed striking.

One important point has to be paid attention to before leaving the document. The October resolution was given retrospective force. The local soviets were ordered to revise the case of every family that had previously been placed in a class category where it did not belong according to the reso-lution. This sort of re-grouping of the families could be complicated enough in itself, and insuperable problems might be encountered when it came to undoing the confiscation and redistribution of land and articles which had followed from wrong class categorisation. It was not anticipated that all the wrong acts of confiscation could be redeemed. The problem was, perhaps, least as far as immovable property was concerned. The resolution stated that all the arable land, hills and woodlands, ponds, houses and gardens which had been taken from families rightly to be classified as middle or poor peasants, as workers or as "poor people" (p'in-min), were to be returned to the original owners. * However, other property confiscated from members of these classes was to be handed back, or compensated by articles correctly taken from class enemies, "only to the extent to which it was possible." Less concern was shown for what had wrongly been confiscated from rich peasants - even their immovable property should be returned, or compensated for, "only to the possible extent."[101]

During the period from mid October 1933 to mid March 1934 the class policy pursued at the local levels must have varied very much from county to county and from district to district. First, there were a few places where the class struggle was continued during a large part of the period; second, there were apparently localities where the soviets felt too busy with other tasks to take any more measures on the class issue; and thirdl there were a number of local soviets that, on the urging of the October resolution, engaged in a massive revision of earlier class decisions and a massive rehabilitation of families unjustly treated.

---

* Compensation was possibly meant to be an alternative.

Our sources on the implementation of the revision are unfortunately not very plentiful. Our material stems wholly from accounts dating from a period immediately following the one under discussion, accounts characterised by a stark condemnation of the class policy which had been pursued by various local soviets. The objectivity of these reports may well be questioned, but let us see what we can get out of them - and what we can get out of our reasoning on the topic.

If the class struggle had been a very complicated matter, so was the revision. Tremendously strong personal feelings were again involved. A disaster had swept over the families classified as landlords, and very heavy blows had been dealt to those put in the rich peasant category. Now the authorities admitted that many mistakes had been made, and the atmosphere of struggle was replaced by an atmosphere of revision. The cadres had at their hand more detailed regulations for class differentiation than had been the case earlier, but the rules were by no means perfectly clear. There was still some room for manoeuvring, and what may have been as important, there was room for distortion of facts concerning the background of individual families. It is not strange that in many places there had not been a cool and consistent class differentiation during the time of struggle, when the revolutionary fervour of the cadres and the masses had been raised to great heights; nor is it strange that there was not everywhere a cool and well regulated revision in the moderate period, when those who felt that they had been unjustly treated saw a chance to rehabilitate themselves. The former propertied families often possessed a shrewdness which might achieve very much once it was given the scope. The later reports that large numbers of real landlords and rich peasants had managed to rehabilitate themselves during the moderate period are perhaps exaggerated, but they probably contain some truth.

Through the October resolution the local soviets had been instructed to correct earlier mistakes, and they had been given some additional standards for class differentiation, but how were they to proceed in carrying out the revision? Where could they obtain the basic data required for determining to which class a given family belonged according to the rules? In some places the cadres reportedly called on those who had been classified as landlords and rich peasants to supply honest information on their own background, and later to fight for their cause at mass meetings. [102] Of course this might be a dangerous method to apply, from the point of view of the regime. If distortion of facts had been likely to occur in the previous period, in the places where the work of class differentiation had been carried on in an atmosphere of struggle and revolutionary fervour; so there was now likely to be distortion of facts in the atmosphere of revision, in the places where the cadres to a considerable extent relied on the honesty of landlords and rich peasants.

The accounts say that the reactionary class elements in the moderate period staged a massive counter-attack in order to recover lost land and lost property. They made use of various means. They had their henchmen in certain local soviets, and in some cases they managed to provide the means for bribes. Through the spreading of rumours they tried to make public opinion suit their purposes.[103] A certain scepticism toward the objectivity of these reports is well warranted; but on the other hand it is not at all surprising that the landlords and the rich peasants - when their most vital interests were concerned - should have resorted to the old Chinese art of intrigues.

The application of the criteria for class differentiation was the main bone of contention. A family that made its living through agrarian exploitation and failed to have one member who engaged in major productive labour for at least four months of the year belonged, according to the October resolution, to the landlord class. One way of misapplying the provision was for instance to reckon book-keeping as major productive labour, which might help landlords to step over into the rich peasant group. The October resolution said that a family which fulfilled the above labour requirement but yet relied on agrarian exploitation for more than 15 per cent, or in special circumstances for more than 30 per cent of its income, was to be put in the rich peasant category. In the moderate period there were reportedly cases of misrepresentation of the proportions of exploitation that had been practised, and this meant that rich peasants luckily were re-classified as middle peasants.[104] It should be recalled that the labour and exploitation criteria pertained to the state of affairs for three consecutive years before the Communist take-over, and in some districts of the Central Soviet Area the Communist take-over lay more than four years back in time. Proportions and percentages might be misrepresented simply through a slip of memory and a wilful misrepresentation could be very difficult to disprove.

Some local soviets were prepared to go very far to meet the demands of those claiming to have suffered from injustice. They did not content themselves with redeeming errors committed during the Land Investigation Movement, but proceeded to revise large numbers of cases of assumed injustice inflicted before the movement had started. In the county of Shengli the number of "landlord" and "rich peasant" families that got their cases revised in the moderate period seems to be much more than double the number of families having been labelled as landlords or as rich peasants during the first phase of the Land Investigation Movement.[105] The problems which arose when it came to returning or compensating land and other property thought to have been wrongly confiscated, proved to be extremely difficult to solve. The land and the property had mostly been redistributed among the masses of the people, and the masses naturally expected to keep what they had got. This sort of concrete redemption had been carried into effect in some cases, in other cases it was apparently only in the process of being effected, when Chang Wen-t'ien in March 1934 ordered an abrupt swing toward the left in class policy. [106)

## The Land Investigation Movement - Its Second Phase

We must admit that it was a difficult situation that confronted Chang Wen-t'ien on the issue of class policy when he took over as head of the Council of People's Commissars. Many errors had been committed during the first phase of the Land Investigation Movement, and the attempt made at correcting them through the October resolution had produced new mistakes. Chang's approach to the problems was radically different from Mao's. He sought to remedy the situation - not through detailed regulations - but through sweeping revolutionary statements.

Although the new radicalisation of class policy was carried into effect by Chang Wen-t'ien, he was not alone in bearing responsibility for it. At the Fifth Plenum of the CCP Central Committee, held in Juichin in January 1934, Mao Tse-tung was severely criticised for the moderate provisions embodied in the October resolution, and accordingly the top party organs decided on a new intensification of the class struggle. [107) Chang Wen-t'ien started to carry out this decision of the party centre in March, after he had to some extent become familiar with his new position as chairman of the Council of People's Commissars.

The reversal of the class policy came through an instruction of the Council of People's Commissars, dated March 15th 1934. [108) This instruction was a very thinly veiled attack on the October resolution. It had been correct to issue an edict of that kind, said now the Council of People's Commissars, but the October resolution had been wrongly applied. The local soviets were warned against applying certain articles of the resolution "mechanically", and it was stated that the resolution contained some ambiguous phrases. Through its instruction of March 15th the Council of People's Commissars ordered a large-scale cancellation of class decisions taken during the moderate period, and most important in this respect were the instruction's articles 1 and 2.

The second article was the more moderate of the two:

> "In rectifying individual mistakes committed in the Land Investigation Movement, only the individual cases of the landlord and rich-peasant elements whose status has been decided as such in the past but is being

doubted or criticised by the masses may be reconsidered. If not doubted or criticised by the masses, no status can be changed, no matter what evidence the landlords or rich peasants may produce. Such changes as have already been made are null and void."[109]

Article 1 of the instruction, relating to class decisions taken before the Land Investigation Movement had started, was quite categorical:

"Landlords and rich peasants whose status was decided as such following the uprising and before the Land Investigation Movement must not be allowed to change their status, no matter what evidence they may produce. Such changes as have already been made are null and void."

Article 1 turned out to be too categorical for actual life. It created a dilemma for a certain "comrade Wang", who decided to clear up his problem through correspondence with Chang Wen-t'ien. Comrade Wang wondered if there were not after all exceptional cases, when the great majority or the whole of the local masses held the opinion that certain persons had been wrongly classified as landlords or as rich peasants before the Land Investigation Movement.[110] Chang Wen-t'ien had to make a retreat, stating that revisions which had taken place in these circumstances could be recognised as valid. But the reasons he gave for not having included such a modifying clause in the instruction of March 15th are characteristic of his general attitude. A modification of this kind, said Chang, could have "confused the line of vision" of the masses, and have created unnecessary worries about class decisions of the past. He continued:

"Rebellion is the highest manifestation of bitter class struggle, it is the life and death struggle between revolution and counter-revolution At such times every action that can promote the victory of the revolution is necessary and proper. At such times there may occur [son cases of] "injustice" toward particular elements (ch'eng-fen). But this sort of "injustice" is unavoidable in every rebellion, because rebellion is after all rebellion and not reckoning of accounts! There is after all not much of this kind of "injustice", and it is not worth g attention from our side."[111]

The details of the rural class policy pursued during the second phase of t Land Investigation Movement, from March 1934 onward, are unfortunate rather obscure. Certain trends of the policy can, however, be discerned

The new instructions of Chang Wen-t'ien and the Council of People's Commissars placed the emphasis on revolutionary fervour and agitated mass sentiments rather than on observance of detailed rules and regulations, and this meant a radical swing toward the left in class differentiation. There was a wave of what we may call "anti-revisionism" - a large number of families whose lot had changed for the better during the moderate period were again labelled as landlords or as rich peasants. Other families, having not been affected by the first phase of the movement, now received such labels for the first time. 112)

With regard to the treatment given to reactionary class elements, the policy during the second phase of the Land Investigation Movement followed a pattern which was very much like that of the administration of justice in the same period. First Chang Wen-t'ien was vigorously pushing the policy toward the left. Many local cadres went still further, and the landlords and the rich peasants had a harder time than ever before. In June Chang found that the cadres had gone too far, and produced a vehement attack on the "extreme leftists".

The drafting of rich peasants for hard labour brigades is one example. It will be recalled that the October resolution had been very moderate on his point, stating the principle that the drafting should not be carried so far as to interfere with productive work on the rich peasant families' own fields of land. In a May 1934 article Chang Wen-t'ien declared that he urgent need for labour in the extremely critical military situation had made this principle obsolete - the limitation should no longer be observed. However, there was still to be a difference in the labour burdens laid on the two main reactionary classes respectively. At least by the time the above article was written there were two principal types of hard labour brigades for reactionary class elements - one for male landlords and one for male rich peasants. The former were supposed to serve permanently, and the latter only temporarily. 113) In June Chang Wen-t'ien complained that many local cadres were forcing rich peasants en masse into the brigades for permanent labour service, which were designed for landlords. *114)

In June Chang Wen-t'ien stated that in exceptional cases it was correct to lump together rich peasants and landlords in the same labour brigades. This should be done in the "direct war zones", and if the military situation so warranted also in the close rear. (Doc. 52)

There was also supposed to be a difference in the treatment of the dependents of landlords and rich peasants respectively. According to Chang's articles, published in May and in June 1934, the dependents of the former should be evicted from all war zones and driven either to white areas or to other soviet districts. The dependents of the latter, however, should normally be allowed to remain in the war zones which they inhabited, although it was permissible to evict them in exceptional

The policy of expropriation followed the pattern as well. The October resolution had laid down that the special levies imposed on rich peasant families should not exceed 40 per cent of their holdings of "circulating capital". In May 1934 Chang Wen-t'ien made it clear that the restriction was abolished, and said that empty bellies among the rich peasants were better than empty bellies among the Red Army men. [115] In June, howeve Chang made a complaint similar to one found already in the October resolution – the local "extreme leftists" had failed to observe the difference in treatment between landlords and rich peasants in this respect, confisc ing even the grain holdings of the latter hundred per cent. [116]

We then come to the most serious matter of all, the killing of landlords and rich peasants. Some examples of death penalties, which have been recorded in the chapter on administration of justice, [117] strongly sugges that in February and March 1934 members of these classes needed not t commit very grave offences to put their lives in peril. From March we have also a report of a horrible scene when reactionary class elements were evacuated by force from the border area of Loan. Some landlords made a sort of sit-down strike on the road, at the same time trying to persuade others to break away and flee to the mountains. The fate of the troublemakers was to be killed by spears, an act which was approved of by the organ of the Kiangsi party committee. [118] Moreover, in May Cha Wen-t'ien authorised executions in the war zones and the border areas of persons from reactionary classes merely on suspicion of counter-revolutionary activity. [119]

We are in no position to evaluate the scale on which the killing was carri on, but Chang's complaints in June of the "extreme leftists'" excessive desire to kill seem to have very grave implications. He wrote:

> "However, the tension of the revolutionary war, and the stepping up of the counter-revolutionary activity of landlords and rich peasants, have made some unstable elements in our party mad and confused (k'uang-luan). They not only want to use red terror to deal with counter-revolutionary landlords and rich peasants, they want to use red terror to deal with all landlords and rich peasants. They want to arrest all landlords and rich peasants, and to kill all of them. They think that only in this way can they finally extinguish the counter-revolutionary activity of the landlords and the rich peasants. For in stance, the urgent order of May 23rd from the Kiangsi Security Bureau is a concrete manifestation of this tendency." [120]

---

cases. In June Chang complained that the "extreme leftists" were evicting rich peasant dependents en masse from war zones and even from other districts. (Docs. 51 and 52. See also doc. 46 B art. 29).

Finally we have the policy toward the cadres. In May 1934 Chang Wen-t'ien urged the party branches and the local soviets to undertake radical purges of foreign class elements and other bad, corrupt and vacillating persons within their own ranks, especially in the war zones and in the border areas. [121] In June, however, he found reason to make the same complaint as Mao had put forward already in August of the preceding year - the "extreme leftists" were purging all soviet cadres who came from landlord or rich peasant families, also those who had made great contributions to the revolutionary cause. [122] And the situation had evidently become much graver than it was when Mao voiced his opinion on the topic. Chang reveals that the "extreme leftists" had in many localities obtained an enormous power by June 1934. According to his account they would say: "Whoever opposes me, he is the running dog of the landlords, the rich peasants and the capitalists." When the leftists made excessive use of terror in the struggle against counter-revolution, the more moderate cadres did not dare to interfere - in fear of their lives. [123]

An attempt to outline the trends of the rural class policy can to a large extent be based on historical data, but we also have to make use of our imagination.

By 1930 Mao Tse-tung and his men had decided on a class policy which might well seem radical at the time, but which was nevertheless moderate compared with later developments. Their confiscation policy was radical - all land was confiscated from landlords and rich peasants - but their redistribution policy was rather moderate. Rich peasants and their families were allotted shares of land, equally with the revolutionary masses, and so were the dependents of the landlords provided they stayed in the village. Even some of the landlords themselves received plots of land, but very often this question did not arise because they had been killed or had fled during the insurrection. [124]

The land law of November 1931 meant a swing toward the left in rural class policy. Henceforth the landlords and their dependents were as a rule not entitled to any land whatsoever, while only poor land was given to rich peasants. This swing toward the left was not the work of Mao, but of members of the 28 Bolshevik group and their associates, who acted under strong influence from Moscow. [125]

Nevertheless it was Mao who, in his capacity of head of the Central Government, was entrusted with supervising the implementation of the new radical line. He did execute the new policy, but up to the summer of 1933 he apparently did not pursue it very vigorously. Poor health may to some

extent have accounted for his lack of vigour in this respect,[126] but we
may also assume that he was lacking enthusiasm for the new principles.

A tremendous vigour was shown in the class struggle during the first phase
of the Land Investigation Movement, from June 1933 onward. Our sources
tell that Mao Tse-tung played a very prominent part in the movement, and
Hsiao Tso-liang has concluded that Mao initiated it.[127] However, the whole
pattern of the development seems to show that important things were going
on behind the scenes. Presumably the party leadership of the 28 Bolsheviks and their supporters had been criticising Mao for not executing the
official policy thoroughly enough; they probably demanded a radicalisation
of the class struggle. There is every reason to accept the account of the
ex-Communist Chen Jan, saying that the party leaders urged a reluctant
Mao to carry the movement through by means of the soviet apparatus.[128]

There were apparently mixed motives lying behind Mao's vigorous conduct
of the class struggle during the first phase of the Land Investigation Movement. If the party leadership, as we have assumed, demanded it, this would
be an extremely strong factor - open defiance of the party directives might
have led to an even earlier removal of Mao from power. On the other hand,
Mao seems to have been genuinely attracted by some aspects of the struggle.
His fight, during the Land Investigation Movement, against subversive activity carried on in revolutionary organs by reactionary class elements has
a parallel in his policy of 1930.[129] Moreover, he was certainly attracted by
the prospect of raising the revolutionary fervour of the masses of the people.

Mao was very radical during the first phase of the Land Investigation Movement, yet, his radicalism had its limitations. He wanted the class struggle
to conform to certain rules. Before long, he became more concerned with
correcting the excesses of local cadres than with encouraging the struggle.

Accordingly, the radical period was followed by a moderate one, from
October 1933 onward. From mid January 1934 Mao's moderation was
heavily criticised by the top party organs, and two months later the new
chairman of the Council of People's Commissars, the "Bolshevik" Chang
Wen-t'ien, carried through a new radical swing toward the left in class
policy. Chang's sweepingly revolutionary statements were interpreted very
radically by many local cadres, and large-scale killing and starving of
reactionary class elements followed. Finally, in June 1934 Chang found that
he had to warn against the excesses of the "extreme leftists".

The rural class policy followed a zigzag course, but its general tendency
was toward the left.

# CHAPTER VII.   FINANCES

From 1931 to 1934 the economic burdens laid on the population of the Central Soviet Area increased tremendously. Perhaps this had to be so, and perhaps not. It depends mainly on whether or not the cost of war per head of the population could have been reduced if a more elastic method of warfare had been adopted. Anyhow, the 28 Bolsheviks, Chou En-lai and the Comintern adviser Li T'e (Otto Braun) prevailed in their insistence on a head-on clash with the Kuomintang forces, in defiance of Mao Tse-tung's advocacy of a more flexible warfare; and the war expenditure per head of the population became high indeed. Whether Mao would have been able to reduce the cost of war, or whether he could have got control over a larger area and a larger population to shoulder the expenses - these remain themes for speculation.

The increase in the economic burdens will be the focus of the present chapter. However, quite a range of questions is involved. In order to describe these burdens it is by no means sufficient to study the tax system. We must also make clear the significance of such factors as currency, rice prices, sale of government bonds, food supply to the Red Army, and the confiscation policy; and the whole complex can only be understood if we acquaint ourselves with the structure and the functions of the financial apparatus at the central and local levels.

## Currency

According to Kung Ch'u the Communist authorities in Kiangsi began to issue their own currency in early 1931. Presumably there was a bank of some kind at the time, taking charge of this most important matter. The state bank was founded toward the end of the same year, soon after the formal establishment of the republic. [1]

Having established its own state bank and assumed control of its own currency, the soviet government did not necessarily feel bound to observe all the restrictions which in normal times are laid on the financial policy of a nation. But it was evidently caught in a dilemma. On the one hand was the temptation to try in the short run to finance the war through inflation,

i. e. through a very extensive issue of banknotes, and on the other were the worries about the complications to which this might lead. An undated Comintern document instructed the Chinese Communists to show great caution with regard to banknote printing. [2] A resolution adopted by the Second National Soviet Congress in January 1934 likewise emphasised the need to show restraint in this regard, but nevertheless it stated that "in the circumstances of a protracted internal war increased issue of paper money is a method often [used for] filling the gap in the finances between expenditure and income."[3] It is obvious to everyone that what the government gained by this method the population had to pay for through the decreased value of their money holdings. Reliable data on the amount of soviet money put into circulation seem not to be available[*]; nevertheless there is no doubt that inflation of the currency was one of the means used for making the people pay for the war.

There was naturally, side by side with the soviet banknotes, also a certain amount of Kuomintang silver money in circulation, [4] but it gradually disappeared. Much of it was sent out of the soviet area in order to cover the import surplus, [5] part of it was acquired through various means by soviet organs, [6] and private persons having got hold of silver coins would not let them go. [7] Mao Tse-tung informs us that in Ts'aihsi in Fukien the silver money had completely disappeared from circulation by late 1933. [8]

The policy was to uphold, within the territory of the Central Soviet Area, the exchange rate of one soviet yüan to one Kuomintang yüan in silver. [9] This rate became, however, very artificial, and some private traders failed to observe it. From early 1934 we know examples of business men being shot for having speculated in currency exchange by paying from three to seven yüan in soviet banknotes for each Kuomintang yüan in silver. [10]

In the late period of the republic the Kuomintang silver money was in the process of disappearing, and confidence in the soviet money was declining.[1] In this situation rice, which in the Central Soviet Area was the most indispensable of all commodities, to some extent acquired the role of a currency. By that time the Central Government was making efforts to secure its revenue, not in the form of money, but in rice.

## Rice Prices

Rice was always indispensable, but the balance of its supply and demand

---

[*] For KMT estimates see Tsao Po-i, 1969, p. 360.

varied tremendously from season to season. Accordingly there were enormous fluctuations in the rice prices. This was a well known phenomenon in the old society of China, but in the Central Soviet Area the distance between the ups and downs was probably larger than the average.

Some data are available on the price fluctuations, but their interpretation is somewhat problematic. In Want'ai, Kanhsien and Kunglüeh the price of unhulled rice (ku) sank after the autumn harvest in 1932 more or less generally to 0.50-0.70 yüan per picul, and the very lowest price reported from these places at the time was 0.25 yüan per picul.[12] In the spring and early summer of 1933 there was a bad food shortage, and in such counties as Yangyin, Juichin and Ch'angt'ing the price of hulled rice (mi) then rose to more than 20 yüan per picul[13] - i.e. more than 80 times the very lowest price noted for unhulled rice in the surplus districts after the autumn harvest of the previous year. Of cource there were various factors lying behind this proportion. The work of hulling the rice counted for some, and removal of the hulls to a certain extent affected the weight. Furthermore, there was the storage and there was the transportation from the surplus districts to the districts of shortage. * Nevertheless, the price increase was fantastic, and the extent to which capitalist exploitation by private rice dealers was carried on under the eyes of a Communist-controlled regime was found to be shocking.

After the autumn harvest of 1933 the price sank again, but not so low this time. For a short period unhulled rice was changing hands at 1.70-1.80 yüan per picul in some surplus districts, but the price rose quickly to 2 or 3 yüan.[14] The increase continued during the autumn and winter, although it varied from locality to locality. By early March 1934 private dealers in Kanhsien were selling hulled rice at more than 17 yüan per picul.[15] What the top price would be like in the really difficult time, two or three months later, is a matter of speculation.

The poor and middle peasants were reported to be suffering tremendously from the price fluctuations. They sold cheap and bought dear. After the autumn harvest their rice holdings seemed to be rather abundant, but they wanted to buy a few other things needed for daily life, such as salt, vegetable oil and cloth, and some of them had to pay for hired labour. They were desperately in need of cash; accordingly they sold rice, and sometimes they sold too much of it, at the ridiculous autumn prices. If they then ran short of food the following spring or summer, they would try to buy rice on the market, if in one way or another they could scrape together money to buy it, at exorbitant prices. On the other side of the coin was the profit made by professional merchants, and reportedly also by rich peasants

---

* There is also an uncertainty as to which currency was used.

who were able to provide the capital needed to engage in the rice trade. [16)]

From a selfish point of view the soundest policy a peasant could pursue would seem to be to stick stubbornly to a sufficient quantity of his own rice. The government would, however, prefer him partly to use other remedies, to be effected through the food co-operatives (liang-shih ho-tso-she) and the Bureau for the Regulation of Food Supply (Liang-shih t'iao-chi-chü).

In the late summer of 1932 the government began to encourage the establishment of food co-operatives, mainly for dealing in rice, and open to membership for people from non-exploiting classes only. Quite a large number of them came into being, especially from August 1933 onward, but very few actually functioned as they were intended to. The food co-operatives were supposed to buy rice somwhat above the market price in the cheap season, and to sell it somewhat below the market price in the expensive season. Nevertheless they would make a profit, which would partly be paid as dividends to the shareholders (i. e. the members), and partly be used to accumulate capital for a further expansion of the trade. To the individual peasant this system was on the whole much to be preferred to exploitation by private traders, and it would benefit society and the state as well. The co-operatives would have a moderating effect on the seasonal fluctuations of rice prices, and they were supposed to some extent to bridge the gap between the surplus districts and the districts of shortage by transporting rice to places where the price was highest. Moreover, they were expected to build up rice reserves from which the state could purchase at times of necessity, especially for the supply of the Red Army. [17)]

Whereas the food co-operatives were implements to be used by the broad masses for regulating rice prices and for securing an adequate food supply for the Red Army, the Bureau for the Regulation of Food Supply was a government organ charged mainly with the same tasks. Unfortunately we cannot fully trace the history of the latter institution. We know that at the provincial level such a bureau was active in Fukien by 1932. [18)] We also know that there was a Central Bureau for the Regulation of Food Supply attached to the Commissariat for National Economy by the spring of 1933,[19)] and we may assume that it was transferred to the Commissariat for Food when this was established in early 1934. By September 1933 the Bureau had 16 branch offices attached to soviets at the county level. [20)] In order to moderate the price fluctuations and to secure an adequate food supply for the Red Army it was supposed to buy rice partly from the food co-operatives and partly from individual peasants. [21)] Although selling cheaper than the market price in the expensive season the Bureau for the Regulation of Food Supply was in 1933-34 making a certain profit, contributing directly to the state finances. [22)] And it must have been saving the state very considerable amounts of money through securing for it the necessary stocks of rice some months in advance - during times of rapidly increasing prices.

## The Financial Apparatus and the Unification of Finances

The building up of an effective financial system was one of the most urgent tasks confronting the new republic in 1931-1932. The apparatus had in the main to be built from the ground up. To be sure, funds had been raised in the Central Soviet Area before the republic was officially established, but the old procedures had to be revolutionised.

An account of the "financial" state of affairs before the establishment of the republic is found in a resolution adopted by the first representative soviet congress of Kiangsi province some time in the spring of 1932. Here, as in several other documents criticising the errors of the past, we may allow for a certain amount of exaggeration, but nevertheless it seems clear that the situation was actually pretty bad. The resolution states:

"Before [the establishment of] the Central Government the soviets of the various levels had no finances to speak of. They collected in a confused way and spent in a confused way, and they wasted as they pleased. Still less were there any budgets, accounts or plans to speak of."[23]

The resolution further says that many soviets used to rely for their revenue exclusively on confiscation of money and valuables from "local tyrants", which in this context obviously meant the landlords. When that source was exhausted, they began to attack the rich peasants, but even their assets did not in the long run meet the demands of the wasteful local soviets. The next victims were therefore the middle peasants, and in one period even the small savings of some poor peasants were exploited. No wonder that this policy of grabbing the money where it could be found resulted in a reduced confidence in the soviet apparatus among the masses.

Before the establishment of the republic, the resolution goes on, there were no fixed tax regulations. Some local soviets ignored the task of tax collection altogether, while others demanded taxes that were too high. Perhaps the gravest error of all was that some local soviets spent everything they collected, failing to send any money upward through the governmental hierarchy.[24]

If the state of affairs was approximately like this, how could the regime subsist? Most of all, how could the war be financed? Our sources tell us that before the summer of 1932 the Red Army was largely self-financing. Even the army raised its own money in the course of the struggle against "local tyrants", which first of all meant landlords. In 1932 it was argued that there had to be a change in this, because the Red Army had too much to do - on the one hand it had to struggle against the external enemy, which required concentration of its units, and on the other it had to raise money through confiscation, which meant dispersion of its forces. To correct this abnormality the Commissariat of Finances assumed the responsibility of supporting the Red Army - in principle from July 1932 onward. [25]

In actual fact the change could not take place overnight. When the Commissariat of Finances in July 1932 in principle assumed the heavy responsibility of supporting the Red Army, it had reportedly a staff of one or two persons. [26] But starting from this tiny nucleus it did see a significant expansion during the following months. According to the program the expansion was very significant; in August or September the Council of People's Commissars laid down that the Commissariat of Finances should have seven offices - respectively for accountancy, auditing, general affairs, taxation, government bonds, currency and state property - plus one committee to give guidance to the co-operatives. [27] An office for management of the state treasury was added toward the end of the same year. [28] Although the responsibility for the co-operatives was taken over in the spring of 1933 by the Commissariat for National Economy, [29] the scope of activity of the Finance Commissariat developed further in other respects. [30]

The first Commissar of Finances was Teng Tzu-hui, who was elected in November 1931, immediately after the First National Soviet Congress. He had a hard job indeed to do, and when he felt the full responsibility of supporting the rapidly expanding Red Army, he is reported to have despaired. He fell into disgrace sometime in 1933, accused among other things of pessimism, opportunism, and of placing the financial burdens on the common people rather than on the exploiting classes. It has to be noted that the attack on Teng Tzu-hui was part of the drive against the "Lo Ming line", which was largely an indirect fight by Mao Tse-tung's opponents against Mao. Perhaps one of Teng's most serious "faults" at the time actually was being too closely associated with Mao. Anyhow, Teng Tzu-hui was demoted to Vice-Commissar of Finances in August 1933. [31] Lin Po-ch'ü became the new Finance Commissar, and he was re-elected after the Second National Soviet Congress, in February 1934. [32]

A difficult task was the building up of finance departments at the various local levels. The Commissariat of Finances was very modest in its com-

plaint when it stated that many workers and peasants did not know how
to write and how to calculate; [33] really qualified personnel must have
been extremely scarce. Nevertheless, a somewhat differentiated local
apparatus is reported to have been established by November 1932 - the financial departments at the county level had at that time one section for
the cashier, one for accountancy and one for taxation. [34] The local machinery was further developed later. [35]

In January 1933 a national treasury was founded, controlled by the Commissariat of Finances and attached to the state bank. It had branches at
the provincial and the county levels; these branches were incorporated
in the branch state banks, where such existed, otherwise they were attached
to the local finance departments. [36]

By means of this apparatus the Chinese Communists hoped to establish a
centralised financial system to replace the earlier haphazardness and
confusion. The Central Government endeavoured to obtain full control of
all available sources of revenue, as well as of the expenditure of the local
soviets and the military organs. Shortly after the birth of the republic too
much optimism was shown toward the prospects in this regard - it was
declared that the "unification of finances" (ts'ai-cheng t'ung-i) should be
carried into effect by January 1932. [37] About a year later, however, the
aim was still far from having been fully attained; but it was now hoped
that - through the establishment of central and local state treasuries
and through the implementation of rather complex accountancy procedures
- the unification of finances could be fully realised from January 1933. [38]
In actual fact there were even several months after that serious problems
remaining to be solved. [39]

The early attempts at establishing a unified system were most of all based
on the requirement that the local soviets should send money upward - the
flow of money should go from the district financial department to the financial department of the county, from the latter to the financial department
of the province and from there to the Commissariat of Finances. Of course
allowance was made for a certain expenditure by the various local soviets,
but only in accordance with specific permission from the financial organ
at the level above. [40] In essence the system continued after January 1st 1933;
from this date onward the money was partly vested in the county and provincial branches of the state treasury, but the Commissariat of Finances
could at any time draw on the holdings of the branches through the central
treasury. [41]

Central control of expenditure obviously necessitated a budgetary system.
With the exception of the lowest levels the soviets were ordered to submit,
not annual, but monthly budgets; the financial department of the county must

191

on behalf of its soviet organisation submit monthly budgets to the financial department of the province, while the latter each month had to submit a budget for the expenditure at the various local levels to the Commissariat of Finances. Approval of the budgets, in their original or in their cut form was in the final instance the prerogative of the commissariat. [42]

Our next step must be to look into the sources of revenue of the Chinese Soviet Republic. The available material does not, however, enable us to make a full survey in this respect. Some items will just be mentioned before we proceed to deal somewhat more in detail with a few others.

Customs and export duties were significant to the extent to which it was possible to break through the Kuomintang blockade. Our sources tell us that in the spring of 1933 efforts were made at building up a customs system, [43] but we do not know the amount of money that was raised in this way.

Nor do we know how much money was raised through the renting out on lease of shops and workshops which had been confiscated from landlords and certain other reactionaries. This source of revenue was probably not a major one. [44]

Finally, we are ignorant of the amount of money raised through taxation of private trade. We do know some regulations showing that the tax rates for traders were progressive, varying in accordance with the amount of their basic capital. On the whole the rates were rather moderate; very small-scale trade was exempt from taxation altogether, while for example merchants with a basic capital of 1,000-1,500 yüan had after July 1932 to pay 10 per cent of their gross profit. [45] Since the material is rather limit there seems to be no point in trying to go further into detail on this item, and we therefore proceed to the obviously much more significant land tax.

The Land Tax

The land tax was important for the state revenue, although it was less important than one might think. Its rates were on the whole rather moderate, and agricultural by-products were not taxed at all. [46] Moreover, there were some social groups that enjoyed tax exemption. Among these were th former farm labourers and other workers who had been allotted land, provided they did not explicitly express a desire to be allowed to contribute to the revolutionary cause through tax paying. [47] The families of Red Army men were also exempt, [48] while employees in the soviet apparatus and certain other cadres at least from 1933 onward had only to pay land tax at half rate. [49] Poor and middle peasants paid the tax, while the land tax rates for the unfortunate rich peasants were especially high.

General regulations for the land tax were adopted by the Central Executive Committee as early as late November 1931. It was left to the various provincial soviets to fix the rates in accordance with local circumstances, but the rates at that time in force in Kiangsi were appended to the CEC's edict to serve as a guide for other provinces. They are reproduced in table 17.

Sometime in 1932 the soviet of Kiangsi province announced that various local soviets, revolutionary organisations and the masses themselves had found these rates to be too low; they were demanding a higher land tax in order to contribute more to the revolutionary cause. [50] Of course we are entitled to question the spontaneity of demands of this sort - a problem which we will revert to below. Anyhow, the rates for Kiangsi were in 1932 increased, as can be seen from table 18.

However, even in 1932 the land tax rates were fixed separately for each province. In Fukien they were higher than in Kiangsi, except for very abundant crops (cf. table 19).

In the autumn of 1933 the land tax rates were for the first time made uniform for the whole of the Central Soviet Area. [51] Generally speaking this meant a very slight increase of the rates in Kiangsi, but for the poor and middle peasants it meant a reduction in Fukien (cf. table 20). Moreover, from that time onward the tax was to a larger extent than before collected in kind, i. e. in the form of unhulled rice, instead of in money, [52] which would protect the government from the tremendous price fluctuations. Finally, the unified rates remained unchanged in 1934, the most conspicuous trait for this year being that the government hurried up collecting the tax in order to get it before the territories were lost to the advancing Kuomintang forces. [53]

Table 17

The land tax rates for Kiangsi, as shown in an appendix to the Provisional Tax Regulations of the Chinese Soviet Republic of November 28th 1931.

| Estimated crop of dry, unhulled rice per person in a given family | Tax to be paid by poor and middle peasants, in percentages of the rice crop | Tax to be paid by rich peasants, in percentages of the rice crop |
|---|---|---|
| Less than 2 piculs | No tax | No tax |
| 2 piculs | No tax | 1 % |
| 3 " | No tax | 2 % |
| 4 " | 1 % | 3 % |
| 5 " | 2 % | 4 % |
| 6 " | 3 % | 5 % |
| 7 " | 4 % | 6. 5 % |
| 8 " | 5 % | 8 % |
| 9 " | 6. 5 % | 9. 5 % |
| 10 " | 8 % | 11 % |
| 11 " | 9. 5 % | 12. 5 % |
| 12 " | 11 % | 14. 5 % |
| 13 " | 12. 5 % | 16. 5 % |
| 14 " | 14. 5 % | |
| 15 " | 16. 5 % | |

Source: Doc. 81A pp. 14-15.

Notes

1. It is uncertain whether or not the footnote to table 18 applies to the present table as well.

2. From November 1931 and up to the time of the evacuation of the Central Soviet Area tax was also laid on such products as tea, fruits, etc., but only provided they had acquired a major significance in the peasants' economy. The tax rates for these products seem in the main to have corresponded well to those imposed on rice production. (Doc. 81 A art. 9; doc. 82 A art. 9; doc. 83 art. 4; doc. 90 D with appendix).

Table 18

Land tax rates for Kiangsi in 1932.

| Estimated crop of dry, unhulled rice per person* in a given family | Tax to be paid by poor and middle peasants, in percentages of the rice crop | Tax to be paid by rich peasants, in percentages of the rice crop |
|---|---|---|
| 1 -  2 piculs | No tax | 4    % |
| 2 -  3  " | No tax | 5    % |
| 3 -  4  " | 4    % | 6    % |
| 4 -  5  " | 5    % | 7    % |
| 5 -  6  " | 6    % | 8    % |
| 6 -  7  " | 7    % | 9    % |
| 7 -  8  " | 8    % | 10    % |
| 8 -  9  " | 9    % | 11    % |
| 9 - 10  " | 10    % | 12. 5 % |
| 10 - 11  " | 11    % | 14    % |
| 11 - 12  " | 12    % | 15. 5 % |
| 12 - 13  " | 13. 5 % | 17    % |
| 13 - 14  " | 15    % | 18. 5 % |
| 14 - 15  " | 16. 5 % | 20    % |
| 15 - 16  " | 18    % | 22    % |

Sources: Doc. 115; doc. 90 C, vol. 2, pp. 56–58.

---

* Every person in a poor or middle peasant family counted in this respect, whereas in a rich peasant family only the persons capable of work were taken into consideration. (Doc. 82 A art. 7). This arrangement meant heavier rates of taxation for rich peasant families.

Table 19

Land tax rates for Fukien in 1932.

| Estimated crop of dry, unhulled rice per person in a given family | Tax to be paid by poor and middle peasants, in percentages of the rice crop | Tax to be paid by rich peasants, in percentages of the rice crop |
|---|---|---|
| 1 - 2 piculs | No tax | 5 % |
| 2 - 3 " | 5 % | 6 % |
| 3 - 4 " | 6 % | 7 % |
| 4 - 5 " | 7 % | 8. 5 % |
| 5 - 6 " | 8. 5 % | 10 % |
| 6 - 7 " | 10 % | 11. 5 % |
| 7 - 8 " | 11. 5 % | 13 % |
| 8 - 9 " | 13 % | 14. 5 % |
| 9 - 10 " | 14. 5 % | 16 % |
| 10 - 11 " | 16 % | 18 % |
| 11 - 12 " | 16 % | 20 % |

Source: Doc. 90 C, vol. 2, pp. 59-60

Note

The footnote to table 18 applies to the present table as well.

Table 20

Land tax rates for the whole of the Central Soviet Area 1933-34.

| A. Estimated crop of dry, unhulled rice per person in a given family | Tax due to be paid by a poor or middle peasant family of five members, reckoned in percentages of the rice crop | Tax due to be paid by a rich peasant family of five members, reckoned in percentages of the rice crop |
|---|---|---|
| 1 - 2 piculs | No tax | 4.8 % |
| 2 - 3 " | 1.9 % | 6.3 % |
| 3 - 4 " | 4.2 % | 7.8 % |
| 4 - 5 " | 5.4 % | 9.3 % |
| 5 - 6 " | 6.4 % | 10.8 % |
| 6 - 7 " | 7.4 % | 12.3 % |
| 7 - 8 " | 8.4 % | 13.8 % |
| 8 - 9 " | 9.4 % | 15.3 % |
| 9 - 10 " | 10.4 % | 16.8 % |
| 10 - 11 " | 11.4 % | 18.3 % |
| 11 - 12 " | 12.4 % | 19.8 % |
| 12 - 13 " | 13.4 % | 21.3 % |
| 13 - 14 " | 14.4 % | 22.8 % |
| 14 - 15 " | 15.4 % | 24.3 % |
| 15 - 16 " | 16.4 % | 28.8 % |

Notes

. To some extent the footnote to table 18 applies to section A of the present table as well. For details see doc. 116 B.

. In 1933 the government instituted a second type of progressive land tax rates, which in fact ran contrary to our own system of family allowances. Large families, i. e. families with many members to whom land had been allotted (children born before the land redistribution inclusive), had to pay tax at a slightly higher rate than small families. The former, possessing a larger acreage of land and normally a more abundant labour power, were thought to be better off than the latter. Section B of this table will show how the system worked if the harvest is kept constant and the size of the family is varied.

| B. Number of family members to whom land had been allotted | Crop per person, reckoned in dry, unhulled rice | Tax due to be paid by poor and middle peasant familie reckoned in percentages of the rice crop |
| --- | --- | --- |
| Single person | 7 - 8 piculs | 8. 0 % |
| 2 | 7 - 8 " | 8. 1 % |
| 3 | 7 - 8 " | 8. 2 % |
| 4 | 7 - 8 " | 8. 3 % |
| 5 | 7 - 8 " | 8. 4 % |
| 6 | 7 - 8 " | 8. 5 % |
| 7 | 7 - 8 " | 8. 6 % |
| 8 | 7 - 8 " | 8. 8 % |
| 9 | 7 - 8 " | 9. 0 % |
| 10 | 7 - 8 " | 9. 2 % |
| 11 | 7 - 8 " | 9. 4 % |
| 12 | 7 - 8 " | 9. 6 % |
| 13 | 7 - 8 " | 9. 8 % |
| 14 | 7 - 8 " | 10. 0 % |
| 15 | 7 - 8 " | 10. 2 % |

Source: Appendix to doc. 83.

———————

On the whole the land tax collected by the soviet government was rather light, and he revenue which it brought the state was limited. For the year 1932 the government had calculated on an income from this source amounting to the modest figure of one million yüan, and less than 800, 000 yüan were in actual fact raised. [54] Unfortunately no corresponding figures are available for 1933, but we know that the land tax constituted only a small part of the revenue raised shortly before the evacuation of the Central Soviet Area in 1934. [55]

In order to obtain a picture of the enormous increase in economic burdens laid on the population we have to broaden our survey of the sources of revenue. We proceed to study the sale of government bonds.

Government Bonds

The net income which the sale of government bonds brought the state was significant indeed. It is true that the first modest issue of bonds, sold in the summer of 1932, was soon redeemed; but the buyers got nothing in return for the bonds of the second issue, amounting to about 1, 200, 000 yüan, or for those of the third issue - approximately three million yüan.

In theory there was all the difference in the world between taxation and sale of government bonds, but in practice the two to some extent tended to converge. Tax was tax, and the bonds were supposed to make up state loans. In any case, the larger part of the loaned money was never returned. Tax was of course supposed to be, if necessary, enforced, while purchase of government bonds was in the main meant to be a voluntary matter. In any case, a good deal of force was actually applied in the sale of bonds at the most local levels, in defiance of the instructions from above.

The conflict between the principle of voluntariness in the purchase of government bonds on the one hand, and the forcible methods often actually used on the other, is a very interesting matter. In order to comprehend this conflict it is necessary to look briefly into the marketing system applied.

The main channels for the sale of bonds were the local soviets and their finance departments. The county soviet was charged directly by the Central Government with the responsibility for the sale of a definite quota of bonds, and through the county financial department the quota was further shared out among the various districts. The district financial department allotted quotas to the different hsiang soviets, and the hsiang soviet might share its quota out among its cadres. [56] Then the real difficulty might occur - because there the allotment of quotas was in the main supposed to stop, and the real sale was expected to begin. A great temptation for cadres who found no other way out was to continue the sharing out of quotas right down to the individual, to order each person or each family to buy government bonds for a certain amount of money. This, said the Central Government, was in general a very wrong thing to do. It is true that there were exception - it was permissible to order such reactionary class elements as rich peasants and big or middle traders to buy certain amounts of bonds; but force must not be applied to the workers and ordinary peasants, who were supposed to shoulder the larger part of this burden.

In 1932 the government harboured the false hope that the financial difficulties necessitating the sale of bonds were of a very temporary nature. Its handling of the first issue of bonds, in the summer of that year, is illustrative. The state was badly in need of money, because the Kuomintang was initiating its Fourth Encirclement Campaign, and the Red Army was in need of supplies. Yet what was deemed necessary was a very short-term state loan - redemption of the bonds was promised after six months only. [57] During that period it was expected that collection of the land tax and military victories would change the financial situation.

According to the original scheme the first issue was expected to bring in 600,000 yüan, but because the planned sale of a part of the bonds in the soviet areas of Hsiangkan and Hsiangokan failed to materialise, only about 500,000 yüan were actually raised. In the Central Soviet Area the sale seems to have proceeded more smoothly than on later occasions, although even at this time there were occurrences of force applied to the common people. There was one provision which at the same time facilitated the sale and contributed to make the whole thing much of a financial fiasco: if the purchasers were willing to forgo a certain interest, otherwise payab after six months, they could use the bonds as a substitute for cash in payment of taxes and rents due to the state. [58] As a result the bonds came pouring back to the government long before the six months period had expired, and as early as October almost the whole of them had actually been redeemed. [59] But the state finances were no better off.

Once more the Central Government faced the danger of state bankruptcy, and a solution for the crisis was sought through a second issue of bonds, from late October 1932 onward. The aim of this second sale was to raise 1,200,000 yüan, exactly double the figure originally set for the first one. However, optimism about the future persisted, and redemption was promised for the summer of 1933. But this time the purchasers were not given the option of returning the bonds at earlier dates. [60]

Many local soviets were probably staggered by the new quotas which were sent them from above. "Whatever happens", instructed the Central Executive Committee, "the sale must everywhere be carried through within the time limits." Yet, for the common people, who were supposed to shoulder the larger share of the burden, the purchase was to be a voluntary matter. The people were not always willing to buy, and what then? "Make use of the methods of propaganda and agitation", said the CEC. [61] Such an approach led to success in some places, but not everywhere. Many local cadres felt they were on the horns of dilemma - either non-fulfilment of the quota, or sharing out the bonds among the people and ordering them to buy. The latter sin might appear to be the lesser one, and the Finance Commissariat found that various soviets were involved in it. [62] A picturesque example of the use of threat in this respect is described in a notice in Hung-se Chung-hua of December 5th 1932:

> "The second time I passed the northern gate* was on my way to Kaot'ien. Again I met a man beating a big gong. What he shouted this time was: "Those buying government bonds must pay half the money today. Those who do not pay will be put in jail!""[63]

Probably the second issue of government bonds was sold out in spite of resistance among the people - we know for sure that the sale was more than one million yüan. [64] From a financial point of view the sale was a success, but, it might seem, a very temporary success. During the spring of 1933 military activity was increasing, and finances were further strained; in these circumstances it was very unpleasant for the government that the dates fixed for redemption of the bonds were approaching. There was a new crisis, and a solution was sought through an appeal to the people. The slogan was: "Return your bonds without asking the government for redemption!" The bonds were, in other words, to be converted into gifts to the state and net contributions to the support of the Red Army. Reportedly the slogan was first put forward by some trade unions, [65] but Hungs-se Chung-hua, the organ of the Central Government, took it up and instituted a national campaign. It began mainly as a movement among workers and cadres, and was later broadened to include the peasant population. [66] In the meantime the dates for redemption were postponed, so that the conversion of bonds into gifts to the state could continue beyond the summer of 1933. [67] By May 1934 a total amounting to more than 900,000 yüan had been handed back by people renouncing their right to get anything in return. Redemption of the remainder, representing less than 300,000 yüan, would seem to be a relatively easy matter, and the Commissariat of Finances was reported to have intended to carry it into effect in June 1934. If so, deed did not follow intention; the Finance Commissar declared that he was responding

---

* This was the northern gate of Shihch'eng.

to the demands of the masses when he postponed the redemption still further. After that the question was never raised. The bonds of the second issue were worthless, or perhaps the Finance Commissariat would say it was not quite so - they could be used to pay for government bonds of the third issue. 68)

Drives for large-scale financial support for the regime were in several cases represented as based on demands from the masses or from local cadres. Undoubtedly there was a great deal of enthusiasm at the lower levels; nevertheless we must make a reservation when relating the accounts of our sources in this respect. Such demands were certainly on occasions - and perhpas they were quite often - induced from above, which will be shown through examples later in this chapter. In any case, the request that the Central Government make a third issue of bonds was put forward in the resolution of the Land Investigation Conference of soviet cadres from eight counties in June 1933. 69) The actual sale began in August of that year, and the third issue was thus marketed long before the final word had been said on the second issue.

The third issue was designated as "economic reconstruction bonds" (ching-chi chien-she kung-chai). As the name indicates, the avowed purpose was this time not, in the first place, the direct financing of the war. To be sure, the Red Army would get its share, which was set at one million yüan out of the total of three million which the sale aimed at. Of the remainder one million would be used as capital for the building up of commercial, productive, and credit co-operatives, and one million was to finance the development of the Bureau for the Regulation of Food Supply and the External Trade Bureau (Tui-wai mao-i chü) with their respective branches. The "economic reconstruction" referred to naturally included work for increased production, but this was by no means the main thing. What mattered much more was the building up of a trade system - especially for export and import - which would restrict the exploitation practised by private merchants. 70)

The Kuomintang had long since made efforts to blockade the Central Soviet Area, but the blockade was not fully effective. Rice was exported, and salt and cloth were imported. This trade had so far been conducted by private merchants; their service was to some extent appreciated by the Communists, but their extraordinary profits were resented. In the autumn of 1932 there were reported cases when unhulled rice was bought for 40-50 cents a picul in the Central Soviet Area, and sold eight or ten times as expensively in nearby white districts. And the transactions did not end there once in the white districts the merchants could buy salt or cloth, which might be sold with a new enormous profit after being taken to the soviet territory. This degree of capitalist exploitation of the soviet population wa found intolerable. Co-operatives and certain state organs had to be developed with a view to taking over the foreign trade to the largest possible extent, and a very substantial part of the initial capital required was to be provided through the sale of "economic reconstruction bonds."[71]

On one point the government was this time more cautious than on previous occasions. No early redemption of the "economic reconstruction bonds" was envisaged. Even the first instalment of interest was not scheduled to be paid until October 1934, which turned out to be exactly the month of evacuation of the Central Soviet Area. And the principal was to be repaid over five years beginning in October 1936 - when in actual fact the Communist headquarters were destined to be established in far-off Shensi. [72] Obviously there was no possibility of repayment at these dates, and nothing has been heard of any later redemption.

The population of the Central Soviet Area, having already seen that the pledge given for redemption of the bonds of the second issue was not fulfilled as scheduled, may from the outset have been sceptical toward the possibility of getting anything in return for the new "economic reconstruction bonds". This was probably one of the reasons for the difficulties encountered in selling them, another cause being that the target set was much higher than on earlier occasions. At the beginning there were signs of optimism and enthusiasm among the central and local cadres; a proposal was put forward for raising the amount aimed at from the original three million yüan to five million. [73] In principle the Central Government adopted the proposal, [74] but later it reverted to the original figure. [75] In fact it proved very hard to attain even the three million - the deadline for the sale was put off more than once, [76] and the bonds were still on the market in May 1934. [77]

It was during the winter of 1933-34 that the campaign for the sale of "economic reconstruction bonds" was conducted most vigorously. Many local cadres were struggling very hard with the problem of getting rid of their quotas. Some of them complained openly that they had no other way out than sharing the bonds out among the masses and ordering them to buy. This was a manifestation of opportunism and bureaucratism said the Central Government and the party leadership, insisting on the use of propaganda and agitation to rouse the enthusiasm of the masses for contribution to the revolutionary cause. [78] The local soviet apparatus as well as various mass organisations were to be set in motion for the campaign. The workers' and peasants' willingness to buy should be secured through propaganda at mass meetings, and their spirit was to be further raised through competitions in the sale between different localities. Finally, there was the agitation directed at the individual, a method which the Council of People's Commissars described in the following way:

" [As for] those who are buying much, their names and the amounts of government bonds which they have bought must be made known through a placard at the gate of the hsiang soviet, so that they can serve as models. [With regard to] those who do not want to buy, one must by no means force them to buy; the delegates to the hsiang soviet, the delegates to the women's representative congress and the members of the trade unions and the poor peasants' unions must go and persuade them to buy, and agitate to get them to buy. One can require that those who have bought government bonds go and persuade those who have not bought any." [79]

Perhaps the individual in certain cases would have preferred to receive some sort of reasonable order rather than be the object of an agitation like this. Anyhow, the use of mass propaganda and individual agitation did promote the sale in some places, and the Central Government was anxious to make these successful districts serve as models for others. [80] But quite often the local cadres found it necessary to resort to illegal methods, using orders and force on the common people, and sometimes their orders were by no means reasonable. The following grim example is recorded in Hung-se Chung-hua of February 16th 1934:

"There was for instance in Chut'ien hsiang in the Ch'iho district of Hsichiang a soviet employee who demanded that a farm labourer should buy government bonds for 10 yüan. The farm labourer agreed. The second day [the soviet employee] would add [government bonds for] 10 yüan; this farm labourer again fully agreed. The third day [the soviet employee] would once more add [government bonds for] 10 yüan and make the purchase amount to a total of 30 yüan. The farm labourer said: "I have no money!" This [soviet] employee said: "If you do not buy for 30 yüan, then you are a landlord!" The result of such orders and force was that the farm labourer hanged himself." [81]

Without giving any further explanation the journal concluded that this particular soviet employee represented the "foreign class elements". But no suggestion was made of class enemies being involved in some other cases of suicide by people who had been ordered to buy bonds, or by cadres who had run into trouble during the sale. [82] It is true that the number of suicides reported in this connection is very limited; nevertheless it is evident that a large number of people felt badly affected by the commandism of the cadres. In an article published in March 1934 Mao Tse-t'an (Mao-Tse-tung's brother) describes a cadre in the county of Juichin who at a mass meeting tried to make use of the method of orders and force to make those present buy bonds, with the result that the lot of them ran away. [83] In other cases the villagers attacked cadres who had made themselves unpopular in this way. [84] The Central Government was undoubtedly right in maintaining that the commandism practised at the local levels, with regard to the sale of government bonds as well as in other respects, had the very unfortunate effect of alienating the masses from the regime. [85]

Nevertheless, after the general radicalisation of the political climate in February 1934 the Central Government gave its blessing to a somewhat different type of force, which was being applied in some places in Fukien. Certain persons said to be sabotaging the sale of government bonds were singled out and shot. This helped, for the sale proceeded more smoothly after that. [86] We may accept that one reason really was that the sabotage had been done away with, but there must also have been an additional cause for more willingness to buy bonds after such events. The local people must have been panic-stricken and thus easier to persuade.

As pointed out above, only one third of the income from the sale of "economic reconstruction bonds" was supposed to be used for the direct financing of the war, while two thirds were to benefit the development of the economy and trade. It is very improbable that this ratio was actually observed. In the extremely critical year of 1934 the war seemed to devour all available resources.

We cannot tell exactly the figure which the sale of "economic reconstruction bonds" actually amounted to; perhaps the original target of three million was reached. In fact it was not in the first place a question of cash income to the state. Although the bonds were reckoned in money, they were to a very large extent paid for in rice. [87] The sale thus constituted a very essential part of the rice collection campaign in the winter of 1933-34.

Rice Collection Campaigns

There were various reasons for the efforts made by the government in 1933-34 to collect most of its revenue in rice rather than in money. To hold stores of rice was a very sound short-term investment, as the price of this commodity was certain to rise tremendously between the autumn harvest and the summer shortage of the next year. Rice could, at least in some periods, be exported, and to keep up a certain amount of foreign trade was of the most vital significance for the regime. And most important of all – a large quantity of rice was needed to feed the rapidly expanding Red Army.

The use made of rice in payment of land tax and in buying "economic reconstruction bonds" has been mentioned above, but we have not completed the picture. There were other drives for loans and contributions of rice, drives which we can deal with very briefly because we have already been acquainted with the technique applied and the problems involved.

A campaign for a loan from the people to the Red Army of 200,000 piculs of unhulled rice was launced in February or March 1933. The loan was announced as a short-term one, to be paid back in the second half of the same year. [88] Before long, however, a slogan was raised - exactly as in the case of the government bonds of the second issue - for converting the loan into a gift. [89]

A very significant rice collection campaign was carried on in the winter of 1933-34. We have already been sufficiently acquainted with its content - it was a drive for collection of rice as tax payment and as payment for "economic reconstruction bonds". The campaign was intensive indeed, although the Food Commissar's insistence that it should be so predominant as to relegate temporarily all other soviet activity to a secondary role, brought a sharp rebuke from Chang Wen-t'ien. [90]

Again there was a major campaign to feed the Red Army in the very difficult months of June and July 1934. About 200,000 piculs of unhulled rice were provided through loans, contributions and confiscation. [91] Once more the well known procedure of converting the loan into a gift was applied to a large extent, although a small portion of the borrowed rice was redeemed in the autumn, through deductions in the land tax. [92]

Finally, the people lent the state about 600,000 piculs of unhulled rice after the autumn harvest of 1934, [93] and the promised redemption one or two years later[94] was of course impossible to carry into effect. What became of the very substantial rice stores at the time of evacuation of the Central Soviet Area, is a matter for speculation.

There seems to be no point in going much more into details of financial policy. There are, however, a few items which are too significant to go unmentioned. First, the resources of the people were further strained through a drive shortly before the Long March for collection or purchase of various articles required for equipment of the army, from bedclothes to implements containing iron or copper. [95] Secondly there were the effort made to save on administrative expenditure; such efforts were made throughout the period of the republic, and they were highly intensified in 1934. [96]

The confiscation from reactionaries has been dealt with in the chapter on rural class policy, but a few words may be added on its purely financial aspect. When Lin Po-ch'ü became Finance Commissar in August 1933, he was charged with the task of placing the economic burdens more heavily on the reactionary classes. [97] He did put forward an ambitious plan in this regard, saying that during the coming six months about six million yüan should be raised through confiscation from landlords and special levies imposed on rich peasants[98] - six million yüan, that was (with every reservation regarding inflation and types of currency) more than seven times as much as the total income from land tax for the year 1932. Such was the program; the actual amount extracted from reactionaries during the period is not known, but it must have been very much less. We do know that the rate of confiscation largely followed the intensity of the class struggle; the flow into the state treasury of confiscated money was quite strong during the first phase of the Land Investigation Movement, much weaker in the subsequent months, and stronger again from April 1934 onward. [99]


The Principle of Voluntariness

The present chapter concentrates on the economic burdens shouldered by the common people. One conspicuous feature in this regard is that most contributions from the worker and peasant masses were in theory of a voluntary nature. How voluntary were they in actual fact? We can do more than speculate on the matter; our sources give us a certain insight.

Payment of land tax was of course supposed to be obligatory, nevertheless there was said to be an element of voluntariness also in this respect. Moreover, an announcement issued by the soviet of Kiangsi province sometime in 1932 seems even to suggest a certain spontaneity, stating that the land tax rates were being increased in response to the demands of the masses.[100] However, a party document of June the same year puts the whole thing in a very different light, obviously killing the notion of spontaneity:

"With regard to the decree of the Central Government through which it was decided to increase the land tax, one must mobilise the masses to support its execution enthusiastically, through their representative congresses. Moreover, it is even more important, before the decree of the Central Government has arrived*, to mobilise the masses to resolve, through their representative congresses, to demand from the Central Government the increase of the land tax ...."[101]

---

* Underlined by T. L.

Passages like this must necessarily make us sceptical toward reports of demands from the masses to be allowed to make sacrifices in order to support the regime. The quoted instance was not the only one when the people were mobilised to demand a measure which had already been decided upon at the top level; we have a similar example in the rice loan in the spring of 1933. [102] In such cases the sacrifices were not made spontaneously, nevertheless they might be made voluntarily. Voluntariness attained through propaganda and agitation may still be voluntariness.

Very significant voluntary contributions may indeed have come from people whose enthusiasm had been roused for participation in the revolutionary cause. But there was a limit. 1933 and 1934 were very hard years; and any normal mother, and probably father too, would, after all, care more for feeding their own children than for feeding the Red Army. It is true that the limit was a rather fluid one - good propaganda could result in a tremendous increase in the voluntary contributions, while neglect of the propaganda work had the opposite effect.

In any case, the "voluntary" contributions were on the whole less voluntary in practice than they were according to the programs. We have seen a conflict with regard to the purchase of government bonds - on the one hand the Central Government's principle of voluntariness, and on the other the forcible methods actually resorted to by many local cadres - in fact the same problem presented itself in various rice collection campaigns. [103] We have also seen that in early 1934 people in some localities of Fukien bought bonds because they were panic-stricken through executions of alleged saboteurs; we have examples of a similar procedure in the rice collection campaign in the summer of the same year. [104] Moreover, we have suggested that personal agitation could be so intense that it was well on the way to acquiring the character of force; let us dwell a little more on this last point.

The agitation was extremely intensive in the campaign of the summer of 1934. In one hsiang the cadres are reported to have singled out the "hard nuts" (wan-ch'iang ti fen-tzu) among the population, i. e. those most unwilling to lend rice to the Red Army, spending two or three hours to persuade them. [105] In another locality teams composed of women from Red Army men's families were organised, and charged with the tasks of propaganda and agitation; these ladies were in truth persistent, talking two or three times if necessary with people reluctant to make their contribution of rice, and if this did not help, the hard nuts were "struggled" against at meetings. [106] A tape recording of these events would have made most interesting material - in any case, the existing sources make it clear that the objects of such agitation and struggle might be in a very pitiful situation.

We can safely conclude that there were various degrees of voluntariness in the people's economic contributions to the state. There was certainly a great deal of revolutionary ardour among the worker and peasant masses, that, thanks to the regime, had been delivered from the traditional class exploitation; there were undoubtedly those who felt glad and proud to make some personal sacrifice in order to contribute to the revolutionary cause. Others would bring forth their contributions only if exposed to a certain amount of moral pressure, while finally some recalcitrants would yield only to threats. The methods applied for collecting "voluntary" contributions ranged from the most genuine voluntariness to the use of brute force.

In two previous chapters we have seen two aspects of a general swing toward the left in the policy of the Chinese Soviet Republic, aspects relating respectively to the administration of justice and to dealing with reactionary rural classes. Can the financial policy be said to fit into the same pattern of radicalisation?

In general, yes. The term radicalisation is one of the most flexible words in the language, so we may even speak of a radicalisation in the policy of placing economic burdens on the people. It is true that the financial methods mainly applied in 1931 and early 1932, characterised by unsystematical expropriation undertaken by local soviets and army units, can hardly be fitted into any pattern. Our establishment of a pattern can start only with the more regular financial measures, prepared during the same confused period and subsequently implemented gradually. These more regular measures at first implied relatively light burdens for the people, but later the burdens increased tremendously. For the worker and peasant masses the increase to a very large extent came as "voluntary" contributions. It should, however, be clear from what has been said above that the contributions did represent burdens, in spite of the principle of voluntariness.

# CONCLUSION

The Chinese soviet regime was - during its life and death struggle with the vastly superior Kuomintang forces - desperately in need of active support from the masses of the people. Passive obedience would not suffice in these circumstances; a really active co-operàtion was required.

The land redistribution and the abolition of the old usury system did certainly create a basis among the masses for such an active support; these measures were most significant factors for the development of a harmonious relationship between the people and the regime. But the harmony had to be nourished - and it should not be disturbed.

The system of government was of course of cardinal importance for maintenance of the harmony. There was a need for governmental organs which were acquainted with, and which would take account of, the will and the sentiments of the masses of the people.

The governmental organs of the Central Soviet Area were designed with a view to channelling the popular voice upward; we may assume that to a certain extent they actually fulfilled this mission - at least in the most advanced districts - but the process was probably not carried very far. The will of the people was supposed to be carried through the basic and the intermediate soviets right up to the central level; in practice, however, this transmission was very likely to be distorted in the process. The easiest part of it was to carry the will of the masses up to the basic soviets at the hsiang level, and this was at least something; but we must remember the subordination of lower organs to higher ones.

It was much simpler to use the hierarchy for channelling decisions taken at higher levels downward. This was a relatively simple thing to do, but it might be dangerous. If the authorities did not show great caution with regard to the instructions sent downward, they might disturb the harmony and alienate the masses.

As time went on the instructions and directives dispatched from higher levels downward became more and more marked by the general radicalisation of policies. What effect did this radicalisation have on the relationship between the regime and the masses?

In some respect mass sentiments might seem to be in harmony with radicalism. An agitated crowd which at a mass meeting demanded the most ruthless class war, or which at a public trial shouted that an alleged counter-revolutionary must die, might feel completely at one with the regime. Nevertheless, the overall effect of the most radical measures would be very much to the detriment of the revolutionary cause. A too harsh treatment of reactionary class elements would cause the resentment even of many middle and poor peasants, whose clan or family ties went across the class barrier. A too zealous fight against counter-revolution was likely to lead to killing of some innocents by mistake, thereby causing widespread panic among the population.

Even radical measures in the financial field might have some appeal. Some arduous revolutionaries would gladly take on heavy economic burdens in order to contribute to the revolutionary cause. However, it would probably be a more common occurrence that people, for whom it was difficult to find the means for feeding their own families, had their revolutionary ardour cooled off by increasing economic burdens.

If radicalisation was carried very far - as it was in the late period of the republic - a serious deterioration of the relationship between the regime and the masses would result. This does not mean that a majority of the population would shift their allegiance and begin to support the enemy. In the most radical period most people would probably think that the Communist regime was hard, but that it would be still worse to have back the Kuomintang. Nevertheless, in some districts part of the middle or poor peasantry did prefer to fly to white areas, thanks to the radicalisation. It is evident that many more were those who stayed but had their revolutionary ardour cooled off.

According to the official Chinese historiography policy was pushed toward the left by the party leadership of the 28 Bolsheviks and their supporters, while Mao represented a more moderate line. Our study of certain spheres of policy does confirm this tenet - but with every reservation stated earlier. The matter is much more complicated than it appears from official Chinese history books.

The leftist line of the party leadership had extremely grave consequences. It undermined the very base which the regime was built upon - namely the mass support.

# CHRONOLOGY OF SOME KEY EVENTS

**1931**

| | |
|---|---|
| January | The Fourth Plenum of the CCP Central Committee is held in Shanghai |
| " | The Central Party Bureau for the Soviet Areas is established. |
| November | The First Party Conference of the (Central) Soviet Area. |
| 7-18 November | The First National Soviet Congress is held in Juichin. |
| 27 November | Mao Tse-tung is elected chairman both of the Central Executive Committee and of the Council of People's Commissars. |

**1932**

| | |
|---|---|
| August | The Ningtu Party Conference. |

**1933**

| | |
|---|---|
| February | Fight against the Lo Ming line begins. |
| Spring | The KMT is defeated in the final battles of the Fourth Encirclement and Annihilation Campaign. |
| June – October | The first phase of the Land Investigation Movement |
| October | The leaders of the KMT Nineteenth Route Army in Fukien prepare a revolt against Chiang Kai-shek, and conclude an agreement with the Communists. |
| October 1933 – March 1934 | Interlude in the class struggle, because of Mao Tse-tung's moderation of class policy. |

**1934**

| | |
|---|---|
| January | The Fukien rebels are defeated by Chiang Kai-shek. The main assaults of the Fifth KMT Encirclement and Annihilation Campaign against the Central Soviet Area begin. |
| 18 January | The Fifth Plenum of the CCP Central Committee convenes in Juichin. |

| | |
|---|---|
| 22 January – 1 February | The Second National Soviet Congress is held in Juichin. |
| 3 February | Chang Wen-t'ien replaces Mao Tse-tung as chairman of the Council of People's Commissars. Mao Tse-tung is re-elected as chairman of the Central Executive Committee. |
| March | Second phase of the Land Investigation Movement begins. |
| April | Kuangch'ang falls to the KMT. The military situation for the Communists becomes very critical. |
| February-June | A period of red terror. |
| Late June | Chang Wen-t'ien blames the "ultraleftists" for carrying red terror too far. |
| October | The main body of the Red Army pulls out of the Central Soviet Area to start the Long March. |

NOTES

## Introduction

1) See for example Ch'en, Jerome, 1965, and Schram, 1966.
2) Hung-se Chung-hua 4. 8. 1933 p. 1 and 16. 8. 1933 p. 3 (from doc. 125); Tou-cheng No. 20 p. 13 (from doc. 109).
3) Ch'en, Jerome, 1965, pp. 170-72, 176-77 and 180-82; Schram, 1966, pp. 171-76; doc. 14.
4) Sheng Yueh, 1971, pp. 205-261; Hsiao Tso-liang, 1961, pp. 12-13 and 115-116; Thornton, 1969, pp. 208-209 (including the footnote).

Several lists of the 28 Bolsheviks have appeared, and they vary to a considerable extent. Professor Jerome Ch'en has very kindly brought to my attention the following sources for identification of the members of the group: 1) She-hui hsin-wen, Shanghai, XII, No. 2, 11. 7. 1935, p. 59; 2) ibid. I, No. 20, 30. 11. 1932, p. 431; 3) Wang Chien-min, 1965, vol. 2 p. 100. Further, a list is given by Warren Kuo, 1968, (Analytical Hist. . . . .), vol. 2, p. 234. I have, however, chosen to rely on the following list of the 28 Bolsheviks, published by a member of the group, Sheng Yueh, 1971, p. 216:

| | |
|---|---|
| Chang Ch'in-ch'iu (Mme. Shen Tse-min) | Shen Tse-min |
| Chang Wen-t'ien (alias Lo Fu or Szu Mei) | Sheng Chung-liang (Sheng Yueh) |
| Ch'en Ch'ang-hao | Sun Chi-min |
| Ch'en Shao-yü (alias Wang Ming) | Sung P'an-min |
| Ch'en Yuan-tao | Tu Tso-hsiang (Mme. Ch'en Ch'ang-hao) |
| Ch'in Pang-hsien (alias Po Ku) | Wang Chia-hsiang (Wang Chia-ch'iang) |
| Chu Ah-ken | Wang Pao-li |
| Chu Tzu-shun (female) | Wang Sheng-ti |
| Ho K'e-ch'uan (alias K'ai Feng) | Wang Sheng-yung |
| Ho Tzu-shu | Wang Yun-ch'eng |
| Hsia Hsi | Yang Shang-k'uen |
| Hsiao T'e-fu | Yin Chien |
| Li Chou-sheng | Yuan Chia-yung |
| Li Yuan-chieh | |
| Meng Ch'in-shu (Mme. Ch'en Shao-yü) | |

214

5) Schram, 1966, p. 154, footnote.
6) Ibid. p. 154, footnote, and pp. 181-182; Mao Tse-tung hsüan-chi, Peking 1958, vol. 3 p. 968 (from doc. 133).
7) Hsiao Tso-liang, 1961, p. 115.
8) See Kung Ch'u, 1954, p. 256.
9) Hsiao Tso-liang, 1961, pp. 108-13 and 150-53; Mao Tse-tung hsüan-chi, Peking 1958, vol. 3 p. 967 (from doc. 133).
10) Chang Kuo-t'ao and Kung Ch'u have both stated that the central headquarters of the CCP moved to Kiangsi in the summer or early fall of 1931. (Hsiao Tso-liang, 1961, pp. 161-62). However, a Mao-sponsored party resolution of April 1945 says that the party centre was not transferred until the beginning of 1933, while apparently contradicting itself by stating that the centre held a conference in Ningtu in Kiangsi in August 1932. (Mao Tse-tung hsüan-chi, Peking 1958, vol. 3 p. 968 - from doc. 133). The fact that the First National Soviet Congress in November 1931 found it necessary to send a telegram to the party centre (doc. 66), suggests that the formal seat of the Central Committee was at that time still at a considerable distance from the red capital, Juichin.

More sources are cited by Hsiao Tso-liang, 1961, p. 162.

John Rue states that Ch'in Pang-hsien (Po Ku), Chang Wen-t'ien and most of the other Politburo members returned from Juichin to Shanghai after the First National Soviet Congress in November 1931. He does not, however, offer any documentation. (Rue, 1966, p. 250).
11) Kung Ch'u, 1954, pp. 303-04. Kung Ch'u also tells that he had met Chang Wen-t'ien somewhat earlier in the soviet area of western Fukien. (Ibid. pp. 264-65).

According to Hung-se Chung-hua of 18.12.1931 (pp. 1-2) the Ningtu Uprising took place on December 14th 1931. Kung Ch'u has misdated the event.

According to Mao Tse-tung, Chang Wen-t'ien and Chou En-lai were present at the Ningtu Conference (in Kiangsi) in August 1932. (Jerome Ch'en, 1969, p. 95).
12) Mao Tse-tung hsüan-chi, Peking 1958, vol. 3 pp. 964 -91 (from doc. 133)
13) See for example Rue, 1966, p. 7, footnote, and compare with note 4 to this introduction.
14) Rue, 1966, pp. 258-59 and 269.
15) Reischauer, Fairbank and Craig, 1965, pp. 100-03; Linebarger, Djang and Burks, 1954, pp. 60-65; van der Sprenkel, 1962, pp. 42-49 and 80-111.

16) See Carr: <u>The Bolshevik Revolution,</u> London 1950, vol. 1 pp. 130 - 31.

## Chapter I. The Hsiang Soviet

1) Doc. 6 art. 38; doc. 9 A p. 18.
2) The decision to abolish the village soviet is reported to have been taken by the First National Soviet Congress. (Doc. 8 p. 7; <u>Sovety v Kitae</u> p. 435. See also doc. 1 art. 1).
3) Doc. 49 art. 1.
4) Lenin: <u>Sobranie Sochineniy</u>, Moscow 1924-26, vol. 6 pp. 136-37 and 380. Lenin normally used the term "The Workers' and Peasants' Revolutionary Democratic Dictatorship."
5) Doc. 2 arts. 5-6; doc. 4 arts. 4-5.
6) <u>Istoriya sovetskoy konstitutsii</u>, pp. 154-55 (from the 1918 constitution of the RSFSR), and pp. 543-44 (from the 1925 constitution of the RSFSR).
7) <u>Mao Tse-tung hsüan-chi</u>, Peking 1958, vol. 3 pp. 974-75 (from doc. 133).
8) <u>Hung-se Chung-hua</u> 6.9.1933 p. 2 (from doc. 134).
9) Doc. 4 art. 21. In small <u>hsiang</u> this ratio could be lowered to 1 to 8 for workers and 1 to 32 for others. One alternate delegate was elected for every five ordinary delegates. (Doc. 4 art. 31; doc. 2, note to art. 35).
10) Doc. 135 <u>leaf</u> 48.
11) Doc. 139B p. 103.
12) Doc. 136
13) <u>Hung-se Chung-hua</u> 6.9.1933 p. 2 (from doc. 134).
14) Doc. 137.
15) <u>Hung-se Chung-hua</u> 6.9.1933 p. 2 (from doc. 134).
16) Doc. 2 arts. 7-10; doc. 3; doc. 4 arts. 45-55.
17) Doc. 137.
18) Doc. 139 B pp. 104-05. An instruction issued by the Organisation Bureau of the Chinese Communist Party on August 1st 1933 said, in a parenthesis, that the list of candidates should be decided upon by the county branch of the party and thereafter adopted by the "party fraction" (<u>tang-t'uan</u>) and the soviets. (See <u>Hung-se Chung-hua</u> 6.9. 1933 p. 3). On this point the instruction seems to be in disagreement with documents referred to in note 19 to this chapter.
19) Doc. 24 pp. 8-9; doc. 139 B p. 105; <u>Hsüan-chü yün-tung chou-pao</u> No. 2 (10.9.1933) p. 7 (refers partly to doc. 138)
20) Doc. 139C p. 136.

21) Doc. 2 art. 21; doc. 4 art. 10.
22) Doc. 2 art. 31; doc. 4 art. 15.
23) Doc. 2 art. 32.
24) Doc. 4, note 1 to art. 18.
25) Ibid. arts. 11-12.
26) Hung-se Chung-hua 27.10.1933. p. 3, 11.11.1933 p. 3 and
    17.11.1933 p. 3.
27) Doc. 18; doc. 31 pp. 7-8; doc. 61 pp. 1-2; Hung-se Chung-hua
    11.11.1933 p. 3.
28) Doc. 3 art. 13; doc. 4 art. 51.
29) Hsüan-chü yün-tung chou-pao No. 2 p. 6 (from doc. 138).
30) Doc. 24 pp. 3-4 and 9-10; Hung-se Chung-hua 6.9.1933 p. 2 (from
    doc. 134).
31) Hung-se Chung-hua 11.11.1933 p. 3; doc. 139B pp. 99 and 104-05.
32) See this thesis pp. 103-04.
33) Hung-se Chung-hua 6.9.1933 p. 2 (from doc. 134)
34) Doc. 1 art. 1; doc. 8. p. 7.
35) See doc. 139A pp. 55-56.
36) Doc. 136.
37) Doc. 6 art. 51. See also doc. 34 art. 10.
38) Mao Tse-tung reports that the chairman, the vice-chairman and
    the clerk in Ch'angkang hsiang were elected at a meeting of the
    representative congress in November 1933. (Doc. 139B p. 105).
39) The draft bill for local soviets of December 1933 said that the chair-
    man and the vice-chairman were to be elected by the presidium.
    (Doc. 6 art. 35).
40) Doc. 9A pp. 6-8.
41) Ibid. p. 8.
42) Ibid. pp. 8-9.
43) Ibid. pp. 8-9.
44) Buck, 1956, p. 373. The table referred to shows small percentages
    of "unknown" (with regard to schooling0.7 per cent for males and
    0.1 per cent for females, and with regard to literacy 0.2 per cent
    for males and 0.1 per cent for females).
45) Sovety v Kitae p. 421; doc. 10 p. 3.
46) The 1931 regulations of local government said explicitly that the
    hsiang soviet was not supposed to have a presidium. (Doc. 34 art.
    6). Nevertheless, Mao Tse-tung says that in Ch'angkang hsiang
    there had been a presidium (although it was called a "standing com-
    mittee" - ch'ang-wei-hui) ever since the hsiang soviet was establish-
    ed. (Doc. 139B p. 100). Provisions for a hsiang presidium are em-
    bodied in the draft bill for local soviets of December 1933, and in
    Mao Tse-tung's instructions of April 1934. (See notes 47-50 and 52
    to this chapter).
47) Doc. 6 art. 33; doc. 9A p. 11.

48) Doc. 6 art. 34; doc. 9A p. 3.

49) Doc. 6 art. 34; doc. 9A p. 3.

50) Doc. 9 A p. 6.

51) Doc. 139B p. 100. In Ch'angkang the institution was called "standing committee", but Mao recommended that the name be changed to "presidium". (Ibid. p. 102).

52) Doc. 9A pp. 3-6.

53) Doc. 139B p. 100.

54) Doc. 139C pp. 133-34.

55) Doc. 2, note to art. 35; doc. 4 art. 31.

56) Doc. 4 art. 31.

57) Doc. 6 art. 48.

58) Doc. 139C p. 134.

59) Doc. 5C p. 54.

60) Doc. 139C p. 135. At this page the election is dated differently, as October 1932 and as November 1932. I assume October is a misprint

61) Ibid. p. 135. The percentages are calculated on the basis of the numbers which Mao gives for delegates from the two sexes. The percentages as represented by Mao, are, according to these numbers not exact.

62) Doc. 9A p. 9.

63) Ibid. pp. 15-16.

64) Ibid. p. 12; doc. 6 art. 47. In Ts'aihsi such meetings were in 1933 normally held every five days. (Doc. 139C p. 134).

65) Doc. 9A p. 17.

66) Ibid. p. 12; doc. 139B p. 98.

67) See doc. 6 art. 36.

68) Doc. 9A pp. 13-14; doc. 139B pp. 98-99.

69) Doc. 9A p. 13.

70) Ibid. pp. 12-14.

71) Ibid. p. 14.

72) Doc. 139B p. 100.

73) Ibid. p. 100; doc. 9A pp. 14-15.

74) Doc. 9A pp. 15-16.

75) Doc. 6 art. 37; doc. 5C pp. 55-56.

76) Doc. 9A p. 18; doc. 6 art. 38.

77) Doc. 9A p. 18.

78) Doc. 139B p. 97; doc. 139C p. 133. The figure for Ch'ankang includes the persons who had left the hsiang to join the Red Army or to take up civil appointments. Whether or not these people are included in the figures given for Ts'aihsi is not clear.

79) Doc. 6 art. 38; doc. 9A pp. 18-21; doc. 139B p. 100.

80) Doc. 9A pp. 25-27; doc. 6 art. 38.

81) Doc. 5C p. 55; doc. 9 A pp. 25-26; doc. 139B pp. 103 and 105.

82) Doc. 6 art. 39.

83) Doc. 139B p. 101.
84) Doc. 139C p. 134.
85) Doc. 9A p. 23.
86) Ibid. pp. 23-24.
87) Ibid. p. 22.
88) Ibid. pp. 24-25.
89) Ibid. p. 22.
90) Doc. 139B p. 101; doc. 139C p. 134. In Ts'aihsi the system was introduced in 1932.
91) Doc. 139B pp. 105-08.
92) Ibid. pp. 105 and 108.
93) Doc. 9A pp. 29-30.
94) Ibid. p. 27; doc. 6 art. 40.
95) Doc. 9A pp. 4-5 and 31.
96) Ibid. p. 27; doc. 6 art. 40.
97) Doc. 6 arts. 40-41.
98) Doc. 9A p. 30.
99) Doc 139B pp. 98-108; doc. 139C pp. 133-38.
100) Hung-se Chung-hua 1.1.1934 p. 4.
101) Doc. 5D pp. 135-38; doc. 5J pp. 189-90.
102) Doc. 139C p. 136.
103) Doc. 5D p. 128.
104) Doc. 5C p. 57.
105) Doc. 5J p. 195.
106) Doc. 9A p. 22. See also doc. 6 art. 39 and doc. 5J p. 194.
107) Doc. 5J p. 194.
108) Fainsod, 1959, p. 141.
109) Carr: Socialism in One Country, vol. 2 p. 307.
110) See ibid. p. 309.
111) Ibid. pp. 335-356 and 362-372. Fainsod, 1959, pp. 141-152.

## Chapter II. The Intermediate Soviets

1) See doc. 6, note at the beginning of chapter 2.
2) Ibid. arts. 4-5. The same document, in its note at the beginning of chapter 2, characterises in general the hsiang soviets and the town soviets as the "basic organisations of soviet power". I think this is misleading as far as larger towns are concerned.
3) Ibid. arts. 16-18 and 26. This document said that the permanent staff for an urban district inside the town wall (ch'eng-nei) was to count five persons, and for an urban district outside the town wall (ch'eng-wai) from two to four persons. The permanent soviet staff

of a town placed on the same level as a <u>hsiang</u>, which would mean that it was attached to a district, was to count four persons.

4) In July 1933 it was laid down that a town or city soviet could administer a rural area at a distance of up to five <u>li</u>. (Doc. 22).

5) We know that the cities of Ningtu (Posheng), Juichin and Yütu were placed on the district level, and subordinated to the counties of the same names. (<u>Hung-se Chung-hua</u> 21.4.1932 p. 6, 13.1.1934 p. 3, 13.3.1934 p. 3 and 29.3.1934 p. 6; doc. 5D p. 135).

6) Doc. 6 art. 95. A city on the county level would be subordinated to a province, and a city on the provincial level would be directly subordinated to the Central Government.

7) Doc. 6

8) Doc. 139B p. 108; doc. 139C p. 138.

9) Doc. 34.

10) Doc. 6 arts. 8, 9, 56, 57, 60, 68, 69, 72, 81, 82 and 85.

11) Ibid. arts. 12, 61, 73 and 86. With regard to the cities it was not said explicitly that it was the presidium that should elect the chairman and the vice-chairman.

12) See this thesis pp. 53, 108-114, 160-161 and 191

13) Doc. 6 art. 95.

14) Ibid. art. 96. Franz Schurmann has dealt in some detail with the same problem in China in the nineteen fifties. (Schurmann, 1966, pp. 188-94).

15) Doc. 6 art. 97.

16) In this regard there is an interesting difference between the draft bill and the Russian constitutional model. The 1925 constitution of the Russian Socialist Federative Soviet Republic stated that the executive committees at the lower levels of the <u>okrug</u> and the <u>uezd</u> could stop the carrying out of instructions from the departments of local soviets on a higher level in exceptional cases, when they were found to be in obvious contradiction to earlier instructions from certain superior organs. An executive committee or a presidium on a higher local level had under certain circumstances the same right even with respect to instructions from a People's Commissariat of the RSFSR. (<u>Istoriya sovetskoy konstitutsii</u> pp. 542-43 (from the 1925 constitution of the RSFSR)). With regard to the authority of the local and central soviet organs of the RSFSR at an earlier stage see Carr: <u>The Bolshevik Revolution 1917-1923,</u> vol. 1, pp. 217-19.

17) Doc. 9B pp. 42-43.

18) Doc. 6 chapter 4.

19) Ibid. art. 197.

20) See this thesis pp. 49-50.

21) See <u>Istoriya sovetskoy konstitutsii</u> p. 152 (art. 53 of the 1918 constitution of the RSFSR), and pp. 539-40 (art. 51 of the 1925 constitution of the RSFSR).

22) Towns attached to the district are not mentioned in this connection in the electoral regulations of 1931. (See doc. 2 art. 36).

23) Doc. 2 arts. 36-38 and 42; doc. 4 arts. 26-28. The former document said that the "workers' and peasants' armed units" (kung-nung wu-chuang) and the Red Army were to take part in the elections.

24) Doc. 6 art. 6.

25) Duverger, 1954, p. 140.

26) Rousseau: Du contract social, livre II, chapitre I.

27) Ibid., livre III, chapitre IV.

28) An instruction of the CEC, dated August 9th 1933, deals with the reports which were required in connection with soviet elections at all levels. The soviets at the central and the intermediate levels were supposed to report on their work to the representative congresses at the level immediately below. The basic soviets were to report to mass meetings. The report should be discussed at the lower level, and the conclusion reached at the discussion was to be reported back to the superior soviet. This system was to be practised in the whole soviet hierarchy, from top to bottom, and it was one of the means for channelling the opinions of the people upward. (Doc. 24 pp. 12-13.)

With regard to the report system see also this thesis pp. 49-50.

29) Doc. 1 arts. 1-2. This resolution stated that its intention was to reduce the size of the administrative units. However, the maximum size it allowed for the district was large in comparison with the size of Yungfeng district in Hsingkuo about a year earlier. Yungfeng was then reported to comprise 4 hsiang and to have a total population of 8,800. (Doc. 139A p. 7).

30) Doc. 22. In the summer of 1933 one district in Juichin was reported to have as much as 12 hsiang (Hung-se Chung-hua 23.7.1933 p. 6), while another one in the same county had 11 hsiang (Tou-cheng No. 24, 29.8.1933, p. 5).

31) If we assume an average hsiang population of 1,500, and an average number of 7 hsiang in a district.

32) Doc. 6 arts. 61-62. The chairman and the vice-chairman were to be elected from the members of the presidium, and the secretary and the clerk(s) were to be engaged by the presidium.

33) Hung-se Chung-hua 31.3.1934 p. 3. Juichin is here, as very often in Communist sources of the time, called Juiching. The syllable ching means capital.

34) Doc. 23.

35) Chang Wen-t'ien likewise mentioned these departmental meetings (pu-wu hui-i). He said they were also to be attended by certain persons not belonging to the departmental staff. (Doc. 9B p. 47).

36) The heads of the departments seem very often to have been members

of the presidium. Chang Wen-t'ien said that if the head of a department did not have a seat in the presidium, then there should be a
presidium member in the committee attached to the department.
(Doc. 9B p. 46).

37) This was in fact more rare than prescribed by the draft bill for
local soviets of December 1933, which said that meetings of the
presidium should normally be called every three days. (See this
thesis table 6, p. 52)

38) Doc. 9B pp. 42-43.

39) Professor E. H. Carr has pointed out that this was the way in which
disputes of the same kind were solved in Russia at an early stage
of the soviet regime. (See Carr: The Bolshevik Revolution 1917-1923,
vol. 1 pp. 217-19).

40) According to Hsieh Jan-chih's article (doc. 23) Shangshe district
had its special institutions for the purpose of supervising the work
at the hsiang level, and these were the four "groups" (tsu), each of
which was composed of two hsiang placed under the leadership of
two members of the district presidium. Chang Wen-t'ien recommend
that similar groups be introduced generally. (Doc. 9B p. 51).

41) According to Chang Wen-t'ien's instructions an inspector should
normally belong to the "group" which was responsible for supervision
of the soviet work in the hsiang concerned. (Doc. 9B p. 52). See
also note 40 to this chapter.

42) Doc. 9B pp. 49-50. See also ibid. pp. 52-53.

43) Hung-se Chung-hua 25.5.1932 p. 8

44) Ibid. 16.3.1932 p. 8.

45) Ibid. 21.11.1932 p. 6 (from doc. 12).

46) Ibid. 22.8.1933 p. 4 and 31.8.1933 p. 5.

47) Wang Chien-min has listed in all 17 counties which he says were
created by the Communists. (Wang Chien-min, 1965, vol. 2 p. 327).
At least 14 of them can with certainty be said to have belonged to the
Central Soviet Area. Among these 14 there are 5 which are not mentioned in the sources referred to in note 46 to this chapter. But one
of these 5, Posheng, is in fact identical with the old county of Ningtu.
(See Hung-se Chung-hua 14.1.1933 p. 1).

48) See Hung-se Chung-hua 18.12.1931, p. 4. Shortly before the evacuation of the Central Soviet Area three additional counties were directl
subordinated to the Central Government, but we do not know which
they were. (See ibid. 8.8.1934 p. 4).

49) Doc. 6 arts. 73-75. The chairman and the vice-chairman (-men) we
to be elected from the members of the presidium. The inspectors we
to be engaged (jen-yung) by the executive committee, but they were
supposed to inspect and supervise the carrying out of the instruction
of the presidium. The secretary (-ies) and the clerk(s) were to be
engaged by the presidium.

50) See doc. 15.
51) Hung-se Chung-hua 31.3.1934 p. 3.
52) Doc. 16.
53) See for example doc. 5D pp. 134-39.
54) Hung-se Chung-hua 8.3.1934 p. 3 and 13.3.1934 p. 3; doc. 17.
55) Doc. 18. The words written in capital letters in the quotation are
    in the original stressed by the use of large Chinese characters.
56) Tou-cheng No. 21 p. 11 (from doc. 19).
57) Hung-se Chung-hua 21.4.1932 p. 5
58) Ibid. 25.5.1932. p. 5.
59) See ibid. 20.12.1933 p. 2 and 13.1.1934 p. 3.
60) Ibid. 20.12.1933 p. 2.
61) Ibid. 23.3.1932 p. 7; doc. 21 pp. 20-21; doc. 76 leaf 6.
62) Hung-se Chung-hua 31.8.1933 p. 5.
63) Ibid. 29.4.1933 p.1.
64) See this thesis p. 62.
65) Ibid. p. 62.
66) Ibid. p. 62.
67) See Hung-se Chung-hua 29.4.1933 p. 1, ibid. 28.4.1934 p. 3 and
    doc. 13.
68) Hsüan-chü yün-tung chou-pao No. 2 (10.9.1933) p. 8.
69) Doc. 6 arts. 86-88. The chairman and the vice-chairmen were to
    be elected from the members of the presidium. The inspectors were
    to be engaged by the executive committee, but they were supposed
    to inspect and supervise the carrying out of the instructions of the
    presidium and the various departments. The secretary (-ies) and
    the clerk(s) were to be engaged by the presidium.
70) Doc. 15.
71) Hung-se Chung-hua 3.3.1934 p. 3 (from doc. 20).
72) The first representative soviet congress of Fukien province was in
    session 18-21 March 1932. (Hung-se Chung-hua 23.3.1932 p. 7).
73) The second representative soviet congress of Kiangsi province was
    in session for nine days in December 1933. (Hung-se Chung-hua
    4.1.1934 p. 3).
74) Hung-se Chung-hua 1.1.1934 p. 1.
75) Ibid. 4.1.1934 p. 3.
76) Ibid. 1.1.1934 p. 1; doc. 110. According to Jerome Ch'en, Wu
    Liang-p'ing belonged to the "International faction", which included
    the 28 Bolsheviks and their supporters. (China Quarterly No. 40
    (October-December 1969) pp. 19-20 - from Jerome Ch'en's
    commentary to the resolutions of the Tsunyi Conference).
77) Doc. 20.
78) Doc. 15.
79) A revolutionary committee, which was an organ of provisional govern-
    ment, was established for the province of Minkan as late as April
    1933. (Hung-se Chung-hua 29.4.1933 p. 1.).

80) Hung-se Chung-hua 1.1.1934 p. 1
81) Ibid. 31.8.1933 p. 5.
82) Doc. 21 pp. 20-27.

## Chapter III. The Central Government

1) Hsiao Tso-liang, 1967, p. 424 (from doc. 65).
2) Western Fukien was at the time of the First National Soviet Congress still a more or less separate soviet area. (See this thesis p. 60).
3) According to Chinesische Arbeiter Korrespondenz of January 9th 1932 it was the Korean Communist Party that was represented. (See quotation in Sovety v Kitae p. 417).
4) Doc. 66.
5) See this thesis pp. 44-45 and tables 3-4 (pp. 48-49).
6) Doc. 4 art. 29.
7) Hung-se Chung-hua 31.1.1934 p. 4 and 1.2.1934 p. 3.
8) Ibid. 24.1.1934 p. 1.
9) Doc. 66; Hsiao Tso-liang, 1961, p. 172.
10) Docs. 37 and 68.
11) Docs. 67 and 114. See also Sovety v Kitae p. 418.
12) Doc. 11.
13) Docs. 37 and 66; Hsiao Tso-liang, 1961, p. 172; Sovety v Kitae p. 418.
14) Hsiao Tso-liang, 1961, p. 171; doc. 69.
15) Doc. 37 p. 1.
16) See Hsiao Tso-liang, 1961, p. 173, and Rue, 1966, pp. 248-249.
17) According to Tsao Po-i, 1969, p. 458, the conference was held on November 1st 1931. See also Mao Tse-tung hsüan-chi, Peking 1958, vol. 3, p. 968 (from doc. 133).
18) See docs. 76 and 77, and also Hsiao Tso-liang, 1961, pp. 164-169.
19) A similar criticism of the state of affairs within the Central Soviet Area had been made by the party leadership already in September 1931 (doc. 25). What was new in November was that the party organisation of the Central Soviet Area adopted the leadership's criticism as self-criticism.

   See also Hsiao Tso-liang, 1961, pp. 164-167.
20) See doc. 78 (reproduced by Hsiao Tso-liang, 1967, pp. 366-73). Of special interest is the fact that the Comintern Presidium in this letter mentioned Mao Tse-tung by name, and praised him for his organisation of short-term training courses to train prisoners of war. (See Hsiao Tso-liang, 1967, p. 370).

21) Compare doc. 71 to doc. 70B, doc. 72 to doc. 70C, doc. 73A to doc. 70A, and doc. 74 to doc. 70D. See also Hsiao Tso-liang, 1961, pp. 178-184.

22) Docs. 11 and 70E.

23) Sovety v Kitae p. 417.

24) Preface to doc. 70.

25) See preface to doc. 62.

26) For information on the Chinese Communist Party's Central Bureau for the Soviet Areas see Hsiao Tso-liang, 1961, pp. 150-153. Chou En-lai is reported to have taken over the functions as secretary of the Central Bureau shortly after the First National Soviet Congress. (Warren Kuo, Analytical Hist...., 1968, vol. 2, p. 382).

27) Doc. 75 pp. 2-3.

28) Hung-hsing 28.1.1934 p. 1.

29) Hung-se Chung-hua 24.1.1934 p. 2; Hung-hsing 28.1.1934 p. 1.

30) Hung-hsing 28.1.1934 p. 1.

31) Hung-se Chung-hua 26.1.1934 p. 1.

32) Hung-hsing 28.1.1934 p. 1; Hung-se Chung-hua 28.1.1934 p. 3.

33) Hung-se Chung-hua 28.1.1934 p. 3; Hung-hsing 4.2.1934 p. 1.

34) Hung-se Chung-hua 31.1.1934 pp. 1-4; Hung-hsing 4.2.1934 p. 1.

35) Hung-se Chung-hua 1.2.1934 pp. 2-3; Hung-hsing 4.2.1934 p. 1.

36) Hung-se Chung-hua 1.2.1934 pp. 1-2; Hung-hsing 4.2.1934 p. 1.

37) Hung-se Chung-hua 1.2.1934 p. 2; Hung-hsing 4.2.1934 p. 1.

38) Hung-se Chung-hua 1.2.1934 p. 2; Hung-hsing 4.2.1934 p. 1.

39) Hsiang Ying on this occasion told the congress that he had not received the whole of the draft prepared by the party "centre", for reason of communications. (Hung-se Chung-hua 3.2.1934 p. 3). This reason seems to be a rather strange one, as one would expect the party centre at the time to have its seat in Juichin.

40) Hung-se Chung-hua 3.2.1934 pp. 3-4; Hung-hsing 4.2.1934 p. 1.

41) The latter telegram is mentioned in Hung-hsing of February 4th 1934 (p. 1), while Hung-se Chung-hua of February 3rd 1934 (p. 1) only tells about the two other ones.

42) Hung-se Chung-hua 3.2.1934 pp. 1-2.

43) See ibid. 1.2.1934 p. 2.

44) According to Hung-hsing of February 4th 1934 (p. 1) 50 among the 175 full members of the Central Executive Committee, which the congress elected, were from the Red Army.

45) Doc. 5C.

46) The reports of Chu Te, Lin Po-ch'ü and Wu Liang-p'ing are summarised in Hung-se Chung-hua of February 1st 1934, p. 2.

47) Mao's opening speech is printed in Hung-se Chung-hua of January 24th 1934, p. 1.

48) Mao's speech at the close of the congress is printed in Hung-se Chung-hua of February 3rd 1934, p. 1.

49) Doc. 5D.
50) Doc. 14.
51) Hung-se Chung-hua 24.1.1934 p. 2.
52) Ibid. 3.2.1934 p. 1.
53) Doc. 5B.
54) See Hsiao Tso-liang, 1961, pp. 261 and 264-265.
55) See Hung-se Chung-hua 28.1.1934 p. 3.
56) Hung-se Chung-hua of January 28th 1934 (p. 3) informs us that in
    the discussion groups of delegates from the Red Army there was a
    struggle against a tendency to lack confidence in one's own ability to
    speak.
57) Hung-se Chung-hua 28.1.1934 p. 3.
58) Doc. 5D p. 125.
59) Ibid. pp. 125-127.
60) Ibid. pp. 126-127. At a later stage, when Mao was more free to
    express hos own views, he said that the Communists should have
    united with the Fukien rebels in 1933. However, he apparently meant
    this would have been correct only as a tactical manoeuvre. The Mao-
    sponsored Tsunyi Resolutions continued to maintain that the Fukien
    rebels were a reactionary clique. (Snow, 1946, p. 179; Jerome
    Ch'en: Resolutions of the Tsunyi Conference (Translation with a
    Commentary), the China Quarterly No. 40 pp. 1-38).
61) Doc. 5D p. 128.
62) Hung-se Chung-hua 1.2.1934 p. 2.
63) See ibid. 3.2.1934 p. 3. A drafting committee for the Second Nationa
    Soviet Congress had been appointed by the Council of People's Com-
    missars as early as August 16th 1933. (See ibid. August 31st 1933 p.
    5). It should also be remembered that it was the party "centre" that
    worked out the draft of the General Principles of the Constitution.
    (See this thesis p. 77).
64) See Hung-se Chung-hua 16.1.1934 p. 2, 19.1.1934 p. 2, 22.1.1934
    p. 3, 1.2.1934 p. 3 and 3.2.1934 p. 3.
65) Ibid. 3.2.1934 p. 3.
66) Ibid. 3.2.1934 p. 3.
67) Ibid. 3.2.1934 p. 3.
68) See Hsiao Tso-liang, 1961, p. 281.
69) Hung-se Chung-hua 3.2.1934 p. 1.
70) Ibid. 3.2.1934 p. 1.
71) Doc. 49 art. 3; doc. 5F art. 3.
72) Doc. 5G art. 24.
73) Doc. 49. See also doc. 66.
74) Doc. 2 arts. 1 and 5-7. See also Hsiao Tso-liang, 1961, p. 177.
75) Compare doc. 4 art. 5 (including the note) to art. 6 of doc. 2.
76) Hung-se Chung-hua 3.2.1934 p. 3.
77) See Carr, The Bolshevik Revolution 1917-1923, London, 1950, vol.
    1 pp. 144-146, and doc. 8 pp. 11-12.

78) Carr, op. cit. pp. 147–148 and 215–216.
79) Chang Kuo-t'ao's vice-chairmanship did enhance his personal prestige, but it cannot have meant much for the policy of the Central Government. Chang seems never to have been to the Central Soviet Area. (See note 2 to chapter V).
80) Doc. 37 p. 1; doc. 66.
81) Doc. 37 p. 1.
82) Doc. 38.
83) Hung-se Chung-hua 6.2.1934 p. 1. It is not clear whether this proportion referred only to the full members, or to the alternates as well.
84) Doc. 38 p. 2.
85) See Hsiao Tso-liang, 1961, p. 281, and Rue, 1966, p. 261.
86) Doc. 73A p. 5. See also Hung-se Chung-hua 14.2.1934 p. 4.
87) See Hsiao Tso-liang, 1961, p. 281, and Rue, 1966, pp. 261–262.
88) See note 4 to the introduction to this thesis.
89) Doc. 38 p. 2.
90) Doc. 5G arts. 9–10. The law allowed for extraordinary sessions, as well as for postponement of ordinary ones, when the circumstances so warranted.
91) Doc. 37 p. 1.
92) Doc. 38 p. 2.
93) Hung-se Chung-hua 28.12.1931 p. 1.
94) Doc. 49 art. 3; doc. 5F art. 3.
95) On one occasion, in February or March 1932, the CEC revised four sentences passed by the Provisional Supreme Court, thus claiming to posses the supreme judicial power as well. (Doc. 47).
96) Doc. 5G art. 12.
97) Ibid. art. 24.
98) In setting up the list the Chinese Communists have borrowed extensively from art. 49 of the 1918 constitution of the Russian Socialist Federative Soviet Republic. It may be of interest to note that art. 50 of this Russian constitution stated that apart from the powers listed in its art. 49 the All-Russian Soviet Congress and the Central Executive Committee had the right to deal with "all questions which they consider to be subject to their decision." The text of the 1918 constitution of the RSFSR is found in Istoriya sovetskoy konstitutsii.
99) Doc. 73A p. 5.
00) Hung-se Chung-hua 14.2.1934 p. 4.
01) Ibid. 6.2.1934 p. 1.
02) Ibid. 12.4.1934 p. 2.
03) Doc. 38 p. 2.
04) Doc. 5G art. 17. Such a provision is also found in art. 27 of the 1925 constitution of the RSFSR and in art. 29 of the 1924 constitution of the Soviet Union.

Art. 23 of doc. 5G said that the presidium was responsible to the CEC.

105) Doc. 5G arts. 18, 20 and 21. For comparison see arts. 30-33 of the 1924 constitution of the Soviet Union.

106) Hung-se Chung-hua 4.1.1934 p. 2. The same document has also been designated as the CEC's decree (ming-ling) No. 26. (See doc. 46E).

107) Examples: Docs. 4, 5G, 6, 40, 46A and 46B.

108) Doc. 37 p. 1.

109) Hung-se Chung-hua 2.3.1932 p. 5.

110) Ibid. 3.3.1933 p.1.

111) Ibid. 29.4.1933 p.1.

112) Ibid. 6.3.1933 p.5.

113) Ibid. 25.8.1933 p.1.

114) Doc. 38 p. 2.

115) See note 4 to the introduction to this thesis.

116) According to Jerome Ch'en, Hsiang Ying, Liang Po-t'ai and Wu Liang-p'ing belonged to the "International faction", which implies that they were supporters of the 28 Bolshevik group (See the China Quarterly No. 40 (October - December 1969) pp. 19-20 - from Jer Ch'en's commentary to the Tsunyi Resolutions).

117) See Warren Kuo, Analytical Hist...., 1968, vol. 2 p. 566.

118) See Hung-se Chung-hua 21.9.1933 p.1.

119) Ibid. 28.12.1931 p. 4, 10.2.1932 p. 8, 2.3.1932 p.5, 9.3.1932 p. 6, 16.3.1932 p.6 , 16.6.1932 p.5, 14.7.1932 p.4, 4.8.1932 p.4, 16.10.1932 p.8 (reports from two meetings), 28.11.1932 p. 6, 28.1.1933 p.8, 10.2.1933 p.1 (reports from two meetings), 22.2. 1933 p.1 (reports from two meetings), 3.3.1933 p.1, 6.3.1933 p. 5 21,3.1933 p.2, 8.4.1933 p.1, 17.4.1933 p.4, 29.4.1933 p.1, 11.5 1933 p.1, 17.7.1933 p.1, 22.8.1933 p.4, 25.8.1933 p.1, 31.8.19 p.5, 15.9.1933 p.2 and 21.9.1933 p.1.

120) Ibid. 10.2.1932 p.8.

121) With regard to appointments of vice-commissars see ibid. 17.4.19 p.4, 29.4.1933 p.1, 11.5.1933 p.1, 17.7.1933 p.1 and 25.8.1933

122) Ibid. 31.8.1933 p. 5.

123) Ibid. 2.3.1932 p.5, 16.3.1932 p.6, 16.6.1932 p.5, 4.8.1932 p.4, 16.10.1932 p.8, 28.1.1933 p. 8, 22.2.1933 p.1, 6.3.1933 p.5 and 31.8.1933 p. 5.

124) Ibid. 10.2.1933 p. 1, 29.4.1933 p.1 and 11.5.1933 p.1.

125) Ibid. 10.2.1933 p.1, 3.3.1933 p.1, 6.3.1933 p.5, 21.3.1933 p.2 8.4.1933 p.1.

126) Ibid. 28.11.1932 p.6, 21.3.1933 p.2, 8.4.1933 p.1, 29.4.1933 p. 11.5.1933 p.1 and 22.8.1933 p.4.

127) Ibid. 21.3.1933 p.2, 8.4.1933 p.1, 29.4.1933 p.1 and 25.8.1933

128) Ibid. 3.3.1933 p.1, 6.3.1933 p.5, 8.4.1933 p.1, 17.4.1933 p.4,

29.4.1933 p.1, 11.5.1933 p.1, 17.7.1933 p. 1 and 25.8.1933 p.1.

129) The same references as for note 119 to this chapter.
130) Doc. 79.
131) Hung-se Chung-hua 2.7.1933 p. 6.
132) Doc. 80.
133) Hung-se Chung-hua 14.4.1934 p.4.
134) Ibid. 16.5.1934 p. 3.
135) Doc. 49 art. 3; doc. 5F art. 3.
136) Doc. 5G.
137) Ibid. arts. 14, 21, 30 and 33.
138) Ibid. art. 28.
139) Carr: The Bolshevik Revolution 1917-1923, London 1950, vol. 1 p. 216. See also the 1918 constitution of the RSFSR, art. 41 with note.
140) See Hung-se Chung-hua 2.3.1932 p. 5, 16.6.1932 p. 5 and 16.10. 1932 p. 8.
141) Ibid. 28.1.1933 p. 8, 10.2.1933 p.1, 3.3.1933 p.1, 6.3.1933 p. 5, 21.3.1933 p. 2, 8.4.1933 p.1 and 17.4.1933 p.4.
142) See ibid. 21.9.1933 p.1.
143) Ibid. 3.3.1933 p.1.
144) Ibid. 17.4.1933 p.4.
145) Ibid. 2.3.1932 p.5, 29.4.1933 p.1, 11.5.1933 p.1, 17.7.1933 (the same issue is also dated 23.7.1933) p.1 and 25.8.1933 p.1.
146) Examples: Docs. 4, 5G, 71 and 72.
147) Docs. 46B, 46C, 46D and 46E.
148) Hung-se Chung-hua 18.12.1931 p. 4.
149) Docs. 2.
150) Docs. 81A, 82A and 83.
151) Hung-se Chung-hua 23.3.1932 p. 7.
152) Ibid. 30.6.1932 p.4.
153) Ibid. 28.11.1932 p. 6.
154) Ibid. 20.6.1933 p. 5.
155) Doc. 79.
156) Hung-se Chung-hua 20.3.1934 p.1.
157) For examples see ibid. 23.3.1932 p. 7, 25.5.1932 p. 6, 14.7.1932 p.4, 20.9.1932 pp. 1-3, 7.1.1933 p.3, 20.6.1933 p. 5 and 6.9.1933 p. 7.
158) Doc. 5C p. 115.
159) Doc. 5J p. 191.
160) See the communique on the 26th ordinary meeting of the Council of People's Commissars in Hung-se Chung-hua of October 16th 1932 p. 8, and the CEC's decree No. 12 published in the same issue pp. 1-2. See also the communique on the 30th ordinary meeting of the council in Hung-se Chung-hua of January 28th 1933 p. 8, and the CEC's decree No. 15 in the same journal of January 14th 1933 p. 1. Such an example might also have been read out of ibid. June 16th

1932 p. 5, had it not been for the puzzling fact that the CEC's edict in this case is dated earlier than the meeting at which the council is reported to have made its request.

161) The persons who were elected members of the Council of People's Commissars in November 1931, as well as those elected in Februar 1934, were all members of the CEC (docs. 37 and 38); and the Organic Law for the Central Soviet of February 17th 1934 laid down that this had to be so. (Doc. 5G art. 16).

162) See Hung-se Chung-hua 13.1.1934 p. 1 and 16.1.1934 p. 1.

163) Ibid. 18.2.1934 p. 1.

164) Tou-cheng No. 58 (5.5.1934) pp. 1-7.

165) Hung-se Chung-hua 30.6.1934 p. 1 and 7.7.1934 p. 2. The edict published on July 7th was issued by the party's Central Committee, the Council of People's Commissars and the Revolutionary Military Committee.

166) Ibid. 26.7.1934 p. 1.

167) Ibid. 30.6.1934 p. 1.

168) See this thesis p. 54 , and also Hung-se Chung-hua of 24.7.1934 p.

169) Hung-se Chung-hua 28.6.1934 p. 1 (from doc. 52).

170) Docs. 48, 51, 52 and 53.

171) Tou-cheng No. 49 (2.3.1934) p. 6 (from doc. 48).

172) Examples: Docs. 5G, 46A and 46B.

173) See Hung-se Chung-hua 30.8.1934 p. 1.

174) Doc. 9A.

175) Hung-se Chung-hua 28.4.1934 p. 4 and 1.8.1934 p. 2.

176) Kung Ch'u claims that Mao in the summer of 1934 was utterly in disgrace. We are even told that his party membership was put on p bation. (Kung Ch'u, 1954, pp. 395-400). Otto Braun (Li T'e) gives a rather different story. (See The China Quarterly No. 46, April/June 1971, p. 284 - from Dieter Heinzig, The Otto Braun Memoirs and Mao's Rise to Power). Otto Braun's account of his experiences as Comintern adviser in China is published in Horizont (East Berlin 1969, Nos. 23-38.

In 1966 Mao stated that Chang Wen-t'ien (Lo Fu) tried to have him expelled from the party at the Ningtu Conference in August 1932. (See Jerome Ch'en, 1969, p. 95 (translation)).

Chapter IV. Counter-Revolution and Corruption

1) Kung Ch'u,1954, pp. 267-68 (note); Li Ang, 1946, pp. 159-60; Tsa Po-i, 1969, pp. 420-21.

2) See Smedley, 1956, pp. 280-81, 286, 293 and 301; Hsiao Tso-liang, 1961, p. 100.
3) Doc. 25 pp. 22-25.
4) Doc. 26 pp. 2-3.
5) Doc. 139A p. 57.
6) Docs. 27, 28 and 29.
7) Docs. 27, 28 and 29.
8) Doc. 29.
9) Docs. 27, 28 and 29.
10) Doc. 27.
11) See Hung-se Chung-hua 14.6.1933 p. 4.
12) Tou-cheng No. 7 (5.4.1933)p. 12; Hung-se Chung-hua 2.5.1933 p. 3.
13) Hung-se Chung-hua 21.5.1934 p. 2.
14) Ibid. 14.6.1933 p. 4.
15) Ibid. 5.5.1933 p. 3 and 18.3.1933 p. 2; doc. 30. By 1931 the Social Democrats seem to have been especially active in Fukien. Later reports tell that they were also operating in Kiangsi. (See Tou-cheng No. 7 (5.4.1933) p. 12).
16) Hung-se Chung-hua 28.4.1934 p. 3. The man found to belong to the Big Sword Society was described as the "chairman of the hsiang" (hsiang chu-hsi).
17) Doc. 31 p. 8.
18) For examples see Hung-se Chung-hua 25.2.1933 p. 1, 29.5.1933 p. 2 and 21.6.1934 p. 2.
19) Ibid. 5.12.1932 p. 5.
20) Ch'ing-nien shih-hua vol. 2, No. 3 (29.1.1933) pp. 29-30.
21) Doc. 32. At least three of the four defendants at this trial had been arrested in October 1931. See also doc. 30. Kung Ch'u denies that there were any Reorganisationists in the Seventh Red Army. (Kung Ch'u, 1954, pp. 243-44.)
22) Hung-se Chung-hua 18.3.1933 p. 2, 14.4.1933 p. 3 and 26.4.1933 p. 4.
23) Doc. 33 p. 4. Examples of alleged ideological infiltration by Trotskyists in the Central Soviet Area are described in Tang ti chien-she Nos. 5 (10.10.1932) and 6 (30.11.1932).
24) There seems to have been a strong affinity between the Third Party and the Social Democratic Party. (See Linebarger, 1941, pp. 178-79 and 181, and Sovety v Kitae p. 515 (index)). Sometimes the two are confused in Chinese Communist sources. (See doc. 26 p. 8 and doc. 33 p. 3).
25) Tou-cheng No. 7 (5.4.1933) p. 12; Hung-se Chung-hua 17.6.1933 p.3 (at p. 3 the issue is, probably wrongly, dated 14.6.1933).
26) In our sources there are numerous references to military units of this kind. For examples see Hung-se Chung-hua 14.6.1933 p. 2, 1.8.1933 p. 2 and 18.2.1934 p. 1. The Young Boys' Army seems to have belonged

under the Big Sword Society. (See ibid. 25.2.1933 p. 1 and 5.12.
1933 p. 2).

27) Ibid. 8.3.1934 p. 3; Shih-hua No. 10 (30.11.1932) p. 16.
28) Hung-se Chung-hua 3.3.1934 p. 3.
29) Ibid. 10.3.1934 p. 1.
30) See ibid. 25.5.1932 p. 6 and 16.2.1934 p. 1.
31) Ibid. 2.4.1933 p. 4. and 22.2.1934 p. 3.
32) Ibid. 16.8.1933 p. 7 and 12.4.1934 p. 2.
33) Ibid. 16.6.1932 p. 6.
34) Ibid. 10.3.1934 p. 3 and 20.3.1934 p. 3; Ch'ing-nien shih-hua,
vol. 3, No. 15 (undated) pp. 18-20.
35) Hung-se Chung-hua 6.2.1934 p. 4, 24.2.1934 p. 3 and 3.3.1934
p. 3.
36) Doc. 116C pp. 2-3.
37) Doc. 35A pp. 5-6.
38) Hung-se Chung-hua 4.1.1934 p. 2.
39) Ibid. 20.12.1933 p. 3.
40) Ibid. 20.2.1934 p. 3.
41) Ibid. 3.3.1934 p. 3.
42) Ibid. 29.3.1934 p. 5 (from doc. 17). The Yütu scandal is also described in ibid. 8.3.1934 p. 3 and 13.3.1934 p. 3, and in Tou-
cheng No. 53 (31.3.1934) pp. 1-5.
43) Doc. 17.


Chapter V. Administration of Justice

1) Doc. 37 p. 1.
2) Chang Kuo-t'ao moved from Shanghai to the Oyüwan (Hupei-Honan-
Anhui) Soviet Area, probably sometime in 1931. (See Hsiao Tso-
liang, 1961, p. 162). This soviet area was, because of the military
situation, not able to send any delegates to the First National Soviet
Congress in November 1931. (Ibid. p. 172). In 1932 Chang Kuo-t'ao
moved, together with the troops at his disposal, to the border region
of Szechuan and Shensi, and founded a new soviet area there. (Wang
Chien-min, 1965, vol. 2 pp. 207-12 and 217-37).
3) Hung-se Chung-hua 29.4.1933 p. 1. Liang Po-t'ai was as early as
December 1931 appointed a member of a judical committee at the
central level. (Hung-se Chung-hua 18.12.1931 p. 4). However, up
to the summer of 1933 this committee seems to have existed only
in name (Doc. 36 p. 3).
4) Doc. 38 p. 2.
5) The monthly expenditure of the commissariat was too small to suppo

so large a staff. The joint expenditure of the Commissariat of Justice and the Commissariat of Internal Affairs was <u>331.48 yüan</u> in February 1934, and only <u>197.49 yüan</u> in March 1934. (<u>Hung-se Chung-hua</u> 14.4. 1934 p. 5).

6) Doc. 36 pp. 3-4.
7) Doc. 46A art. 6.
8) Doc. 5G art. 34.
9) Doc. 47.
10) See docs 27 and 32.
11) Doc. 38 p. 2.
12) Docs 27 and 32.
13) Doc. 5G arts. 34-36 and 38-39. The Committee was to be headed by the chief of the court.

Prior to the promulgation of the <u>Organic Law for the Central Soviet</u> the court was in general called <u>Lin-shih tsui-kao fa-t'ing</u> (Provisional Supreme Court). (Docs. 27, 32 and 38). The Organic Law, however, designated it as <u>Tsui-kao fa-yüan</u> (Supreme Court), and used the word <u>fa-t'ing</u> for its chambers.

14) Doc. 5G art. 40.
15) Docs. 39 and 40.
16) Doc. 39.
17) Doc. 41 pp. 8 and 16.
18) Doc. 6 art. 152.
19) Ibid. art. 150; doc. 39.
20) Docs 28, 29, 30, 39, 63 and 64; <u>Hung-se Chung-hua</u> 6.4.1932 p. 4 and 16.6.1932 p. 6.
21) Doc. 39.
22) Doc. 39.
23) Doc. 42. Regarding civil courts see also doc. 6 art. 151.
24) Doc. 6 art. 151; doc. 39.
25) Doc. 41 p. 18. This source refers to an earlier decree from the Commissariat of Justice concerning labour courts. The earlier decree has not been found.
26) Doc. 36 p. 4; doc. 6 art. 151.
27) Doc. 6 art. 151; doc. 46C art. 7.
28) Doc. 41 pp. 9, 17 and 19.
29) Doc. 6 art. 148. Regarding the organisation of the judicial committees see ibid. arts. 148-49.
30) See for instance <u>Hung-se Chung-hua</u> 14.7.1933 p. 6, 1.3.1934 p. 1 and 20.3.1934 p. 3.
31) Docs.39 and 40.
32) Doc. 54.
33) Doc. 41 pp. 7 and 15-16.
34) Ibid. pp. 3-12 and 21.

35) Ibid. p. 10.

36) Ibid. p. 12.

37) Hung-se Chung-hua 7.11.1932 p. 8 (from doc. 39); doc. 41 pp. 16-17.

38) Szu-fa hui-k'an (Ts'ai-p'an hui-k'an) No. 2 (9.7.1933) p. 2.

39) Doc. 36 p. 6.

40) Hung-se Chung-hua 7.11.1932 p. 8 (from doc. 39).

41) Ibid. 5.12.1932 p. 8 (from doc. 42).

42) See ibid. 7.11.1932 p. 7 (from doc. 39).

43) Doc. 6 art. 154.

44) Doc. 41 pp. 12-13.

45) Hung-se Chung-hua 7.11.1932 p. 8 (from doc. 39).

46) Doc. 6 art. 154.

47) Hung-se Chung-hua 7.11.1932 p. 8 (from doc. 39); doc. 41 pp. 13-1 See also doc. 43 pp. 52-53.

48) Hung-se Chung-hua 7.11.1932 p. 7 (from doc. 39). See also ibid. 1.3.1934 p. 1 and doc. 43 p. 54.

49) Problemy Kitaya No. 11 (1933) p. 5; Schwartz, 1958, p. 177.

50) Doc. 37 p. 1.

51) Rue, 1966, pp. 267 and 270.

52) See Kung Ch'u, 1954, pp. 247-48.

53) Doc. 37 p. 1; doc. 55 art. 1.

54) Doc. 6 arts. 175-85; doc. 55; Kung Ch'u, 1954, pp. 429-30.

55) Doc. 6 art. 155; doc. 56 pp. 10-11 and 21; Hung-se Chung-hua 16.10.1932 pp. 1-2. Often the local militia is called Ch'ih-shao-tui, and both the Red Guards and the Young Vanguard then seem to be included.

56) Hung-se Chung-hua 21.11.1932 p. 6 (from doc. 12) and 5.12.1932 p. (from doc. 42); doc. 6 arts. 143 and 155.

57) Doc. 6 art. 163.

58) Doc. 40. See also Kung Ch'u, 1954, pp. 247-48.

59) Doc. 41 pp. 9-12.

60) Docs. 40 and 55.

61) See this thesis p. 109.

62) Docs. 27, 28, 29, 30, 32, 57; doc. 41 p. 19; Hung-se Chung-hua 6.4.1932 p. 4 and 5.5.1933 p. 3.

63) Tou-cheng No. 49 p. 7 (from doc. 48).

64) Docs. 27, 32 and 57. Most of these cases, or possibly all of them, were of a military nature.

65) See Hung-se Chung-hua 29.3.1934 p. 3.

66) Doc. 5G art. 37. With regard to the model for the provision see Istoriya sovetskoy konstitutsii p. 468 (from the 1924 constitution of the USSR). The Chinese provision seems not to have conformed fully to that of the Soviet Union.

67) Doc. 5G art. 37. The influence from the Soviet Union is obvious –
see Istoriya sovetskoy konstitutsii pp. 436-38 (from Polozhenie o
Tsentral'nom Ispolnitel'nom Komitete Soyuza SSR – Statute of the
Central Executive Committee of the USSR, dated November 12th
1923). Nevertheless the Chinese stipulation has – possibly because
of a mistake – a content which is different from the much more
complicated provisions of the Soviet Union.

68) Doc. 40 art. 2.

69) Docs. 28 and 29.

70) Doc. 54.

71) Szu-fa hui-k'an (Ts'ai-p'an hui-k'an) No. 2 (9.7.1933) p. 3. This
journal was published by the judicial department of Kiangsi province.

72) Doc. 46A arts. 5-6.

73) Doc. 47; Hung-se Chung-hua 16.6.1932 p. 6, 16.10.1932 p. 8 and
21.11.1932 p. 4.

74) Doc. 46A arts. 5-6.

75) Doc. 41.

76) See doc. 45.

77) Doc. 40 arts. 1, 3, 4, 5 and 6; doc. 55 art. 9.

78) Doc. 46A arts. 1 and 3.

79) Doc. 40 arts. 1, 2 and 5.

80) Doc. 55 art. 10.

81) See Hung-se Chung-hua 18.3.1933 p. 2, 2.4.1933 p. 4, 2.5.1933 p.
3 and 20.2.1934 p. 3.

82) Doc. 58.

83) Tou-cheng No. 49 p. 8 (from doc. 48).

84) Doc. 40. See also Hung-se Chung-hua 25.5.1932 p. 6.

85) No quotation marks are used by Chang Wen-t'ien, but the style of
the reproduced provisions suggests that they are simply quoted.

86) Tou-cheng No. 49 p. 7 (from doc. 48). The regulations may possibly
have allowed for exceptions to these rules.

87) Doc. 41 pp. 9-10.

88) Tou-cheng No. 49 p. 7 (from doc. 48).

89) Ibid. No. 49 p. 7 (from doc. 48).

90) Ibid. No. 49 p. 7 (from doc. 48).

91) Doc. 46A art. 2.

92) See Sovety v Kitae pp. 316-17.

93) Doc. 40, the preamble and arts. 5-6.

94) Doc. 39. The statement that the soviet courts were working under
the control of the masses was given in connection with the information
that the secondary judges were elected by the mass organisations.

95) Doc. 41 pp. 7, 9 - 11, 15 and 18.

96) Szu-fa hui-k'an (Ts'ai-p'an hui-k'an ) No. 2 (9.7.1933) pp. 1 and
3; Tou-cheng No. 24 pp. 5-6 (from doc. 59).

97) Szu-fa hui-k'an (Ts'ai-p'an hui-k'an) No. 2 (9.7.1933). p. 1.

98) Tou-cheng No. 49 p. 6 (from doc. 48).

99) Hung-se Chung-hua 7.11.1932 p. 7 (from doc. 39).

100) Szu-fa hui-k'an (Chianghsi sheng ts'ai-p'an-pu pan-yüeh-k'an) No. 7 (no date visible) pp. 2-3; doc. 41 p. 7.

101) Szu-fa hui-k'an (Chianghsi sheng ts'ai-p'an-pu pan-yüeh-k'an). No. 7. (no date visible) p. 3.

102) Hung-se Chung-hua 7.11.1932 p. 7 (from doc. 39); doc. 41 p. 16; Szu-fa hui-k'an (Ts'ai-p'an hui-k'an) No. 2 (9.7.1933) p. 1; doc. 6 art. 151.

103) Hung-se Chung-hua 7.11.1932 p. 7 (from doc. 39); doc. 41 pp. 7 and 16.

104) Doc. 60C p. 22; Tou-cheng No. 24 pp. 5-6 (from doc. 59); Szu-fa hui-k'an (Ts'ai-p'an hui-k'an) No. 2 (9.7.1933) pp. 1 and 3; Szu-fa hui-k'an (Chianghsi sheng ts'ai-p'an-pu pan-yüeh-k'an) No. 7 p. 2. (No date of issue of No. 7 is visible on the microfilm, but the article referred to deals with ambulant courts in Kiangsi for the two months of September and October 1933).

105) Doc. 41 pp. 7 and 15.

106) Hung-se Chung-hua 6.4.1932 p. 4 (see note 107), 5.5.1933 p. 3 and 5.12.1933 p. 2; Szu-fa hui-k'an (Ts'ai-p'an hui-k'an) No. 2 (9.7. 1933) p. 3.

107) Hung-se Chung-hua 6.4.1932 p. 4. This trial is also recorded in docs. 28 and 29, which do not designate it as a public trial.

The second example is found in Hung-se Chung-hua of December 5th 1933 p. 2.

108) Ibid. 12.2.1934 p. 2, 14.2.1934 p. 1, 22.2.1934 p. 3, 8.3.1934 p. 3, 22.3.1934 p. 1, 24.3.1934 p. 2, 19.4.1934 p. 2, 5.7.1934 p. 2 and 17.7.1934 p. 3.

Although none of the available reports from 1934 says that a court took part in the proceedings of a "public trial", the following should be noted: Hung-se Chung-hua of May 21st 1934 reported (on p. 3) a case in which the culprit was first sent to a court, and later judged at a public trial organised by the masses. Further, the same journal reported on February 18th 1934 (p. 3) a trial by the Supreme Court of cases which had previously passed through a "public trial"; and on March 1st 1934 it reported that the Supreme Court had approved a death sentence passed at a "public trial".

109) Ibid. 6.4.1932 p. 4.

110) Ibid. 5.5.1933 p. 3; doc. 61 pp. 13-14; Szu-fa hui-k'an (Ts'ai-p'an hui-k'an) No. 2 (9.7.1933) p. 3.

111) Hung-se Chung-hua 12.2.1934 p. 2, 14.2.1934 p. 1, 22.3.1934 p. 1, 21.5.1934 p. 3, 19.6.1934 p. 2, 5.7.1934 p. 2 and 17.7.1934 p. 3.

112) Doc. 60C p. 20.

113) Ibid. p. 20; doc. 61 p. 14; Szu-fa hui-k'an (Ts'ai-p'an hui-k'an) No. 2 (9.7.1933) p. 3.

114) Doc. 61 p. 14.

115) Hung-se Chung-hua 6.4.1932 p. 4, to be consulted in conjunction with docs. 28 and 29. Hung-se Chung-hua 5.5.1933 p. 3; doc. 61 pp. 13-14.

In early 1934 it happened that the Supreme Court dealt with high-ranking cadres who had previously been tried at "public trials", and we are informed that at least four of them were finally sentenced, not to death, but to imprisonment. Whether the public trial of these four was staged in early 1934 or late 1933 is, however, uncertain. (Hung-se Chung-hua 18.2.1934 p. 3. See also ibid. 8.3.1934 p. 3, 13.3.1934 p. 3 and 29.3.1934 p. 7 (from doc. 17)).

116) Hung-se Chung-hua 22.3.1934 p. 1, 24.3.1934 p. 2, 21.5.1934 p. 3, 19.6.1934 p. 2, 5.7.1934 p. 2 and 17.7.1934 p. 3.

117) See, however, note 120 to this chapter.

118) Doc. 49 art. 4; doc. 5F art. 4.

119) Doc. 40 art. 7; doc. 55 art. 11.

120) Doc. 46C. Perhaps it is this statute at a preparatory stage which is referred to in Szu-fa hui-k'an (Ts'ai-p'an hui-k'an) No. 2 (9.7.1933) p. 2.

121) Doc. 46C.

122) Doc. 46D art. 4. Those who refused to return to their units were made liable to pay indemnities for the cost of equipping them etc., and they were deprived of the right to vote. (Ibid. art. 5).

123) Ibid. arts. 1-2.

124) See Hung-se Chung-hua 11.4.1933 p. 4.

125) Doc. 46E arts. 1-2.

126) Doc. 46B.

127) Doc. 27.

128) Doc. 47.

129) Doc. 28. In its criticism of the sentences recorded in docs. 28 and 29 the Supreme Court said that the period for which the right to vote was denied should be reckoned from the day the convict was released from prison. (Doc. 54).

130) Doc. 27.

131) Doc. 30.

132) Doc. 30.

133) Hung-se Chung-hua 2.4.1933 p. 4. With regard to other cases in which capital punishment was inflicted for similar offences, see ibid. 15.3.1933 p. 3 and 22.2.1934 p. 3.

134) Ibid. 16.2.1934 p. 1.

135) Ibid. 1.3.1934 p. 1. The same article informs us that the district of Telien was situated in Chaocheng county in Fukien.

136) Ibid. 22.3.1934 p. 1. Ch'iaoyang was a district in the county of Chienning in the soviet province of Minkan.

137) Docs. 63 and 64 may contain some information of interest in this regard, but, because of unclear print, parts of these documents are extremely difficult to read.
138) Hung-se Chung-hua 17.7.1934 p. 3.
139) Doc. 41 p. 5.
140) Hung-se Chung-hua 14.2.1934 p. 1 and 24.3.1934 p. 2.
141) Ibid. 18.2.1934 p. 3 and 29.3.1934 p. 3.
142) Tou-cheng No. 49 p. 4 (from doc. 48).
143) Doc. 46B.
144) Tou-cheng No. 49 p. 6 (from doc. 48).
145) Doc. 45.
146) Hung-seChung-hua 25.5.1934 p. 1 (from doc. 51).
147) Chang Wen-t'ien later criticised this view. See ibid. 28.6.1934 p. 1 (from doc. 52).
148) Tou-cheng No. 67 pp. 3-4 (from doc. 53). See also doc. 52.
149) Tou-cheng No. 67 p. 4 (from doc. 53).
150) Doc. 40.
151) Kung Ch'u, 1954, pp. 243-48.
152) Ibid. pp. 257 and 266-67.
153) Doc. 25 pp. 22-25.
154) Hsiao Tso-liang, 1961, pp. 159-61.


Chapter VI. Rural Class Policy and the Land Investigation Movement

1) Doc. 84.
2) Doc. 60C p. 15.
3) Hung-se Chung-hua 23.6.1932 pp. 7-8.
4) Mao Tse-tung hsüan-chi, Peking 1958, vol. 1 p. 121; SW, Peking 1964, vol. 1. p. 137.
5) This translation of the term is used in the edition of Mao Tse-tung's Selected Works published in Peking 1964 (vol. 1. p. 137).
6) See Selected Works of Mao Tse-tung, London, 1955, vol. 1 p. 138.
7) See Hsiao Tso-liang, 1961, p. 350 (Glossary).
8) Ch'ü T'ung-tsu, 1962, pp. 168-92; Yang, C.K.: A Chinese Village in Early Communist Transition, p. 112.
9) Doc. 139A p. 22.
10) Tou-cheng No. 15 (15.6.1933) p. 12 (from doc. 85); ibid. No. 20 (5.8.1933) p. 16 (from doc. 86).
11) Ibid. No. 20 p. 16 (from doc. 86).
12) The same references as for note 36 to this chapter.
13) Tou-cheng No. 15 (15.6.1933) pp. 9, 13 and 14 (from doc. 85); ibid. No. 21 (12.8.1933) p. 16 (from doc. 86).

14) Ibid. No. 15 (15.6.1933) p. 13 (from doc. 85).

15) Doc. 79, chapter 3.

16) See ibid. chapter 3 (including the note) and chapter 8 (including the note).

17) Doc. 71.

18) Hsiao Tso-liang, 1961, p. 180. See also ibid. pp. 71-72, and Hsiao Tso-liang, 1967, pp. 195-97.

19) Doc. 87.

20) Doc. 88.

21) Deutscher: Stalin. A Political Biography, London 1967, pp. 319-31.

22) See Hsiao Tso-liang, 1967, p. 563 (from doc. 89).

23) Hung-se Chung-hua 20.2.1934 p. 1; Doc. 90A, vol. 1, pp. 26-27.

24) Doc. 71 art. 3.

25) See ibid. art. 4 and doc. 90A, vol. 1, p. 21.

26) Doc. 71 art. 3.

27) See doc. 90A, vol. 1, p. 24 and Tou-cheng No. 21 (12.8.1933) p. 16 (from doc. 86).

28) Doc. 71 art. 8. As Hsiao Tso-liang has pointed out, the rich peasants were more ruthlessly discriminated against in the final text of the land law than in the draft introduced by the CCP Central Committee. (See Hsiao Tso-liang, 1961, p. 179 and doc. 70B).

29) Doc. 71 arts. 1, 5 and 7.

30) Ibid. art. 8.

31) Ibid. art. 9.

32) Ibid. art. 7.

33) Ibid. art. 5. Such a provision was not included in the draft of the land law (doc. 70B).

34) Hung-se Chung-hua 21.11.1932 p. 5 (from doc. 12). See also Hsiao Tso-liang, 1969, pp. 69-71.

35) See Hsiao Tso-liang, 1969, pp. 64-77.

36) Doc. 81A art. 11; doc. 82A art. 11; doc. 83 art. 6.

37) Hung-se Chung-hua 12.7.1934 p. 1, 24.7.1934 p. 2 and 28.7.1934 p. 2.

38) Doc. 81A art. 13; doc. 82A art. 13; doc. 83 art. 1.

39) Doc. 91 leaves 11-12.

40) Hung-se Chung-hua 28.11.1932 p. 6.

41) Doc. 25 p. 14.

42) In May 1934 Chang Wen-t'ien complained that there were even by that time in the Central Soviet Area many landlords and rich peasants who had not been placed in hard labour brigades. (Doc. 51). See also this thesis p. 175.

43) Tou-cheng No. 24 (29.8.1933) p. 4 (from doc. 59); Hung-se Chung-hua 20.6.1933 p. 3.

44) Kung Ch'u, 1954, the author's preface, p. 11.

45) Ibid. pp. 372-377.
46) Doc. 92.
47) Ibid.
48) Doc. 60A, doc. 60B, doc. 60C and doc. 93.
49) Doc. 60C. The quotations are based on translation by Hsiao Tso-liang, 1969, pp. 228-29, and on the version printed in Hung-se Chung-hua 29. 6. 1933.
50) Doc. 93 p. 2.
51) Doc. 60A.
52) Doc. 60C p. 14.
53) Doc. 60E.
54) Doc. 60B pp. 7-8; doc. 94.
55) Doc. 60B p. 8; doc. 60C p. 14; doc. 60H.
56) Hung-se Chung-hua 14. 6. 1933 p. 3, 20. 6. 1933 p. 3 and 23. 6. 1933 p. 3; doc. 60C pp. 12 and 26.
57) Doc. 60E p. 31.
58) Hung-se Chung-hua 13. 8. 1933 p. 3; Sheng-wei t'ung-hsün 27. 7. 1933 pp. 1-3 and 30. 7. 1933 pp. 1-2.
59) Doc. 60A pp. 3-4; doc. 60B p. 8; doc. 60C p. 15.
60) Doc. 139A pp. 22-28.

Kung Ch'u claims that the peasant masses in what was to become the Central Soviet Area on the whole led a rather pleasant life before the revolution. (Kung Ch'u, 1954, pp. 415-17). Against the background of what we know about exploitation in the Chinese countryside it is not possible to accept Kung Ch'u's account on this point.

61) Doc. 95. In this article Mao also writes that, more exceptionally, one might in the same area find large villages which were relatively advanced, and small villages which were relatively backward.
62) Tou-cheng No. 24 pp. 5-6 (from doc. 59).
63) Ibid. pp. 4-6 (from doc. 59).
64) Hung-se Chung-hua 31. 8. 1933 p. 6, 9. 10. 1933 p. 3 and 20. 11. 1933 p. 3.
65) Ibid. 26. 7. 1933 p. 6, 3. 9. 1933 p. 6, 9. 10. 1933 p. 3 and 14. 11. 1933 p. 3; doc. 31 p. 2.
66) Hung-se Chung-hua 31. 8. 1933 p. 6, 6. 9. 1933 p. 8, 18. 9. 1933 p. 8 and 21. 9. 1933 p. 1; doc. 61 pp. 4-5 and 10-16.
67) Hung-se Chung-hua 13. 8. 1933 p. 3 and 9. 10. 1933 p. 3.
68) Ibid. 13. 8. 1933 p. 3 and 9. 10. 1933 p. 3.
69) Ibid. 31. 8. 1933 p. 6, 9. 10. 1933 p. 3 and 14. 11. 1933 p. 3; doc. 31 p
70) Hung-se Chung-hua 14. 7. 1933 p. 6; doc. 79, note to chapter 7; doc. 93 p. 2.
71) Doc. 79, note to chapter 7.
72) Hung-se Chung-hua 5. 12. 1933 p. 1.
73) Tou-cheng No. 24 p. 7 (from doc. 59).

74) Hung-se Chung-hua 20.11.1933 p. 3.
75) Doc. 93 p. 1; Hung-se Chung-hua 21.9.1933 p. 1.
76) Hung-se Chung-hua 12.10.1933 (on p. 3 the date 6.10.1933 is given) p. 3; doc. 31 pp. 8-9.
77) Hung-se Chung-hua 18.9.1933 p. 8.
78) Doc. 31 pp. 8-9; Tou-cheng No. 24 p. 7 (from doc. 59); Hung-se Chung-hua 12.10.1933 (on p. 3 the date 6.10.1933 is given) p. 3.
79) Hung-se Chung-hua 12.10.1933 (on p. 3 the date 6.10.1933 is given) p. 3 and 11.11.1933 p. 3; doc. 31 pp. 7-8.
80) Tou-cheng No. 24 p. 8 (from doc. 59).
81) Ibid. p. 7; Hung-se Chung-hua 12.10.1933 (on p. 3 the date 6.10. 1933 is given) p. 3 and 11.11.1933 p. 3.
82) Tou-cheng No. 24 pp. 7-10 (from doc. 59); Hung-se Chung-hua 11.11.1933 p. 3 and 16.1.1934 p. 3.
83) Tou-cheng No. 24 p. 8 (from doc. 59).
84) Doc. 60A pp. 3-4; doc. 60B p. 8; doc. 60C p. 15.
85) Doc. 60B p. 9.
86) Tou-cheng No. 24 p. 10 (from doc. 59).
87) See North, 1952, p. 117.
88) Tou-cheng No. 24 p. 10 (from doc. 59).
89) See Hung-se Chung-hua 16.1.1934 p. 3.
90) Ibid. 21.9.1933 p. 1; doc. 79.
91) Hung-se Chung-hua 11.11.1933 p. 3; doc. 31 pp. 7-8; doc. 61 pp. 1-2.
92) Doc. 84.
93) Doc. 79. Mao Tse-tung had this document reissued, with significant modifications, in 1948 and 1950. (See Hsiao Tso-liang, 1969, pp. 111-12).
94) Tsao Po-i, 1969, pp. 471-72; Warren Kuo, Analytical Hist..., 1968, vol. 2 pp. 563-64.
95) Doc. 84.
96) Doc. 79, chapter 1 with note.
97) Doc. 84.
98) Doc. 79, chapter 2 with note, and chapter 3 with note.
99) Ibid., chapter 5 with note.
100) Ibid., chapter 7 with note.
101) Chung-hua su-wei-ai kung-ho-kuo chung-yang cheng-fu jen-min wei-yüan-hui ming-ling ti 49 hao (Decree No. 49 of the Council of People's Commissars, the Central Government of the Chinese Soviet Republic). Printed as a preamble to doc. 79.
102) Doc. 96; Hung-se Chung-hua 14.4.1934 p. 3.
103) Tou-cheng No. 61 pp. 10-11 (from doc. 99); Hung-se Chung-hua 14.4.1934 p. 3; doc. 96.
104) Doc. 96.
105) Hung-se Chung-hua 14.4.1934 p. 3 and 7.5.1934 p. 3; Tou-cheng

No. 61 p. 10 (from doc. 99). The figure given in doc. 96 for revised cases in Shengli is presumably based on incomplete statistics.

106) Tou-cheng No. 61 pp. 10-11 (from doc. 99); Hung-se Chung-hua 14.4.1934 p. 3.

107) Tsao Po-i, 1969, pp. 471-72; Warren Kuo, Analytical Hist..., 1968, vol. 2 pp. 563-64.

108) Doc. 97.

109) This quotation, and the following one, are taken almost verbatim from Hsiao Tso-liang's translation (Hsiao Tso-liang, 1969, p. 283).

110) Doc. 98.

111) Ibid.

112) Hung-se Chung-hua 7.5.1934 pp. 2-3.

113) Doc. 51.

114) Doc. 52; Tou-cheng No. 67 p. 4 (from doc. 53).

115) Doc. 51.

116) Doc. 52. See also Tou-cheng No. 67 p. 4 (from doc. 53).

117) See this thesis pp. 137-38.

118) Sheng-wei t'ung-hsün No. 81 (30.3.1934) p. 8.

119) Doc. 51.

120) Doc. 52.

121) Doc. 51.

122) Tou-cheng No. 67 p. 3 (from doc. 53).

123) Ibid. p. 5 (from doc. 53).

124) Doc. 87 arts, 1, 2, 7, 8 and 10; doc. 139A pp. 30-31; Hsiao Tso-liang, 1967, p. 426 (from doc. 65); Hsiao Tso-liang, 1969, pp. 20-22.

125) Hsiao Tso-liang, 1961, p. 180; Hsiao Tso-liang, 1969, pp. 47 and 5.

126) Mao Tse-tung is reported to have stayed at a hospital in T'ingchou for four months in late 1932. (See Hung-ch'i p'iao-p'iao, vol. 11, 1959, pp. 3-18). Hung-se Chung-hua of 23.6.1933 (p. 3) reports that Mao had recently recovered from an illness.

127) Hsiao Tso-liang, 1969, pp. 80-81.

128) See Warren Kuo, Analytical Hist..., 1968, vol. 2 p. 533.

129) Hsiao Tso-liang, 1969, pp. 168-170 (translation). See also ibid. pp. 34-35.


Chapter VII. Finances

1) Kung Ch'u, 1954, pp. 412-13; Hung-se Chung-hua 7.11.1932 p. 7 (from doc. 108).

2) Doc. 102, leaf 57.

3) Doc. 5 I pp. 184-85. This resolution also made it clear that there had been an excessive issue of banknotes in the Hsiangokan soviet ar

4) See Hung-se Chung-hua 30. 6. 1932 p. 4.
5) See Tou-cheng No. 20 p. 13 (from doc.109).
6) See Hung-se Chung-hua 31. 8. 1933 p. 3.
7) See Tou-cheng No. 20 p. 13 (from doc. 109).
8) Doc. 139C p. 147.
9) Hung-se Chung-hua 30. 6. 1932 p. 4; doc. 103.
10) Hung-se Chung-hua 20. 2. 1934 p. 3 and 22. 2. 1934 p. 3.
11) See ibid. 31. 8. 1933 p. 3.
12) Ibid. 4. 6. 1933 p. 6 and 23. 6. 1933 p. 6.
13) Ibid. 23. 6. 1933 p. 6 and 14. 7. 1933 p. 5.
14) Tou-cheng No. 29 p. 12 (from doc. 105).
15) Hung-se Chung-hua 6. 3. 1934 p. 3.
16) Doc. 101A pp. 3-5; Hung-se Chung-hua 23. 6. 1933 p. 6.
17) Doc. 101A pp. 7-12; doc. 101B pp. 14-16; doc. 101C; Hung-se Chung-hua 7. 11. 1932 p. 7 (from doc. 108), 23. 6. 1933 p. 6 and 15. 3. 1934 p. 2; Tou-cheng No. 56 pp. 16-18 (from doc. 106). The members were to be given preferential treatment with regard to permission to sell to, as well as for permission to buy from, the food co-operatives.
18) Doc. 101A pp. 6-7. There is a possibility that the docuement in this connection refers to a time previous to 1932.
19) Hung-se Chung-hua 8. 5. 1933 p. 5. The Central Bureau for the Regulation of Food Supply was apparently at that time transferred from the Commissariat of Finances.
20) Tou-cheng No. 29 p. 12 (from doc. 105). There were also a number of branch offices at a lower level than the county.
21) Hung-se Chung-hua 20. 5. 1933 p. 5 and 14. 7. 1933 p. 5.
22) Ibid. 6. 3. 1934 p. 3 and 31. 3. 1934 p. 6. Tou-cheng No. 29 p. 12 (from doc. 105). To some extent the Bureau for the Regulation of Food Supply was also dealing in commodities other than rice.
23) Doc. 104 p. 87.
24) Ibid. pp. 87-88.
25) Hung-se Chung-hua 7. 11. 1932 p. 3 (from doc. 107) and p. 6 (from doc. 108).
26) Hung-se Chung-hua 7. 11. 1932 p. 6 (from doc. 108).
27) Doc. 90B art. 5.
28) Doc. 111B.
29) Hung-se Chung-hua 8. 5. 1933 p. 5. Tsao Po-i runs into difficulties on this point because he misdates doc. 90 B. (Tsao Po-i, 1969, p. 350). For approximate dating of the document see the bibliography to this thesis.
30) See Hung-se Chung-hua 15. 9. 1933 p. 2.
31) Doc. 110; Hung-se Chung-hua 25. 8. 1933 p. 1 and 3. 9. 1933 p. 2; Hsiao Tso-liang, 1961, pp. 230-47.
32) See this thesis p. 89.

33) Hung-se Chung-hua 7.11.1932 p. 7 (from doc. 108).
34) Ibid. p. 7 (from doc. 108).
35) See doc. 6 arts. 119-23.
36) Doc. 111B; Hung-se Chung-hua 7.1.1933 p. 3.
37) Doc. 112B pp. 29-30.
38) Docs. 111A, 111B and 111C.
39) Doc. 113, chapter 5.
40) Docs. 112A and 112B.
41) Doc. 111B.
42) Doc. 111C arts. 15-21 and 49; doc. 112A arts. 3-7. See also
    Hung-se Chung-hua 7.11.1932 p. 6 (from·doc. 108).
43) See Hung-se Chung-hua 21.3.1933 p. 2, 2.5.1933 p. 6 and 11.5.19:
    p. 5. In January 1934 Mao Tse-tung told the Second National Soviet
    Congress that the customs rates ranged from 0 to 100 per cent.
    (Doc. 5C p. 81).
44) Doc. 82B.
45) Doc. 81A pp. 9-12; doc. 82A pp. 1-4; doc. 82C.
46) Doc. 81A art. 8; doc. 82A art. 8; doc. 83 art. 3.
47) See this thesis p. 153.
48) Doc. 114 art. 6.
49) Doc. 83 art. 8; doc. 117D art. 1.
50) Doc. 115 p. 1.
51) Doc. 116B art. 1.
52) The regulations of November 1931 stated that the question whether
    the land tax was to be collected in money or in kind should be decid
    in conformity with the wishes of the peasants (doc. 81A art. 18).
    Payment of the tax in kind was possibly practised to some extent in
    1932 (doc. 101A p. 3), but it was not the rule (doc. 82A art. 18 and
    doc. 116A art. 9). From the autumn of 1933 the government went in
    actively for having a large part of the land tax collected in the form
    of unhulled rice (doc. 116C), although the possibility of paying in
    money was still kept open (doc. 116A art. 7). In January 1934 the
    party and the government ordered that the tax should be paid ex-
    clusively in unhulled rice (doc. 118).
53) Doc. 119.
54) Doc. 116C.
55) Tou-cheng No. 73 p. 9 (from doc. 131).
56) Docs. 120, 121, 122 and 124B. See also Hung-se Chung-hua 14.1.1
    p. 8. Small amounts of bonds were sold in the Red Army and within
    party organisations.
57) Doc. 120, including the appendix.
58) Ibid:, doc. 121; Hung-se Chung-hua 7.11.1932 p. 7 (from doc. 108
    and 28.11.1932 p. 7 (from doc. 12).
59) Hung-se Chung-hua 23.10.1932 p. 1.
60) Doc. 122, including the appendix.

61) Ibid.
62) Hung-se Chung-hua 28.11.1932. p. 6.
63) Ibid. 5.12.1932 p. 5.
64) See ibid. 23.11.1933 p. 3.
65) Ibid. 6.3.1933 p. 3.
66) Numerous reports on this movement are found in Hung-se Chung-hua from March 6th 1933 onward.
67) See ibid. 2.5.1933 p. 2 and 5.5.1933 p. 5.
68) Ibid. 14.5.1934 p. 3.
69) See quotation in this thesis p. 159.
70) Hung-se Chung-hua 26.7.1933 p. 1 and 16.8.1933 p. 3 (from doc. 125).
71) Ibid. 16.8.1933 p. 3 (from doc. 125); doc. 124C.
72) Doc. 124A arts. 4-5.
73) This was proposed in a resolution adopted by a conference on economic reconstruction in August 1933. (Hung-se Chung-hua 19.8.1933 p. 1).
74) See Hung-se Chung-hua 27.10.1933 p. 1 (from doc. 126).
75) Ibid. 1.2.1934 p. 2.
76) Ibid. 27.9.1933 p. 3; doc. 118.
77) Hung-se Chung-hua 14.5.1934 p. 3.
78) Doc. 118.
79) Doc. 124B.
80) Doc. 118.
81) Hung-se Chung-hua 16.2.1934 p. 1.
82) Ibid. 27.9.1933 p. 3 and 17.3.1934 p. 1; doc. 113 pp. 2 and 22.
83) Tou-cheng No. 49 p. 11 (from doc. 127). Another case of mass flight connected with forcible sale of "economic reconstruction bonds" is reported in a letter from the Central Government, printed in Hung-se Chung-hua of September 27th 1933 (p. 3).
84) Hung-se Chung-hua 8.3.1934 p. 3. See also Tou-cheng No. 49 p. 11 (from doc. 127).
85) See for example doc. 18.
86) Hung-se Chung-hua 16.2.1934 p. 1, 1.3.1934 p. 1 and 10.3.1934 p.1.
87) See doc. 118.
88) Hung-se Chung-hua 16.2.1933 p. 3; doc. 129.
89) Hung-se Chung-hua 20.4.1933 p. 3 and 8.5.1933 p. 3.
90) Doc. 130.
91) Hung-se Chung-hua 26.6.1934 p. 1, 30.6.1934 p. 1, 28.7.1934 p. 3 and 8.8.1934 p. 4. The original target was 240,000. - piculs.
92) Ibid. 26.7.1934 p. 2; Tou-cheng No. 73 p. 9 (from doc. 131).
93) Hung-se Chung-hua 24.7.1934 p. 1.; Tou-cheng No. 73 p. 9 (from doc. 131).
94) Doc. 119.
95) Hung-se Chung-hua 19.6.1934 p. 2, 26.6.1934 p. 2, 28.6.1934 p. 3, 10.7.1934 p. 3, 8.8.1934 p. 4 and 18.9.1934 p. 3. We do not know the extent to which the government paid for these articles. In any

case, it was in the circumstances of little consolation for the people
to receive soviet banknotes, which were soon to become invalid.

96) Hung-se Chung-hua 2.3.1932 p. 6, 22.2.1933 p.3, 13.3.1934 pp. 1-2 and 29.3.1934 p.3.
97) Doc. 50.
98) Hung-se Chung-hua 15.9.1933 p. 2.
99) Ibid. 20.8.1934 p. 4.
100) Doc. 115 p. 1.
101) Doc. 132 pp. 2-3.
102) Hung-se Chung-hua 16.2.1933 p. 3; doc. 129.
103) See Hung-se Chung-hua 5.7.1934 p. 2, 30.8.1934 p.4 and 11.9.19 p. 2.
104) Ibid. 19.6.1934 p. 2 and 17.7.1934 p. 3.
105) Ibid. 19.6.1934 p. 2.
106) Ibid. 28.7.1934 p. 3.

SELECTED BIBLIOGRAPHY

A. Chinese Documents

Note 1. Most of the documents are found in the Shih Sou Collection (SSC), microfilms of which can be bought from the Hoover Institution, Stanford University. These documents were collected by Kuomintang troops under the command of General Ch'en Ch'eng in 1934.

Note 2. For some of the documents I have noted that there is "no clear pagination". In these cases the pages referred to are found by counting, the first text page being taken as p. 1. The arrangement of the material does in fact make it necessary also to point out that the pages are to be counted in the order in which they are read.

1. Chung-hua su-wei-ai kung-ho-kuo hua-fen hsing-cheng ch'ü-yü chan-hsing t'iao-lieh. (Provisional Regulations of the Chinese Soviet Republic for Demarcation of Administrative Units). Adopted by the CEC at its first plenary session in November 1931, promulgated in December 1931. Reproduced by Wang Chien-min, 1965, vol. 2 pp. 328-29.

2. Chung-hua su-wei-ai kung-ho-kuo ti hsüan-chü hsi-tse. (Detailed Regulations for Elections in the Chinese Soviet Republic). Adopted by the CEC at its first plenary session in November 1931, promulgated in December 1931. SSC 008. 634/3772 c. 1/0274. Reel 10.

3. Hsüan-chü wei-yüan-hui ti kung-tso hsi-tse. (Detailed Regulations for the Work of the Election Committees). Adopted by the CEC at its first plenary session in November 1931. Printed as an appendix to doc. 2.

4. Su-wei-ai chan-hsing hsüan-chü-fa. (Provisional Law for Soviet Elections). Promulgated by the CEC on August 9th 1933. SSC. 008. 634/4424 c. 1/0276. Reel 10.

5.  Chung-hua su-wei-ai kung-ho-kuo ti-erh-tz'u ch'üan-kuo tai-piao
    ta-hui wen-hsien. (Documents of the Second National Congress of
    the Chinese Soviet Republic).
    March 1934. SSC 008. 61 029/5044/0246. Reel 16.

    The following documents of this collection have been consulted:

    A.  Ti-erh-tz'u ch'üan-kuo su-wei-ai tai-piao ta-hui hsüan-yen.
        (Declaration of the Second National Soviet Congress).
        Dated February 1st 1934. Pp. 1-8.
        (Reproduced by Hsiao Tso-liang, 1967, p. 761).

    B.  Chung-kung wu-chung ch'üan-hui chi erh-tz'u ch'üan-su ta-hui
        tang-t'uan ti chih-ling. (Instructions of the Fifth Plenum of the
        Chinese Communist Party to the Party Corps of the Second Na-
        tional Soviet Congress). Pp.9-21.
        (Reproduced by Hsiao Tso-liang, 1967, pp. 697-98).

    C.  Chung-hua su-wei-ai kung-ho-kuo chung-yang chih-hsing wei-
        yüan-hui yü jen-min wei-yüan-hui tui ti-erh-tz'u ch'üan-kuo su-
        wei-ai tai-piao ta-hui ti pao-kao.
        (Report of the Central Executive Committee and the Council of
        People's Commissars of the Chinese Soviet Republic to the Second
        National Soviet Congress). P. 22-124.
        The report was delivered by Mao Tse-tung to the congress 24-25
        January 1934.
        (Reproduced by Hsiao Tso-liang, 1967, pp. 702-28).

    D.  Kuan-yü chung-yang chih-hsing wei-yüan-hui pao-kao ti chieh-lun
        (Concluding Remarks on the Report of the Central Executive
        Committee).
        By Mao Tse-tung. Pp. 125-39.
        (Reproduced by Hsiao Tso-liang. 1967, pp. 728-31).

    E.  Kuan-yü chung-yang chih-hsing wei-yüan-hui pao-kao ti chüeh-i.
        (Resolution on the Report of the Central Executive Committee).
        Pp. 140-43.
        (Reproduced by Hsiao Tso-liang, 1967, p. 732.)

    F.  Chung-hua su-wei-ai kung-ho-kuo hsien-fa ta-kang.
        (General Principles of the Constitution of the Chinese Soviet Re-
        public). Pp.144-51.
        Approved in principle by the Second National Soviet Congress in

January 1934. (See this thesis p. 84 ). (Reproduced by Hsiao Tso-liang, 1967, pp. 733-34).

G. Chung-hua su-wei-ai kung-ho-kuo chung-yang su-wei-ai tsu-chih-fa. (Organic Law for the Central Soviet of the Chinese Soviet Republic).
Prolumgated by the CEC on February 17th 1934. Pp. 152-66.
(Reproduced by Hsiao Tso-liang, 1967, pp. 735-38).

H. Kuan-yü Hung-chün wen-t'i chüeh-i. (Resolution on the Problem of the Red Army).
Adopted by the Second National Soviet Congress in January 1934.
Pp. 167-75.
(Reproduced by Hsiao Tso-liang, 1967, pp. 739-41).

I. Kuan-yü su-wei-ai ching-chi chien-she ti chüeh-i.
(Resolution on Soviet Economic Construction).
Adopted by the Second National Soviet Congress in January 1934.
Pp. 176-87.
(Reproduced by Hsiao Tso-liang, 1967, pp. 741-44).

J. Su-wei-ai chien-she chüeh-i-an. (Resolution on Soviet Construction. )
Adopted by the Second National Soviet Congress in January 1934.
Pp. 188-98.
(Reproduced by Hsiao Tso-liang, 1967, pp. 744-46. )

6. Chung-hua su-wei-ai kung-ho-kuo ti-fang su-wei-ai chan-hsing tsu-chih-fa (ts'ao-an). (Provisional Organic Law for Local Soviets of the Chinese Soviet Republic . (Draft)).
Published by the CEC on December 12th 1933.
SSC 008. 632/4404 c. 2/0299. Reel 16.

7. Min Kan liang sheng kung-jen tai-piao ta-hui. Hsüan-chü yün-tung kung-tso chih-nan. (The Representative Congress of Workers from the Two Provinces of Fukien and Kiangsi. Guide for the Work of the Election Movement).
Undated. SSC 008. 634/7701/0275. Reel 10.

8. Su-wei-ai cheng-ch'üan. (The Soviet Political Power). Reproduced by the General Political Department of the Chinese Red Army in September 1932.
SSC 008. 63/4424-3 c. 1/0667. Reel 10. (The first of the three documents with the same title).

9. Chang Wen-t'ien and Mao Tse-tung: <u>Ch'ü hsiang su-wei-ai tsen-yang kung-tso.</u> (How the Soviets of the District and the <u>Hsiang</u> Should Work).
Published by the Council of People's Commissars in April 1934.
SSC 008.63/1171/0270. Reel 10.

    A. Mao Tse-tung: <u>Hsiang su-wei-ai tsen-yang kung-tso</u>? (How Should the <u>Hsiang</u> Soviet Work?). Pp. 1-39.

    B. Chang Wen-t'ien: <u>Ch'ü su-wei-ai tsen-yang kung-tso</u>? (How Shou the District Soviet Work?) Pp. 41-63.

10. <u>Kuan-yü ch'üan-kuo su-wei-ai tai-piao ta-hui ti wen-ta.</u>
(Questions and Answers Concerning the National Soviet Congress).
Reproduced by the soviet government of Hsingkuo County, probably in June 1931.
SSC 008.631/8064/0481. Reel 10. No clear pagination.

11. <u>Kung-nung chien-ch'a-pu tsu-chih t'iao-lieh.</u> (Regulations for the Organisation of Departments of the Workers' and Peasants' Inspection).
Published by the Central Government.
SSC 008.632/1054/0925. Reel 10.

The title-page says that the regulations were adopted by the First National Soviet Congress in November 1931. Their adoption by the congress is, however, not mentioned in doc. 66.

12. <u>Chianghsi sheng-su pao-kao.</u> (Report of the Provincial Soviet of Kiangsi).
<u>Hung-se Chung-hua</u> November 21st 1932 pp. 5-6 and November 28th 1932 pp. 7-8.

13. <u>Minkan sheng ko-ming wei-yüan-hui kuan-yü chao-chi ti-i-tz'u ch'üan-sheng kung-nung-ping tai-piao ta-hui chüeh-i.</u>
(Resolution of the Revolutionary Committee of Minkan Province Concerning the Convening of the First Provincial Representative Congress of Workers, Peasants and Soldiers).
June 1933. SSC 008.631/7709/7262. Reel 10. No clear pagination.

14. <u>Kuan-yü chin-chi tung-yüan ti pao-kao.</u> (Report on Urgent Mobilisation).

The report was delivered by Mao Tse-tung at the Second National
Soviet Congress on January 29th 1934.
Hung-se Chung-hua February 1st 1934 p. 1.
(Reproduced by Hsiao Tso-liang, 1967, p. 760).

15. Chung-yang shen-chi wei-yüan-hui shen-ho Yüehkan sheng san-yüeh-
fen yü-suan ti tsung-chieh. Chi Yüehkan sheng-su chu-hsi-t'uan i-
feng hsin. (A Summary of the Central Audit Committee's Investigation
of the March Budget of Yüehkan Province. A Letter to the Presidium
of the Provincial Soviet of Yüehkan).
Hung-se Chung-hua March 22nd 1934 p. 3.

16. Liang-p'ing (identical with Wu Liang-p'ing):
Tsen-yang shih su-wei-ai ch'eng-wei keng yu-li ti tung-yüan ch'ün-
chung ti cheng-ch'üan chi-kuan. (How to Make the Soviets Into Political Power Organs for Still More Effective Mobilisation of the Masses).
Tou-cheng No. 44 (January 26th 1934) pp. 8-12.

17. Hsiang Ying: Yütu chien-chü ti ch'ing-hsing ho ching-kuo.
(The Circumstances and the Proceedings of the Prosecutions in
Yütu).
Hung-se Chung-hua March 29th 1934 pp. 5-8.

18. Jen-min wei-yüan-hui wei Want'ai ch'ün-chung t'ao-p'ao wen-t'i
chi Want'ai hsien-su chu-hsi-t'uan ti chih-shih-hsin.
(A Directive Letter from the Council of People's Commissars to the
Presidium of the County Soviet of Want'ai Regarding the Problem
of Mass Flight from Want'ai. )
Hung-se Chung-hua April 10th 1934 pp. 2-3. The letter is dated
April 3rd 1934.

19. Lo Fu (alias of Chang Wen-t'ien): Erh-tz'u su-ta-hui ti kai-hsüan
yün-tung yü su-wei-ai ti te-mo-k'o-la-hsi. (The Election Movement
for the Second National Soviet Congress and the Soviet Democracy).
Tou-cheng No. 21 (August 12th 1933) pp. 9-15. The article is dated
August 1st 1933.

20. Liang-p'ing (identical with Wu Liang-p'ing): Tsai hsin-ti hsing-shih
hsia ch'e-ti chuan-pien Fuchien sheng-su ti kung-tso. (Thoroughly
Change the Work of the Provincial Soviet of Fukien Under the New
Circumstances).
Hung-se Chung-hua March 3rd 1934 p. 3 and March 6th 1934 p. 3. The
article is dated February 9th 1934.

21. <u>Chianghsi kung-nung-ping su-wei-ai ti-i-tz'u ch'üan-sheng ta-hui</u>
    <u>tui su-wei-ai kung-tso pao-kao ti chüeh-i.</u>
    (Resolution of the First Congress of the Workers', Peasants' and
    Soldiers' Soviet of Kiangsi Province Concerning the Report on
    Soviet Work).
    May 6th 1932. SSC 008. 631/3442/ 0286. Reel 10.

22. <u>Chung-yang chih-hsing wei-yüan-hui kuan-yü ch'ung-hsin hua-fen</u>
    <u>hsing-cheng ch'ü-yü ti chüeh-i.</u> (Resolution of the Central Executive
    Committee Regarding Re-Demarcation of Administrative Areas).
    Dated July 21st 1933.
    <u>Hung-se Chung-hua</u> August 1st 1933 p. 3.

23. Jan-chih (identical with Hsieh Jan-chih): <u>Mo-fan ti Shangshe ch'ü-</u>
    <u>su ti kung-tso.</u> (The Work of the Model District Soviet of Shangshe).
    <u>Hung-se Chung-hua</u> April 21st 1934 p. 3.

24. <u>Chung-hua su-wei-ai kung-ho-kuo chung-yang chih-hsing wei-yüan-</u>
    <u>hui hsün-ling (ti erh-shih-erh hao). Kuan-yü tz'u tz'u hsüan-chü</u>
    <u>yün-tung ti chih-shih.</u> (Instruction of the Central Executive Committee
    of the Chinese Soviet Republic (No. 22). A Directive on the Present
    Election Movement). August 9th 1933. SSC 008. 634/2133/0319. Reel
    10. No clear pagination.

25. <u>Chung-yang tui su-ch'ü chih-shih-hsin.</u> (A Directive Letter from the
    Centre to the Soviet Areas). Dated September 1st 1931. SSC 008. 222/
    5053/0022. Reel 14.
    (Reproduced by Hsiao Tso-liang, 1967, pp. 382-89).

26. <u>Chung-yang-chü chi ko-chi tang-pu ti hsin. Kuan-yü fan AB t'uan</u>
    <u>chi ch'i-t'a fan-ko-ming p'ai-pieh ti tou-cheng wen-t'i.</u> (A Letter
    from the Central Bureau to Party Branches of All Levels. On the
    Problems of the Struggle Against the AB League and Other Cate-
    gories of Counter-Revolutionaries). Reprinted by the Political De-
    partment of the Second Division of the Third Army Corps of the
    Chinese Workers' and Peasants' Red Army. The reprint is dated
    January 4th 1932. SSC 008. 252/7148/0035. Reel 4. No clear pagina-
    tion.

27. <u>Lin-shih tsui-kao fa-t'ing p'an-chüeh-shu. Ti-i hao.</u>
    (The Provisional Supreme Court's Record of Sentences. No. 1).
    The trial was held on February 25th 1932.
    <u>Hung-se Chung-hua</u> March 2nd 1932 p. 7.

28. Chianghsi sheng su-wei-ai ts'ai-p'an-pu p'an-chüeh-shu. Ti-i hao.
(Record of Sentences of the Judicial Department of the Provincial
Soviet of Kiangsi. No. 1).
The trial was held on April 3rd 1932.
Hung-se Chung-hua April 21st 1932 pp. 7-8.

29. Chianghsi sheng su-wei-ai ts'ai-p'an-pu p'an-chüeh-shu. Ti-erh
hao. (Record of Sentences of the Judicial Department of the Provincial Soviet of Kiangsi. No. 2.)
The trial was held on April 3rd 1932.
Hung-se Chung-hua April 21st 1932 p. 8.

30. Min-hsi su-wei-ai cheng-fu ts'ai-p'an-pu p'an-chüeh-shu. Ti-erh
hao. (Record of Sentences of the Judicial Department of the Soviet
Government of Western Fukien. No. 2).
The trial was held 12-13 February 1932.
Hung-se Chung-hua June 23rd 1932 pp. 6-7.

31. Ch'a-t'ien yün-tung ti kai-k'uang. (The General Situation of the
Land Investigation Movement).
Published by the Kiangsi Provincial Committee of the Chinese
Communist Party in September 1933.
SSC 008.741026/4463/1161. Reel 17. No clear pagination.

32. Lin-shih tsui-kao fa-t'ing – P'an-chüeh-shu. Ti-san hao.
(The Provisional Supreme Court - Record of Sentences. No. 3).
The trial was held on February 26th 1932.
Hung-se Chung-hua March 2nd 1932 p. 8.

33. Su-fan wen-t'i t'i-kang. (Outline of the Problem of Exterminating
the Counter-Revolutionaries).
Published by the State Political Security Bureau. Reprinted by the
Department of Education of the Provincial Soviet of Kiangsi in
August 1933.
SSC 008.237/5077/0289. Reel 14. No clear pagination.

34. Ti-fang su-wei-ai cheng-fu chan-hsing tsu-chih t'iao-lieh.
(Provisional Regulations for the Organisation of Local Soviet Govern-
ment).
Adopted by the Central Executive Committee in November 1931.
Printed in Ch'ih-fei fan-tung wen-chien hui-pien pp. 703-20.

35. Liang-shih-pu teng chi-kuan kuan-yü liang-shih wen-t'i ti chih-shih.

(Directives of the Commissariat for Food and Other Organs Con-
cerning the Food Problem).
SSC 008.756/9387/0241. Reel 12. No clear pagination.
Document in this collection which has been consulted:

A. Chung-hua su-wei-ai kung-ho-kuo liang-shih jen-min wei-yüan-
pu kuan-yü liang-shih t'u-chi yün-tung ti chih-shih. Ti-san hao.
(Directive of the People's Commissariat for Food of the Chinese
Soviet Republic Regarding the Surprise Attack Movement for
Food Supply. No. 3). February 20th 1934.

36. Chung-yang szu-fa jen-min wei-yüan-pu wu-ko yüeh kung-tso chi-
hua. (I-chiu san-san, pa yüeh - shih-erh yüeh).
(A Five Months Working Plan for the People's Commissariat of
Justice. (August-December 1933)).
July 30th 1933. SSC 008.548/1027/0760. Reel 6.
No clear pagination.

37. Chung-hua su-wei-ai kung-ho-kuo chung-yang chih-hsing wei-yüan-
hui pu-kao. Ti-i hao. Kuan-yü i-ch'üan ta-hui hsüan-chü chung-yang
wei-yüan yü jen-min wei-yüan. (Proclamation of the Central Executive Committee of the Chinese Soviet Republic. No. 1. On the Election by the First National Soviet Congress of the Members of the Central Executive Committee and of the Council of People's Commissars).
December 1st 1931. SSC (No call numbers visible on the microfilm).
Reel 16.
(Reproduced by Hsiao Tso-liang, 1967, p. 431.)

38. Chung-hua su-wei-ai kung-ho-kuo chung-yang chih-hsing wei-yüan-
hui pu-kao. Ti-i hao. Kuan-yü erh-ch'üan ta-hui hsüan-chü chung-
yang chih-hsing wei-yüan yü jen-min wei-yüan. (Proclamation of
the Central Executive Committee of the Chinese Soviet Republic. No.
1. On the Election by the Second National Soviet Congress of the
Members of the Central Executive Committee and of the Council of
People's Commissars).
February 5th 1934. SSC (no call numbers visible on the microfilm).
Reel 16.
(Reproduced by Hsiao Tso-liang, 1967, p. 762).

39. Szu-fa jen-min wei-yüan-pu i nien lai kung-tso. (The Work of the
People's Commissariat of Justice for One Year.)
The report is dated October 24th 1932.
Hung-se Chung-hua November 7th 1932 pp. 7-8.

40.  Chung-hua su-wei-ai kung-ho-kuo chung-yang chih-hsing wei-yüan-
     hui hsün-ling. Ti-liu hao. (Instruction of the Central Executive
     Committee of the Chinese Soviet Republic. No. 6.)
     The instruction is dated December 13th 1931.
     Hung-se Chung-hua December 28th 1931 pp. 1-2.

41.  Tui ts'ai-p'an chi-kuan ti kung-tso chih-shih. (Directive for the
     Work of the Judicial Organs).
     Published by the People's Commissariat of Justice.
     Signed May 30th 1933, published June 1933.
     SSC 008. 548/3449/0759. Reel 6.

42.  Fuchien sheng-su pao-kao. (Report of the Provincial Soviet of
     Fukien).
     Hung-se Chung-hua December 5th 1932 pp. 7-8.

43.  Chianghsi sheng su-wei-ai cheng-fu wu chih shih liu-ko yüeh kung-
     tso pao-kao kang-yao. (Outline of the Report of the Soviet Govern-
     ment of Kiangsi Province on Its Work During the Six Months from
     May to October).
     Published by the Soviet Government of Kiangsi Province on November
     2nd 1932.
     SSC 008. 61026/3119/0269. Reel 10. No clear pagination.

44.  Chung-hua su-wei-ai kung-ho-kuo chün-shih ts'ai-p'an-so chan-
     hsing tsu-chih t'iao-lieh. (Provisional Regulations for the Organisa-
     tion of the Military Judicial Offices of the Chinese Soviet Republic).
     Published by the Central Executive Committee of the Chinese Soviet
     Republic on February 1st 1932.
     SSC 008. 5525/3754/0553. Reel 7.

45.  Liang Po-t'ai: Ts'ai-p'an chi-kuan ti chu-yao kung-tso fang-hsiang.
     Chen-ya fan-ko-ming. (The Main Working Line of the Judicial Organs.
     Suppress the Counter-Revolution). Hung-se Chung-hua March 1st
     1934 p. 3.

46.  Su-wei-ai fa-tien. Ti-erh chi. (The Soviet Code of Laws. The Second
     Collection).
     July 1934. SSC 008. 542/4424 v. 2/1146. Reel 16.

The following documents of this collection have been consulted:

A.  Chung-hua su-wei-ai kung-ho-kuo szu-fa ch'eng-hsü.
    (The Judicial Procedure of the Chinese Soviet Republic).
    Promulgated by the CEC on April 8th 1934. Pp. 55-59.

B. Chung-hua su-wei-ai kung-ho-kuo ch'eng-chih fan-ko-ming
   t'iao-lieh. (Regulations of the Chinese Soviet Republic for Punish
   ment of Counter-Revolutionaries). Promulgated by the CEC on
   April 8th 1934. Pp. 61-69.

C. Wei-fan lao-tung fa-ling ch'eng-fa t'iao-lieh.
   (Regulations of Punishment for Violation of Laws and Ordinances
   on Labour).
   Promulgated by the CEC on October 15th 1933. Pp. 71-73.

D. Chung-hua su-wei-ai kung-ho-kuo chung-yang chih-hsing wei-
   yüan-hui ming-ling. Ti erh-shih-wu hao. Kuan-yü Hung-chün
   t'ao-p'ao wen-t'i. (Decree of the Central Executive Committee
   of the Chinese Soviet Republic. No. 25. On the Problem of Flight
   from the Red Army).
   December 15th 1933. Pp. 75-76.

E. Chung-hua su-wei-ai kung-ho-kuo chung-yang chih-hsing wei-
   yüan-hui ming-ling. Ti erh-shih-liu hao. (Decree of the Central
   Executive Committee of the Chinese Soviet Republic. No. 26).
   December 15th 1933. Pp. 77-78.

47. Chung-yang chih-hsing wei-yüan-hui tui-yü lin-shih tsui-kao fa-t'ing
    shen-li AB t'uan kai-tsu-p'ai chün-shih-fan teng yao-fan ti p'an-
    chüeh-shu ti chüeh-i-an. (Resolution of the Central Executive Com-
    mittee on the Records of Sentences from the Trials by the Provision
    Supreme Court of Principal Criminals Among Members of the AB
    League, Reorganisationists and War Criminals.)
    Hung-se Chung-hua March 2nd 1932 p. 7.

48. Lo Fu (alias of Chang Wen-t'ien): Wu-ch'ing ti ch'ü tui-fu wo-men
    ti chieh-chi ti-jen. (Deal without Mercy with Our Class Enemies).
    The article is dated February 17th 1934.
    Tou-cheng No. 49 (March 2nd 1934) pp. 3-8.

49. Chung-hua su-wei-ai kung-ho-kuo hsien-fa ta-kang. (General Prin-
    ciples of the Constitution of the Chinese Soviet Republic).
    Approved by the First National Soviet Congress in November 1931.
    Reprinted in Su-wei-ai Chungkuo (Soviet China), Moscow 1933.
    pp. 37-44.

50. Chung-yang cheng-fu kuan-yü cheng-tun ts'ai-cheng-pu kung-tso ti
    hsün-ling. (Instruction of the Central Government on Reforming the
    Work of the Financial Departments).
    Dated August 25th 1933.
    Hung-se Chung-hua September 3rd 1933 p. 2.

51.  Chang Wen-t'ien: Tui-yü wo-men ti chieh-chi ti-jen, chih-yu ch'ou-hen, mei-yu k'uan-shu! (Toward Our Class Enemies there is only Hatred and no Pardon!) Editorial in Hung-se Chung-hua of May 25th 1934 pp. 1-2. The editorial is dated May 22nd 1934.

52.  Chang Wen-t'ien: Shih chien-chüeh ti chen-ya fan-ko-ming hai-shih tsai fan-ko-ming ch'ien-mien ti k'uang-luan? (Should We Resolutely Suppress the Counter-Revolutionaries, or Should We Get Mad and Confused in Face of Them?) Editorial in Hung-se Chung-hua of June 28th 1934 pp. 1-2. The editorial is dated June 25th 1934. (Translated by Hsiao Tso-liang, 1969, pp. 285-90).

53.  Chang Wen-t'ien: Fan-tui hsiao tzu-ch'an chieh-chi ti chi-tso chu-i. (Oppose the Extreme Leftism of the Petty Bourgeoisie). The article is dated June 24th 1934. Tou-cheng No. 67 (July 10th 1934) pp. 2-6.

54.  Lin-shih tsui-kao fa-t'ing hsün-ling. Ti-erh hao. (Instruction of the Provisional Supreme Court. No. 2). The instruction is dated April 20th 1032. Hung-se Chung-hua April 21st 1932 p. 7.

55.  Chung-hua su-wei-ai kung-ho-kuo kuo-chia cheng-chih pao-wei-chü tsu-chih kang-yao. (General Principles for the Organisation of the State Political Security Bureau of the Chinese Soviet Republic). Issued by the CEC in late 1931. Reproduced by Wang Chien-min, 1965, vol. 2 pp. 426-428.

56.  Shao-tui tu-pen. Ti-i ts'e. (Reader of the Young Vanguard. Vol. 1). Published by the Central Office of the Young Vanguard in April 1934. SSC 008.5542/9070 v. 1 c.2/0675. Reel 9.

57.  Lin-shih tsui-kao fa-t'ing - P'an-chüeh-shu. Ti-erh hao. (The Provisional Supreme Court - Record of Sentences. No. 2). The trial was held 25-26 February 1932. Hung-se Chung-hua March 2nd 1932 pp. 7-8.

58.  Chung-hua su-wei-ai kung-ho-kuo lin-shih chung-yang cheng-fu jen-min wei-yüan-hui ming-ling. Ti-wu hao. (Decree of the Council of People's Commissars of the Provisional Central Government of the Chinese Soviet Republic. No. 5).

The decree is dated February 9th 1934.
Hung-se Chung-hua February 20th 1934 p. 3.

59.  Mao Tse-tung: Ch'a-t'ien yün-tung ti ch'u-pu tsung-chieh.
     (Preliminary Summary on the Land Investigation Movement).
     Tou-cheng No. 24 (August 29th 1933) pp. 4-12.

60.  Ch'a-t'ien yün-tung chih-nan. (Guide to the Land Investigation
     Movement).
     Published by the Central Government in 1933.
     SSC 008. 743/4063-3 c. 1/1151. Reel 17.

     A.  Chung-yang-chü kuan-yü Ch'a-t'ien yün-tung ti chüeh-i.
         (Resolution of the Central Bureau on the Land Investigation
         Movement).
         June 2nd 1933. Pp. 1-5.

     B.  Chung-yang cheng-fu kuan-yü Ch'a-t'ien yün-tung ti hsün-ling.
         (Instruction of the Central Government on the Land Investigation
         Movement).
         June 1st 1933. Pp. 7-10.
         The Instruction was issued by the Council of People's Commissa
         (see p. 7).
         (Translated by Hsiao Tso-liang, 1969, pp. 198-202).

     C.  Pa-hsien ch'ü i-shang su-wei-ai fu-tse jen-yüan Ch'a-t'ien
         yün-tung ta-hui so t'ung-kuo ti chieh-lun. (Conclusions Reached
         by the Conference of Soviet Personnel in Responsible Positions
         at the District Level and Above from Eight Counties on the Land
         Investigation Movement). P. 11-26.
         Also in Hung-se Chung-hua of June 29th 1933 pp. 5-7. Translate
         by Hsiao Tso-liang, 1969, pp. 215-30. Hsiao Tso-liang says tha
         the document probably is a statement originally made by Mao Ts
         tung.

         The conference was held 17-21 June 1933.

     D.  Tsen-yang fen-hsi chieh-chi. (How to Differentiate the Classes).
         Pp. 27-30.
         (Also listed as doc. 84).

     E.  Pa-hsien p'in-nung-t'uan tai-piao Ch'a-t'ien yün-tung ta-hui
         ti chüeh-i. (Resolution Adopted by the Conference on the Land

Investigation Movement of Representatives of the Poor Peasant Unions of Eight Counties). Pp. 31-33.

The conference was held from June 25th to July 1st 1933.

F. P'in-nung-t'uan tsu-chih yü kung-tso ta-kang. (General Principles for the Organisation and the Work of the Poor Peasant Unions).
Issued by the Central Government on July 15th 1933. Pp. 35-40.

G. Wei  Ch'a-t'ien yün-tung chi Juichin Huangpo ch'ü-su ti i-feng hsin. (A Letter on the Land Investigation Movement to the Soviet of Huangpo District in Juichin). Pp. 41-47.
The letter was sent by the People's Commissariat for Land, and is dated July 13th 1933.

H. Hsien ch'ü hsiang san-chi ch'a-t'ien wei-yüan-hui ti tsu-chih yü jen-wu. (Organisation and Tasks of the Land Investigation Committees on the County, District and Hsiang Levels). Undated. P. 49.

I. Ch'a-t'ien yün-tung ti k'ou-hao piao-yü. (Slogans and Watchwords for the Land Investigation Movement). Undated. Pp. 51-54.

51. T'aching ch'ü ti chuan-pien. (The Transformation of T'aching District).
Published by the Commissariat of the Workers' and Peasants' Inspection in November 1933.
SSC 008.743/6237/0296. Reel 11. No clear pagination.

52. Chung-hua su-wei-ai kung-ho-kuo ch'eng-chih fan-ko-ming t'iao-lieh. (Regulations of the Chinese Soviet Republic for the Punishment of Counter-Revolutionaries).
Issued by the CEC on March 7th 1934.
SSC 008.542/2837/0281. Reel 6. No clear pagination.

This was a draft for the document listed as No. 46B.

53. Chianghsi sheng Ihuang hsien-su ts'ai-p'an-pu fa-t'ing p'an-chüeh-shu. Ti-wu hao. (Record of Sentences of the Court of the Judicial Department of the Ihuang County Soviet in the Province of Kiangsi. No. 5).

The trial was held on September 6th 1933.
SSC 008.548/3047/0867. Reel 6. No clear pagination.

64.  Chianghsi sheng Want'ai hsien su-wei-ai cheng-fu ts.'ai-p'an-pu
fa-t'ing. Ti san-shih-i hao p'an-chüeh-shu. (The Court of the
Judicial Department of the Soviet Government of Want'ai County
in the Province of Kiangsi. Record of Sentences, No. 31).
Dated September 1st 1933. The trial was held.on August 16th 1933.
SSC 008.548/4457/0917. Reel 6. No clear pagination.

65.  Chianghsi ti chung-yang su-ch'ü. (The Central Soviet Area in
Kiangsi).
Dated September 3rd, 1931.
Reproduced by Hsiao Tso-liang, 1967, pp. 422–429.

66.  Chung-hua su-wei-ai tai-piao ta-hui chi chung-kung chung-yang tie
(Telegram from the Chinese Soviet Congress to the Centre of the
Chinese Communist Party).
Dated November 18th 1931. (See Hsiao Tso-liang, 1961, p. 172).
Signed by the presidium of the congress.
Reproduced by Hsiao Tso-liang, 1967, p. 431.

67.  Kuan-yü Chung-kuo ching-nei shao-shu min-tsu wen-t'i ti chüeh-i
(Resolution on the Problem of National Minorities within China).
Printed in Su-wei-ai Chung-kuo, Moscow 1933, pp. 199-204.
According to this source the resolution was adopted by the First
National Soviet Congress in November 1931.

68.  Chung-hua su-wei-ai kung-ho-kuo cheng-kang. (The Political
Programme of the Chinese Soviet Republic).
Adopted by the First National Soviet Congress in November 1931.
Reproduced by Hsiao Tso-liang, 1967, p. 432. (See also Hsiao
Tso-liang, 1961, pp. 174-175.)

69.  Szu Mei (alias of Chang Wen-t'ien): Ch'ing-chu su-wei-ai ti-i-tz'
ch'üan-kuo tai-piao ta-hui. (Celebrate the First National Soviet
Congress).
Printed in Hung-ch'i chou-pao, October 30th 1931.
Reproduced by Hsiao Tso-liang, 1967, pp. 429-30.

70.  Chung-kuo kung-ch'an-tang chung-yang wei-yüan-hui t'i-ch'u ch'
kuo su-wei-ai ti-i-tz'u tai-piao ta-hui ts'ao-an. (Draft Resolutio
Introduced by the Central Committee of the Chinese Communist P

to the First National Soviet Congress).
Reprinted by the Political Department, Third Army Corps,
First Route Army, Chinese Worker' and Peasants' Red Army.
Undated. SSC 008. 631/8064-2/0267. Reel 16.

A. Hung-chün wen-t'i chüeh-i-an (ts'ao-an). (Resolution on the
   Problem of the Red Army (Draft)).
   Undated. Pp. 1-7.
   (Reproduced by Hsiao Tso-liang, 1967, pp. 435-36).

B. T'u-ti-fa ts'ao-an. (Draft Land Law).
   Undated. Pp. 9-14.
   (Reproduced by Hsiao Tso-liang, 1967, pp. 435-36).

C. Lao-tung-fa ts'ao-an. (Draft Labour Law).
   Undated. Pp. 15-25.
   (Reproduced by Hsiao Tso-liang, 1967, pp. 435-36).

D. Ching-chi cheng-ts'e ts'ao-an. (Draft Resolution on Economic
   Policies).
   Undated. Pp. 27-30.
   (Reproduced by Hsiao Tso-liang, 1967, pp. 447-48).

E. Kung-nung chien-ch'a-ch'u ti tsu-chih hsi-t'ung yü jen-wu (ts'ao-
   an). (The Organisational System and the Tasks of the Workers'
   and Peasants' Inspectorate. (Draft)).
   Undated. Pp. 31-36.
   (Reproduced by Hsiao Tso-liang, 1967, pp. 448-449.)

71. Chung-hua su-wei-ai kung-ho-kuo t'u-ti-fa. (Land Law of the Chinese
    Soviet Republic).
    Adopted by the First National Soviet Congress in November 1931.
    Promulgated on December 1st 1931.
    SSC. Reel 18. No call numbers visible on the microfilm.
    (Reproduced by Hsiao Tso-liang, 1967, p. 437; translated by Hsiao
    Tso-liang, 1969, pp. 186-90).

72. Lao-tung-fa. (The Labour Law).
    Adopted by the First National Soviet Congress in November 1931.
    Reproduced by Hsiao Tso-liang, 1967, pp. 440-443.

73. Chung-hua su-wei-ai kung-ho-kuo lin-shih chung-yang cheng-fu pan-
    pu Hung-chün wen-t'i chüeh-i-an yü Hung-chün fu-hsü t'iao-lieh.

(Resolution on the Problem of the Red Army, and Regulations for Pensions to Red Army Men. Promulgated by the Provisional Central Government of the Chinese Soviet Republic).
No date visible on the microfilm.
SSC 008. 5526/2137-2/0547. Reel 16.

A. <u>Hung-chün wen-t'i chüeh-i-an.</u> (Resolution on the Problem of the Red Army).
Adopted by the First National Soviet Congress in November 1931
Pp. 1-8.
(Reproduced by Hsiao Tso-liang, 1967, pp. 445-447).

74. <u>Kuan-yü ching-chi cheng-ts'e ti chüeh-i-an.</u> (Resolution on Econom Policies).
Adopted by the First National Soviet Congress.
Printed in <u>Su-wei-ai Chung-kuo,</u> Moscow 1933, pp. 147-54.

75. <u>Ch'üan-su ta-hui kuan-yü lao-tung-fa pao-kao.</u> (Report at the Natio Soviet Congress on the Labour Law).
Published by the National Labour Federation's Executive Bureau fo the Soviet Areas.
The report was delivered by Hsiang Ying at the First National Sovi Congress in November 1931.
SSC 008. 786/9923/0931. Reel 12.

76. <u>Su-ch'ü tang ti-i-tz'u tai-piao ta-hui t'ung-kuo cheng-chih chüeh-i an.</u> (Political Resolution Adopted by the First Party Conference of the (Central) Soviet Area).
Published by the Central Bureau for the Soviet Areas in November 1931.
SSC. 008. 235/1833 c. 1/0295. Reel 15.
(Reproduced by Hsiao Tso-liang, 1967, pp. 391-96).

77. <u>Su-ch'ü tang ti-i-tz'u tai-piao ta-hui t'ung-kuo tang ti chien-she wen-t'i chüeh-i-an.</u> (Resolution on the Question of Party Recon-struction. Adopted by the First Party Conference of the (Central) Soviet Area).
Published by the Central Bureau for the Soviet Areas in November 1931.
SSC. 008. 235/9021/0027. Reel 15.
(Reproduced by Hsiao Tso-liang, 1967, pp. 397-404).

78. Kung-ch'an kuo-chi chih-wei chu-hsi-t'uan chi Chung-kuo kung-
    ch'an-tang ti hsin. (Letter from the Presidium of the Executive
    Committee of the Communist International to the Chinese Communist
    Party).
    Dated July 1931.
    (Reproduced by Hsiao Tso-liang, 1967, pp. 366-73).

79. Chung-yang cheng-fu kuan-yü t'u-ti chou-cheng chung i-hsieh wen-
    t'i ti chüeh-ting. (Decisions of the Central Government on Some
    Problems of the Land Struggle).
    Adopted by the Council of People's Commissars on October 10th 1933.
    SSC 008.743/4047/1166. Reel 17.
    (Translated by Hsiao Tso-liang, 1969, pp. 257-82).

80. Chung-hua su-wei-ai kung-ho-kuo chung-yang jen-min wei-yüan-
    hui hsün-ling ti shih-ch'i hao. Kuan-yü chiao-yü kung-tso. (Instruction
    No. 17 of the Central Council of People's Commissars of the Chinese
    Soviet Republic. On Educational Work).
    Dated September 15th 1933.
    SSC 008.431 /4801/0451. Reel 5.

81. Chung-hua su-wei-ai kung-ho-kuo ching-chi cheng-ts'e.
    (The Economic Policies of the Chinese Soviet Republic).
    December 1st 1931. SSC 008/655/2131-2/0212. Reel 11.
    Document in this collection which has been consulted:

    A. Chung-hua su-wei-ai kung-ho-kuo chan-hsing shui-tse.
       (Provisional Tax Regulations of the Chinese Soviet Republic).
       Adopted by the CEC at its first plenary session on November
       28th 1931. Pp. 7-16.

82. Lin-shih chung-yang cheng-fu pan-pu yu-kuan ts'ai-cheng fa-ling.
    (Regulations on Finances Promulgated by the Provisional Central
    Government).
    Published by the People's Commissariat of Finances.
    Undated. SSC 008.662/6413/0224. Reel 10.

    A. Hsiu-cheng chan-hsing shui-tse. (Revision of the Provisional Tax
       Regulations).
       Promulgated by the CEC on July 15th 1932. Pp. 1-7.

    B. Tien-fang mo-shou ho tsu-chieh t'iao-lieh.
       (Regulations for Confiscation and Renting of Shops).
       Issued by the Commissariat of Finances in August 1932. Pp. 9-13.

C. Shang-yeh so-te-shui cheng-shou hsi-tse. (Detailed Regulations for the Collection of Income Tax on Trade). Undated. Pp. 23-28.

83. Nung-yeh-shui chan-hsing shui-tse. (Provisional Regulations for the Agricultural Tax).
Promulgated by the CEC on September 18th 1933.
SSC 008. 663/5532-2/0099. Reel 11. No clear pagination.
Appendix: Nung-yeh-shui shui-lü-piao. (Table of the Rates of the Agricultural Tax)

84. Tsen-yang fen-hsi chieh-chi. (How to Differentiate the Classes). Hung-se Chung-hua June 29th 1933, p. 8. Also included in doc. 60(D). (Translated by Hsiao Tso-liang, 1969, pp. 254-57).

The document was composed by Mao Tse-tung, and in a revised form it is included in the official edition of Mao's Selected Works. (Mao Tse-tung hsüan-chi, Peking 1958, vol. 1 pp. 121-24). It was adopted by the conference of soviet cadres from eight counties, held 17-21 June 1933. (Doc. 60C p. 15). It was approved by the Council of People's Commissars on October 10th 1933. (Doc. 79, the second preamble).

85. Lo Fu (alias of Chang Wen-t'ien): Su-wei-ai cheng-ch'üan hsia ti chieh-chi tou-cheng. (The Class Struggle under the Soviet Power). Tou-cheng No. 15 (June 15th 1933) pp. 9-14.
The article is dated May 26th 1933. Only the last part of it is available.

86. Lo Fu (alias of Chang Wen-t'ien): Lun nung-ts'un chung ti chieh-chi tou-cheng. Ta-fu Li t'ung-chih ti hsin. (On the Class Struggle in the Countryside. A Letter of Reply to Comrade Li). Tou-cheng No. 20 (August 5th 1933) p. 16, continued in ibid. No. 21 (August 12th 1933) pp. 15-16.
The letter is dated July 11th 1933.

87. T'u-ti fa. (Land Law).
Promulgated by the Chinese Revolutionary Military Committee. (Reproduced by Hsiao Tso-liang, 1967, pp. 15-17; translated by Hsiao Tso-liang, 1969, pp. 130-35).
This land law probably dates from 1930.

88. T'u-ti chan-hsing-fa. (Provisional Land Law). Reproduced by Hsiao

Tso-liang, 1967, p. 30; translated by Hsiao Tso-liang, 1969, pp. 127-30.
This land law was adopted by the Li Li-san-sponsored National Conference of Delegates from the Soviet Areas in May 1930.

89. Ch'en Shao-yü: Wei Chung-kung keng-chia pu-erh-se-wei-k'o-hua erh tou-cheng. (Struggle for the More Complete Bolshevisation of the Chinese Communist Party).
Third edition, Yenan 1940.
Reproduced by Hsiao Tso-liang, 1967, pp. 499-609.

90. Ch'ih-fei wen-chien hui-pien. (A Collection of Red Bandit Documents). Published by the Fourth and later the Second Department, Nanchang Headquarters.
July 1933 - October 1934. Vols. 1, 7, 8, 10 and 11.
SSC. Reels 20-21.
The following documents of this collection have been consulted:

A. Chianghsi sheng su-wei-ai cheng-fu tui-yü mo-shou ho fen-p'ei t'u-ti ti t'iao-lieh. (Regulations of the Soviet Government of Kiangsi Province for the Confiscation and Redistribution of Land). Approved by the Provisional Central Government.
Vol. 1 pp. 17-27.

The date of the document is here given as December 1st 1932. However, Hsiao Tso-liang has found that it existed at least by April 1932. (Hsiao Tso-liang, 1969, p. 58). The correct date of the document may possibly be December 1st 1931.
(Translated by Hsiao Tso-liang, 1969, pp. 191-98).

B. Ts'ai-cheng-pu chan-hsing tsu-chih kang-yao.
(Provisional Principles for the Organisation of the Financial Departments).
Adopted by the Council of People's Commissars at its 22nd ordinary meeting.
Vol. 2 pp. 7-12.
Note: We know that the Council of People's Commissars held its 20th ordinary meeting on July 30th 1932 (Hung-se Chung-hua August 4th 1932 p. 4), and its 25th ordinary meeting on September 30th 1932 (Hung-se Chung-hua October 16th 1932 p. 8).

C. T'u-ti-shui cheng-shou hsi-tse. (Detailed Regulations for the Collection of Land Tax).

The land tax rates for Kiangsi and Fukien are appended.
Undated. Vol. 2 pp. 52-60.

  D. Shan-lin-shui cheng-shou hsi-tse. (Detailed Regulations for the
     Collection of Tax on Hills and Woodlands).
     Undated. Vol. 2 pp. 60-72.

91. Posheng hsien su-wei-ai ti-erh tz'u tai-piao ta-hui ko-chung chüeh-
    i-an. (Various Resolutions of the Second Representative Congress
    of the Posheng County Soviet). March 1933. SSC 008.631/4327/0554.
    Reel 10.

92. Mao Tse-tung: Ch'a-t'ien yün-tung shih kuang-ta ch'ü-yü nei ti
    chung-hsin chung-ta jen-wu. (The Land Investigation Movement is
    the Great and Central Task in Vast Areas).
    Hung-se Chung-hua June 17th 1933 (on p. 3 the date June 14th 1933
    is given), p. 3.
    (Translated by Hsiao Tso-liang, 1969, pp. 202-05).

93. Chung-hua su-wei-ai kung-ho-kuo lin-shih chung-yang cheng-fu pu-
    kao. Ti erh-shih-ch'i hao. Wei k'ai-chan Ch'a-t'ien yün-tung.
    (Announcement of the Provisional Central Government of the Chinese
    Soviet Republic. No. 27. On the Development of the Land Investigat
    Movement).
    September 1st 1933. SSC. No call numbers visible on the microfilm
    Reel 17.

94. Mao Tse-tung: Ch'a-t'ien yün-tung ti ti-i pu. Tsu-chih shang ti ta
    kuei-mo tung-yüan. (The First Step of the Land Investigation Move-
    ment. Large-Scale Organisational Mobilisation).
    Hung-se Chung-hua June 20th 1933 p. 3.
    (Translated by Hsiao Tso-liang, 1969, pp. 205-08).

95. Mao Tse-tung: I-chü nung-ts'un chung chieh-chi tou-cheng ti fa-cha
    chuang-t'ai ti ch'a-pieh ch'ü k'ai-chan Ch'a-t'ien yün-tung. (Unfo
    the Land Investigation Movement in Accordance with the Difference
    in the Stages of Development of the Class Struggle in the Countrysi
    Hung-se Chung-hua June 23rd 1933 p. 3.
    (Translated by Hsiao Tso-liang, 1969, pp. 208-10).

96. Wang Kuan-lan: Chi-hsü k'ai-chan Ch'a-t'ien yün-tung yü wu-ch'i
    ti chen-ya ti-chu fu-nung ti fan-kung. (Continue to Develop the Lan
    Investigation Movement and Ruthlessly Suppress the Counter-Attac
    of the Landlords and the Rich Peasants).
    Hung-se Chung-hua March 20th 1934 p. 1.

97. Kuan-yü chi-hsü k'ai-chan Ch'a-t'ien yün-tung ti wen-t'i. Jen-min
    wei-yüan-hui hsün-ling chung-tz'u ti-i hao. (On the Problem of
    Continued Development of the Land Investigation Movement. In-
    struction, Serial Character Chung, No. 1 of the Council of People's
    Commissars).
    Dated March 15th 1934.
    Hung-se Chung-hua March 20th 1934 p. 1.
    (Translated by Hsiao Tso-liang, 1969, pp. 282-84).

98. Kuan-yü k'ai-chan Ch'a-t'ien yün-tung chung i-ko wen-t'i ti ta-fu.
    Chang chu-hsi chi Wang t'ung-chih ti hsin. (Reply to a Question
    Concerning the Development of the Land Investigation Movement.
    A Letter from Chairman Chang to Comrade Wang).
    Dated March 26th 1934.
    Hung-se Chung-hua March 29th 1934 p. 1.

99. Wang Kuan-lan: Shengli hsien chi-hsü k'ai-chan Ch'a-t'ien yün-tung
    ching-yen. (The Experience of the Continued Development of the Land
    Investigation Movement in the County of Shengli).
    Tou-cheng No. 61 (May 26th 1934), pp. 9-14. The article is dated
    May 18th 1934.

100. Ting-i (probably identical with Lu Ting-i): Liang-ko cheng-ch'üan-
     liang-ko shou-ch'eng. (Two Political Powers - Two Results).
     Tou-cheng No. 72 (September 23rd 1934), pp 12-20.

101. Kuan-yü liang-shih ho-tso-she wen-t'i. (On the Problem of Food Co-
     Operatives).
     Published by the People's Commissariat of Finances in September
     1932.
     SSC 008.658/9388/0214. Reel 11.

     A. Tzu-hui (identical with Teng Tzu-hui):
        Fa-chan liang-shih ho-tso-she yün-tung lai kung-ku su-ch'ü ching-
        chi fa-chan. (Develop the Food Co-Operative Movement in Order
        to Consolidate the Economic Development of the Soviet Area).
        Undated. Pp. 1-12.

     B. Jen-min wei-yüan-hui hsün-ling. Ti-ch'i hao. Fa-chan liang-
        shih ho-tso-she yün-tung wen-t'i. (Instruction No. 7 of the Council
        of People's Commissars. On the Problem of the Movement for
        Development of Food Co-Operatives).
        August 21st 1932. Pp. 13-16.

C. Liang-shih ho-tso-she chien-chang. (Outline of Statutes for
Food Co-Operatives).
Undated. Pp. 17-23.

102. Su-wei-ai cheng-ch'üan ti ching-chi cheng-ts'e. (Ts'ao-an).
(Kung-ch'an kuo-chi tung-fang-pu). (The Economic Policy of the
Soviet Power. (Draft). (The Comintern Eastern Department)).
Undated. SSC 008. 655/2131/0211. Reel 11.
Note: It is not clear whether this is a draft submitted to the Comintern
Eastern Department, or a draft which the Eastern Department sub-
mitted to the Chinese soviet government.

103. Chung-hua su-wei-ai kung-ho-kuo jen-min wei-yüan-hui pu-kao.
Ti-i hao. Wei t'ung-i yü liu-t'ung su-wei-ai fu-pi. (Announcement
No. 1 of the Council of People's Commissars of the Chinese Soviet
Republic. On the Standardisation and Circulation of Soviet Coins).
February 5th 1934. SSC reel 16. (No call numbers are visible on the
microfilm).

104. Chianghsi sheng ti-i tz'u kung-nung-ping su-wei-ai ta-hui. Ts'ai-
cheng yü ching-chi wen-t'i ti chüeh-i-an. (The First Congress of
the Workers', Peasants' and Soldiers'Soviet of Kiangsi Province.
Resolution on Problems of Finances and Economy).
Undated. SSC 008. 662/6417/0215. Reel 10.
Note: The congress must have been held sometime in the spring of
1932. (See date of doc. 21).

105. Liang-p'ing (identical with Wu Liang-p'ing): Ching-chi chien-she
ti ch'u-pu tsung-chieh. (Preliminary Summary on Economic Reconstruction).
Tou-cheng No. 29 (October 7th 1933) pp. 9-15.
The article is dated September 30th 1933.

106. Liang-p'ing (identical with Wu Liang-p'ing):
Mu-ch'ien su-wei-ai ho-tso yün-tung ti chuang-k'uang ho wo-men
ti jen-wu. (The Present Situation of the Co-Operative Movement of
the Soviets and Our Tasks).
Tou-cheng No. 56 (April 21st 1934) pp. 16-22.

107. Chung-hua su-wei-ai kung-ho-kuo lin-shih chung-yang cheng-fu
ch'eng-li chou-nien chi-nien hsiang ch'üan-t'i hsüan-min kung-tso
pao-kao-shu. (Report to the Whole of the Electorate by the Provisional
Central Government of the Chinese Soviet Republic on the Occasion

of the Anniversary of Its Foundation).
Hung-se Chung-hua November 7th 1932 pp. 2-4.

108.  Ts'ai-cheng jen-min wei-yüan-pu i nien lai kung-tso pao-kao.
(Report by the People's Commissariat of Finances on Its Work
for One Year).
Hung-se Chung-hua November 7th 1932 pp. 6-7.

109.  Liang-p'ing (identical with Wu Liang-p'ing): Mu-ch'ien su-ch'ü ti
hsien-chin wen-t'i. (The Problem of Silver Cash in the Soviet Areas
at Present).
Tou-cheng No. 20 (August 5th 1933) pp. 13-14.
The article is dated June 22nd 1933.

110.  Liang-p'ing (identical with Wu Liang-p'ing): Fan-tui hsiang kun-
nan t'ou-hsiang ti yu-ch'ing chi-hui chu-i. (Combat Right Opportunism That Submits to Difficulties). Tou-cheng No. 23 (August 22nd
1933) pp. 17-20.
(Reproduced by Hsiao Tso-liang, 1967, pp. 670-71. See also Hsiao
Tso-liang, 1961, pp. 242-43).
The article is dated August 4th 1933.

111.  Ts'ai-cheng jen-min wei-yüan-pu pan-pu yu-kuan ts'ai-cheng kuei-
tse. (Regulations on Finances Promulgated by the People's Commissariat of Finances).
December 1932. SSC 008.662/6415/0225. Reel 10.

The following documents of this collection have been consulted:

A.  Chung-hua su-wei-ai kung-ho-kuo lin-shih chung-yang cheng-fu
ts'ai-cheng jen-min wei-yüan-pu hsün-ling ti shih-erh hao.
T'ung-i k'uai-chi chih-tu.
(Instruction No. 12 of the People's Commissariat of Finances of
the Provisional Central Government of the Chinese Soviet Republic.
Unification of the Accountancy System).
December 16th 1932.

B.  Kuo-k'u chan-hsing t'iao-lieh. (Provisional Regulations for the
State Treasury).
Undated.

C.  Ts'ai-cheng jen-min wei-yüan-pu k'uai-chi kuei-tse.
(Regulations of Accountancy [Issued by] the People's Commissariat
of Finances).
Undated.

112. Chung-hua su-wei-ai kung-ho-kuo lin-shih chung-yang cheng-fu
     pan-pu yu-kuan ts'ai-cheng t'iao-lieh. (Regulations Relating to
     Finances Promulgated by the Provisional Central Government of
     the Chinese Soviet Republic). June 1932. SSC 008. 662/6412/0223.
     Reel 10.

     The following documents of this collection have been consulted:

     A. Chung-hua su-wei-ai kung-ho-kuo chan-hsing ts'ai-cheng
        t'iao-lieh. (Provisional Financial Regulations of the Chinese
        Soviet Republic).
        Promulgated by the CEC in December 1931. Pp. 21-25.

     B. Jen-min wei-yüan-hui hsün-ling ts'ai-tzu ti-erh hao.
        (Financial Instruction No. 2 of the Council of People's
        Commissars).
        December 29th 1931. Pp 27-31.

113. Chianghsi sheng ko hsien chi chung-hsin ch'ü ts'ai-chang lien-hsi-
     hui chüeh-i. (Resolution of the Joint Meeting of the Heads of Financial
     Departments of the Various Counties and the Central Districts in
     Kiangsi).
     Published in October 1933. SSC 008. 661/6421/0240. Reel 10.
     No clear pagination.

114. Ti-i tz'u ch'üan-kuo su-wei-ai tai-piao ta-hui chüeh-i. Hung-chün
     yu-tai t'iao-lieh. (A Resolution of the First National Soviet Congress.
     Regulations for the Privileges of Red Army Men).
     Published by the General Political Department of the Central Re-
     volutionary Military Committee in December 1931.
     SSC 008. 5545/2132/0545. Reel 8.
     This document is also included in Su-wei-ai Chung-kuo, Moscow
     1933, pp. 182-87.

115. Chianghsi sheng su-wei-ai cheng-fu pu-kao. Ti-san hao. Shih-hsing
     cheng-shou chin-nien t'u-ti lei-chin shui. (Announcement No. 3 of
     the Soviet Government of Kiangsi Province. Carry Out the Collection
     of This Year's Progressive Land Tax).
     SSC reel 11. No call numbers or date are visible on the microfilm.

116. T'u-ti-shui cheng-shou hsi-tse chi t'u-ti-shui cheng-shou wen-t'i.
     (Detailed Regulations for the Collection of Land Tax and Problems
     Concerning the Collection of Land Tax).

Undated. SSC 008. 663/4042/0237. Reel 11. No clear pagination.

A. T'u-ti-shui cheng-shou hsi-tse. (Detailed Regulations for the
   Collection of Land Tax).
   Undated.

B. T'u-ti-shui shui-lü-piao chih chieh-shih. (Explanation of the
   Table of Land Tax Rates).
   Issued by the People's Commissariat of Finances.
   Undated.

C. Chung-hua su-wei-ai kung-ho-kuo lin-shih chung-yang cheng-
   fu ts'ai-cheng jen-min wei-yüan-pu hsün-ling. Ti erh-shih-szu
   hao. Wei cheng-shou t'u-ti-shui wen-t'i. (Instruction No. 24 of
   the People's Commissariat of Finances of the Provisional Central Government of the Chinese Soviet Republic. On the Problem
   of Land Tax Collection).
   Undated.
   Note: A separate version of the instruction, found later on the
   same microfilm reel, is dated October 6th 1933. This may
   possibly be the date of a reprint.

117. Nung-yeh-shui chan-hsing shui-tse chi yu-kuan wen-t'i.
     (Provisional Regulations of the Agricultural Tax and Related Pro-
     blems).
     Published by the People's Commissariat of Finances.
     Undated. SSC 008. 663/5532/0242. Reel 11. No clear pagination.

A. The first document in the collection is identical with doc. 83,
   but the appendix is lacking.

B. The second document is identical with doc. 116B.

C. A document containing regulations of tax exemption, promulgated
   by the CEC on October 26th 1933. The title of the document is
   not legible on the microfilm.

D. Chung-hua su-wei-ai kung-ho-kuo chung-yang ts'ai-cheng jen-
   min wei-yüan-pu t'ung-ling. Ti-szu hao. Wei nung-yeh-shui
   mien-shui chien-shui pu-ch'ung t'iao-lieh wen-t'i. (Communication No. 4 of the People's Commissariat of Finances of the
   Chinese Soviet Republic. On Problems Concerning the Supplementary Regulations of Exemption and Reduction of the Agricultural Tax).
   November 8th 1933.

118. Kuan-yü wan-ch'eng t'ui-hsiao kung-chai cheng-shou t'u-ti-shui
shou-chi liang-shih pao-han Hung-chün kei-yang ti t'u-chi yün-tung
ti chüeh-ting. (Decisions on the Surprise Attack Movement to Complete the Sale of Government Bonds, the Collection of Land Tax and
the Collection of Food, to Safeguard the Supply of the Red Army).
Issued by the Presidium of the Second National Soviet Congress and
the Central Committee of the Chinese Communist Party.
Dated January 23rd 1934.
Hung-se Chung-hua January 28th 1934 p. 1.

119. Chung-kung chung-yang wei-yüan-hui, chung-yang jen-min wei-yüan-
hui kuan-yü tsai chin-nien ch'iu-shou chung chieh-ku liu-shih wan
tan chi cheng-shou t'u-ti-shui ti chüeh-ting. (Decisions of the Central
Committee of the Chinese Communist Party and the Council of
People's Commissars Concerning the Loan of 600.000 Piculs of Un-
hulled Rice and the Collection of Land Tax During This Year's Autumn
Harvest).
Dated July 22nd 1934.
Hung-se Chung-hua July 26th 1934 p. 1.

120. Chung-hua su-wei-ai kung-ho-kuo lin-shih chung-yang cheng-fu
pu-kao. Ti-chiu hao. (Announcement No. 9 of the Provisional Central Government of the Chinese Soviet Republic).
Appendix: Fa-hang "ko-ming chan-cheng" tuan-ch'i kung-chai
t'iao-lieh. (Regulations for the Issue of Short-Term "Revolutionary
War" Bonds).

The date given for this document is strangely enough June 25th 1932,
although it is printed in Hung-se Chung-hua of June 23rd 1932 (p. 5).

121. Chung-hua su-wei-ai kung-ho-kuo lin-shih chung-yang cheng-fu chih
hsing wei-yüan-hui hsün-ling. Chih-tzu ti shih-san hao. Wei fa-hang
ko-ming chan-cheng tuan-ch'i kung-chai-chüan shih. Instruction,
Serial Character Chih, No. 13 of the Executive Committee of the
Provisional Central Government of the Chinese Soviet Republic. On
the Issue of Short-Term Revolutionary War Bonds).

The date given for this document is strangely enough June 26th 1932,
although it is printed in Hung-se Chung-hua of June 23rd 1932 (pp.
5-6).

122. Chung-yang chih-hsing wei-yüan-hui ti shih-ch'i hao hsün-ling. Wei
fa-hang ti-erh ch'i ko-ming chan-cheng kung-chai. (Instruction No.

17 of the Central Executive Committee. On the Second Issue of Revolutionary War Bonds).
Dated October 21st 1932.
Appendix: <u>Fa-hang ti-erh ch'i kung-chai t'iao-lieh.</u>
(Regulations for the Second Issue of Government Bonds).
<u>Hung-se Chung-hua</u> November 1st 1932 pp. 1-2.

123. <u>Chung-hua su-wei-ai kung-ho-kuo lin-shih chung-yang cheng-fu pu-kao. Ti erh-shih-liu hao. Wei fa-hang san-pai wan ching-chi chien-she kung-chai.</u> (Announcement No. 26 of the Provisional Central Government of the Chinese Soviet Republic. On the Issue of Government Bonds for Economic Reconstruction to the Amount of Three Million Yüan).
August 28th 1933. SSC reel 10. No call numbers are visible on the microfilm.

124. <u>Fa-hang ching-chi chien-she kung-chai t'iao-lieh chi ch'i yu-kuan wen-chien.</u> (Regulations for the Issue of Government Bonds for Economic Reconstruction and Related Documents).
SSC 008. 662/1222/023d. Reel 10. No clear pagination. The following documents of this collection have been consulted:

A. <u>Fa-hang ching-chi chien-she kung-chai t'iao-lieh.</u>
(Regulations for the Issue of Government Bonds for Economic Reconstruction).
Issued by the Central Government on July 22nd 1933.

B. <u>Chung-hua su-wei-ai kung-ho-kuo chung-yang jen-min wei-yüan-hui hsün-ling. Ti shih-liu hao. Kuan-yü t'ui-hsiao kung-chai ti fang-fa.</u> (Instruction No. 16 of the Council of People's Commissars of the Chinese Soviet Republic. On the Methods of Selling Government Bonds).
According to <u>Hung-se Chung-hua</u> of September 6th 1933 (p. 7) the date of this document is August 28th 1933.

C. <u>Kuan-yü t'ui-hsiao san-pai wan ching-chi chien-she kung-chai ti hsüan-ch'uan ta-kang.</u> (General Principles of the Propaganda for the Sale of Economic Reconstruction Bonds to the Amount of Three Million).
Dated August 28th 1933.

125. Mao Tse-tung: <u>Fen-sui wu-tz'u "wei-chiao" yü su-wei-ai ching-chi chien-she jen-wu.</u> (Smashing the Fifth "Encirclement and Annihilation Campaign" and the Soviet Task of Economic Reconstruction).

This was a report delivered by Mao at a conference on economic reconstruction of cadres from 17 counties.
Hung-se Chung-hua August 16th 1933 pp. 2-4.

126. Chung-hua su-wei-ai kung-ho-kuo lin-shih chung-yang cheng-fu ch'eng-li liang chou-nien chi-nien tui ch'üan-t'i hsüan-min ti kung-tso pao-kao. (Report to the Whole of the Electorate by the Provisional Central Government of the Chinese Soviet Republic on the Occasion of the Second Anniversary of Its Foundation). Dated October 24th 1933.
Hung-se Chung-hua October 27th 1933 pp. 1-2.

127. Mao Tse-t'an: Wei ch'üan-pu wan-ch'eng liang-shih t'u-chi chi-hua erh tou-cheng. (Struggle for the Fulfilment of the Plan for the Surprise Attack in Food [Collection]).
Tou-cheng No. 49 (March 2nd 1934) pp. 8-13.

128. Ch'en T'an-ch'iu: Shou-chi liang-shih t'u-chi yün-tung tsung-chieh. (Summary on the Surprise Attack Movement for Food Collection).
Hung-se Chung-hua March 31st 1934 p. 5. The article is dated March 26th 1934.

129. Chung-hua su-wei-ai kung-ho-kuo chung-yang chih-hsing wei-yüan-hui hsün-ling. Ti erh-shih hao. Wei ko-ming ch'ün-chung chieh-ku kung-kei Hung-chün. (Instruction No. 20 of the Central Executive Committee of the Chinese Soviet Republic. On the Loan of Rice from the Revolutionary Masses to Supply the Red Army). Dated March 1st 1933.
Hung-se Chung-hua March 6th 1933 pp. 5-6.

130. Chang Wen-t ien: Liang-shih t'u-chi yün-tung yü liang-shih-pu ti kung-tso. (The Surprise Attack Movement for Food Collection and the Work of the Food Departments). Editorial in Hung-se Chung-hua of February 27th 1934 (p. 1). The editiorial is dated February 25th 1934.

131. T'an-ch'iu (identical with Ch'en T'an-ch'iu): Ch'iu-shou liang-shih tung-yüan ti tsung-chieh. (Summary on the Mobilisation for Food Collection during the Autumn Harvest).
Tou-cheng No. 73 (September 30th 1934) pp. 8-13.

132. Chung-kung Chianghsi sheng-wei t'ung-chih. Ti erh-shih-liu hao. Ch'ou-tso ching-fei wen-t'i. (Notice No. 26 of the Kiangsi Provinci

Committee of the Chinese Communist Party. On the Problem of
Devising Means for Meeting Expenditure).
Dated June 27th 1932. SSC 008.662/8852/0063. Reel 11.
No clear pagination.

33. Kuan-yü jo-kan li-shih wen-t'i ti chüeh-i. (Resolution on Some
Historical Problems).
Adopted by the Seventh Enlarged Plenary Session of the CCP Sixth
Central Committee (since the Sixth National Congress of 1928), on
April 20th 1945.
Printed in Mao-Tse-tung hsüan-chi, Peking 1958, vol.3, pp. 955-
1002.

34. Mao Tse-tung: Chin-nien ti hsüan-chü. (This Year's Election).
A report delivered at a conference on the election movement of
cadres from 18 counties in the southern part of the Central Soviet
Area.
Hung-se Chung-hua September 6th 1933 pp. 1-2.

35. Kuo-chi tui-yü Chung-kuo su-wei-ai wen-t'i chüeh-i-an.
(A Resolution of the International [Comintern] on the Problem
of the Chinese Soviets).
Undated, but a reference to village soviets (on leaf 48) shows that
the resolution is adopted before November 1931. SSC, reel 16. The
call numbers are not visible on the microfilm.

36. Hsiang Ying: Ch'iang-ku ch'eng hsiang su-wei-ai ti tsu-chih ho
kung-tso. (Consolidate the Organisation and Work of the Town Soviets and the Hsiang Soviets).
Editorial in Hung-se Chung-hua of April 6th 1932 (p. 1).

37. Chung-yang chih-hsing wei-yüan-hui chüeh-i. Kuan-yü ko-chi
hsüan-chü yün-tung ti chien-ch'a. (Resolution of the Central Executive Committee. On the Investigation of the Election Movement
at the Various Levels).
Dated December 1st 1932.
Hung-se Chung-hua December 5th 1932 pp. 2-3.

38. Chung-yang nei-wu jen-min wei-yüan-pu wei chin-hsing hsüan-chü
tui Chianghsi i-feng chih-shih-hsin. (A Directive Letter on the
Election Work from the People's Commissariat of Internal Affairs
to Kiangsi).
Dated September 7th 1933.
Hsüan-chü yün-tung chou-pao No. 2 (September 10th 1933 pp. 6-8).

139.  Mao Tse-tung: <u>Nung-ts'un tiao-ch'a</u>, (Investigations of Rural
      Districts).
      Published by Cieh-fang-she, 1949.
      The following documents of this collection have been consulted:

   A. <u>Hsingkuo tiao-ch'a</u>. (An Investigation of Hsingkuo). The
      investigation was undertaken by Mao in late 1930, by way of
      interviewing eight Red Army men from Yungfeng district in
      Hsingkuo. P. 7-62.

   B. <u>Ch'angkang hsiang tiao-ch'a.</u> (An Investigation of Ch'angkang
      <u>Hsiang.</u>)
      Preface dated December 15th 1933. Pp. 96-132.

   C. <u>Ts'aihsi hsiang tiao-ch'a.</u> (An Investigation of Ts'aihsi <u>Hsian</u>
      The investigation was probably undertaken in late 1933. It
      covered the two <u>hsiang</u> of Upper and Lower Ts'aihsi. Pp. 133
      50.

## B. Journals

<u>Ch'ing-nien shih-hua</u>. (True Words of Youth).
Organ of the Central Bureau for the Soviet Areas of the Chinese
Communist Youth League.
1931-1934. SSC 008.2105/5083. Reels 18-19.

<u>Hsüan-chü yün-tung chou-pao.</u> (Weekly Magazine for the Election
Movement).
Published by the Preparatory Committee for the Second National
Soviet Congress.
1933. SSC 008.63405/3773/0664. Reel 10.

<u>Hung-hsing pao</u>. (The Red Star).
Published by the General Political Department of the Chinese
Workers' and Peasants' Red Army.
1933-1934. SSC 008.1052/2160/0971. Reel 16.

<u>Hung-se Chung-hua.</u> (Red China).
Organ of the Provisional Central Government of the Chinese
Soviet Republic.
1931-1934. SSC 008.1052/2125. Reels 16-17.

Bibliography                                    Journals

Problemy Kitaya. (Chinese Problems).
Published on behalf of Nauchno-issledovatel'skiy institut po Kitayu
(Institute for Scientific Research on China).
Moscow 1929-1935.

Sheng-wei t'ung-hsün. (Correspondence of the Provincial Committee).
Published by the Kiangsi Provincial Committee of the Chinese
Communist Party.
1933-1934. SSC 008. 2105/9023. Reel 17.

Shih-hua. (True Words).
Organ of the CCP Central Bureau for the Soviet Areas.
1932. SSC 008. 2105/3002/1152. Reel 18.

Szu-fa hui-k'an. (Judicial Journal).
Published by the Judicial Department of the Provincial Soviet of
Kiangsi.
1933. SSC 008. 54105/1732/0658. Reel 6.
Note: No. 2 of this journal is entitled Ts'ai-p'an hui-k'an (Judicial
      Journal), and No. 7 is named Chianghsi sheng ts'ai-p'an-pu pan
      yüeh-k'an (Fortnightly Publication of the Judicial Department of
      Kiangsi Province).

Tang ti chien-she. (Party Reconstruction).
Published by the Organisational Department of the CCP
Central Bureau for the Soviet Areas.
1932. SCC, reel 17. (No call numbers are visible on the microfilm).

Tou-cheng. (Struggle).
Organ of the CCP Central Bureau for the Soviet Areas.
1933-1934. SSC 008. 2105/7720. Reel 18.




B. Books

Brandt, Conrad, Schwartz, Benjamin, and Fairbank, John K. A Documentary
History of Chinese Communism. Cambridge, Mass.: Harvard University
Press, 1959.

Buck, J. L. Land Utilization in China. New York, 1956.

Carr, Edward Hallett. The Bolshevik Revolution 1917-1923.
London: Macmillan, 1950-1953. 3 vols.

_____. Socialism in One Country. London: Macmillan,
1958-1964. 3 vols.

Ch'en, Jerome (ed.). Mao. Englewood Cliffs, New Jersey:
Prentice-Hall, Inc., 1969.

_____. Mao and the Chinese Revolution. London:
Oxford University Press, 1965.

Ch'ih-fei fan-tung wen-chien hui-pien. (A Collection of Red Bandit
Reactionary Documents). Compiled under the sponsorship of General
Ch'en Ch'eng, 1935.

Ch'ih-fei wen-chien hui-pien. (A Collection of Red Bandit Documents).
See under Chinese Documents, No. 90.

Ch'ü T'ung-tsu. Local Government in China under the Ch'ing.
Cambridge, Mass.: Harvard University Press, 1962.

Deutscher, Isaac. Stalin. A Political Biography. Second ed., London:
Oxford University Press, 1967.

Duverger, Maurice. Political Parties. London: Methuen, 1954.

Fainsod, Merle. Smolensk under Soviet Rule. London: Macmillan,
1959.

Hinton, William. Fanshen. A Documentary of Revolution in a Chinese
Village. New York: Monthly Review Press, 1966.

Ho Kan-chih. A History of the Modern Chinese Revolution. Peking:
Foreign Languages Press, 1959.

Hsiao Tso-liang. Power Relations within the Chinese Communist
Movement, 1930-1934. Seattle: University of Washington Press, 1961.

_____. Power Relations within the Chinese Communist
Movement, 1930-1934. Vol. II. The Chinese Documents.
Seattle: University of Washington Press, 1967.

_____. The Land Revolution in China, 1930-1934.
Seattle: University of Washington Press, 1969.

Hu Ch'iao-mu. Chung-kuo kung-ch'an-tang san-shih nien.
(Thirty Years of the Chinese Communist Party). Peking: Jen-min
ch'u-pan-she, 1951.

Hung-ch'i p'iao-p'iao (Red Flag Flutters). 17 vols. Peking: Chungkuo ch'ing-nien ch'u-pan-she, 1957-1966.

Istoriya sovetskoy konstitutsii (v dokumentakh) 1917-1956. (A History of Soviet Constitutions (in Documents) 1917-1956). Compiled by A. A. Lipatov and N. T. Savenkov. Moscow: Gosudarstvennoe izdatel'stvo yuridicheskoy literatury, 1957.

Johnson, Chalmers, A. Peasant Nationalism and Communist Power. Stanford: Stanford University Press, 1962.

Klein, Donald W., and Clark, Anne B. Biographic Dictionary of Chinese Communism, 1921-1965. 2 vols. Cambridge, Mass.: Harvard University Press, 1971.

Kuo, Warren. Analytical History of the Chinese Communist Party. 4 vols. Taipei: Institute of International Relations, 1968-71.

Kung Ch'u. Wo yü Hung-chün. (The Red Army and I). Hong Kong: South Wind Publishing Company, 1954.

Lenin, V. I. Sobranie sochineniy. (Collected Works). 20 vols. Moscow 1924-1926.

Li Ang. Hung-se wu-t'ai. (The Red Stage). Peiping, 1946.

Linebarger, Paul M. A. The China of Chiang Kai-shek. Boston: World Peace Foundation, 1941.

Linebarger, P. M. A., Djang Chu and Burks, A. W. Far Eastern Governments and Politics. China and Japan. New York: Van Nostrand, 1954.

Mao Tse-tung. Mao Tse-tung hsüan-chi. (Selected Works of Mao Tse-tung). 4 vols. Peking: Jen-min ch'u-pan-she, 1958-60.

_____. Selected Works of Mao Tse-tung. 5 vols. London: Lawrence & Wishart Ltd., 1955.

_____. Selected Works of Mao Tse-tung. 4 vols. Peking: Foreign Languages Press, 1960-65.

_____. Nung-ts'un tiao-ch'a. (Investigations of Rural Districts). See under Chinese Documents, No. 139.

Myrdal, Jan. Report from a Chinese Village. London: Heinemann, 1965.

North, Robert C. Kuomintang and Chinese Communist Elites. Stanford: Stanford University Press, 1952.

North, Robert C. Moscow and Chinese Communists. Stanford: Stanford University Press, 1953.

Reischauer, E. O., Fairbank, J. K. and Craig, A. M. East Asia. The Modern Transformation. (Vol. 2 of A History of East Asian Civilisation). London: Allen & Unwin, 1965.

Rousseau, Jean Jacques. Du contrat social. Paris 1962.

Rue, John E. Mao Tse-tung in Opposition. Stanford: Stanford University Press, 1966.

Schram, Stuart R. Mao Tse-tung. Penguin Books, 1966.

Schurmann, Franz. Ideology and Organization in Communist China. Berkeley and Los Angeles: University of California Press, 1966.

Schwartz, Benjamin I. Chinese Communism and the Rise of Mao. Cambridge, Mass.: Harvard University Press, 1958.

Sheng Yueh (Sheng Chung-liang). Sun Yat-sen University in Moscow and the Chinese Revolution. A Personal Account. Center for East Asian Studies, The University of Kansas, 1971.

Smedley, Agnes. The Great Road. The Life and Times of Chu Teh. New York: Monthly Review Press, 1956.

Snow, Edgar. Red Star over China. London: Victor Gollancz Ltd., 1946.

Sovety v Kitae. (Soviets in China). Part I is written by E. Johanson and O. Taube. Moscow: Partiynoe izdatel' stvo, 1933.

Su-wei-ai Chung-kuo. (Soviet China). Moscow: Izdatel'stvo inostrannykh rabochikh v SSSR, 1933.

Swarup, Shanti. A Study of the Chinese Communist Movement, 1927-1934. Oxford: Clarendon Press, 1966.

Thornton, Richard C. The Comintern and the Chinese Communists 1928-1931. Seattle and London: University of Washington Press, 1969.

Tsao Po-i: Chianghsi su-wei-ai chih chien-li chi ch'i peng-k'uei. (The Rise and Fall of the Chinese Soviet in Kiangsi, 1931-1934). Taipei: Kuo-li cheng-chih ta-hsüeh tung-ya yen-chiu-so, 1969.

Van der Sprenkel, Sybille. Legal Institutions in Manchu China. A Sociological Analysis. London: The Athlone Press, 1962.

Waller, Derek J. The Kiangsi Soviet Republic: Mao and the National Congresses of 1931 and 1934. Berkeley: University of California, 1973.

Wang Chien-min. Chung-kuo kung-ch'an-tang shih-kao. (A Draft History of the Chinese Communist Party). 3 vols. Taipei 1965.

Wittfogel, Karl A. Oriental Despotism. A Comparative Study of Total Power. New Haven: Yale University Press, 1957.

Yakhontoff, Victor A. The Chinese Soviets. New York: Coward-McCann, 1934.

Yang, C.K. A Chinese Village in Early Communist Transition. Included in C.K. Yang, Chinese Communist Society: the Family and the Village. Cambridge, Mass.: The M.I.T. Press, 1965.


D. Other Sources

Braun, Otto (Li T'e). Von Schanghai bis Jänan. Published in Horizont (East Berlin), 1969, Nos. 23-38.

Ch'en, Jerome. Resolutions of the Tsunyi Conference. (Translation with a commentary). The China Quarterly No. 40, October - December 1969, pp. 1-38.

Heinzig, Dieter. The Otto Braun Memoirs and Mao's Rise to Power. The China Quarterly No. 46, April-June 1971, pp. 274-288.

# INDEX

Great leap forward   158, 160, 165

Hainan   68
Hard labour brigades   93, 114, 115, 154, 170, 175, 181
Heinzig, Dieter   10
Hinton, William   163
Ho K'o-ch'üan (K'ai Feng)   74
Ho Shu-heng   89, 107
Hsiang   15-20, 29, 45-47, 51, 54, 164
Hsiang soviet   14-16, 21-24, 31, 34, 54, 55, 57, 58, 97, 161, 164, 199,
    204, 210; representative congress   21-28, 33-35, 49, 54;   soviet
    delegates   22, 26-31, 33, 35; presidium   21-26, 29, 33-35;   com-
    mittees   23, 32-35;   staff   21-23, 25, 26, 29, 33, 35;   chairman
    21-24, 26, 28, 103;   vice-chairman   21-24, 26;   clerk   22-26
Hsiangkan   68, 69, 200
Hsiangohsi   68
Hsiangokan   68, 69, 200
Hsiang Ying   10, 17, 21, 73, 76, 77, 85, 86, 89
Hsiao Tso-liang   7, 12, 71, 79, 143, 151, 184
Hsiao Tzu-cheng   100, 134
Hsichiang   59, 62, 204
Hsieh Jan-chih   52-54
Hsien
    see County
Hsinch'üan   62, 156
Hsinfeng   156, 166
Hsingkuo   26, 53, 55, 57, 62, 100, 133, 134, 148, 156, 163, 166
Hsinkan   62
Hsink'ang   62
Hsü T'e-li   89
Hsünwu   62, 111, 114, 156
Hu Hai   89, 93
Huich'ang   55, 62, 105, 111, 114, 128, 156, 161, 171
Hunan   7

Ich'ien   102
Ihuang   62, 156
Illiterates   24, 34, 79
Imperialism   35, 97
Intermediate soviets   39, 42;   representative congress   40, 42, 43,
    47-49;   executive committee   40, 42-44;   presidium   40, 43, 44;
    departments   40, 41, 43, 44;   committees   40, 44;   chairman
    40, 43;   inspectors   40, 41
Jails   114
Japanese   9, 97

Java   68
Jent'ien   164, 165
Judges   109, 117, 128
Judical committees   110, 111, 117
Judical departments   87, 103, 108-14, 116-18, 120, 121, 123-27, 134-
    36, 138, 160
Judicial organs   111, 112, 114-16, 118-24, 126, 127, 135, 139, 140,
    142, 143
Juichin   7, 9, 51, 56, 57, 59, 61, 69, 71, 74, 79, 103, 104, 111, 112,
    114, 139, 155, 156, 161, 162, 164, 166, 172, 179, 187, 204, 212, 213


K'ai Feng
    see Ho K'o-ch'üan
Kalinin   75
K'angtu   62
Kanhsien   55, 62, 156, 167, 187
Kao Tzu-li   89
Kiangsi   7-10, 12, 26, 55, 60-62, 64, 65, 69, 72, 74, 100-102, 112-14,
    118, 127, 134, 135, 141, 153, 155, 161, 162, 168, 182, 185, 189,
    193-95, 207
Kiangsi Soviet   9
Korea   68, 69
Kuangch'ang   62, 156, 166, 213
Kulaks   37, 151
Kung Ch'u   11, 99, 142, 143, 155, 162, 185
Kunglüeh   55, 62, 101, 156, 166, 187
Kuomintang (KMT)   7, 9, 35, 46, 75, 76, 78, 97-99, 102, 137, 143,
    144, 185, 186, 192, 193, 200, 202, 210-13
Kwangtung   8, 9


Labour camps   107, 114, 115, 120
Land Investigation Movement   93, 102, 125-27, 137, 145, 151-55, 157-
    72, 178-81, 184, 207, 212, 213
Land laws   71, 73, 151-53, 155, 183
Landlords   19, 25, 31, 80, 99, 102, 103, 115, 118, 122, 125, 129, 135-
    38, 141, 145, 146, 148, 149, 151, 152, 154, 156-58, 160, 162, 164-
    71, 174, 175, 177-83, 189, 190, 192, 204, 207
Legality   139, 140
Lenin   16, 72
Li Li-san   7, 10, 12, 151
Li T'e
    see Braun, Otto
Li Wei-han (Lo Mai)   82, 86
Liang Po-t'ai   75, 89, 107, 120, 126, 139-41
Lich'uan   156